Growth

Dear Ta

Her

2022 !

Best wishes,

Joe.

Nearly half of small consultancies fail within their first five years, but over 250 are sold every month. How do you ensure you are in the right group? How can you successfully grow a consulting firm? How do you maximise the value of your consultancy for an exit or investment?

This is the first evidence-based book to tackle these questions. Based upon interviews with 72 founders who grew and sold their firms, two international surveys, and a long career researching and advising consultancies, Professor Joe O'Mahoney provides a detailed, evidence-based approach to successful growth and exit for consultancy leaders.

Accessible, evidence-based and written by a leading expert in the field, this book is essential reading for anyone looking to set up, grow or sell their own consultancy business.

Prof. Joe O'Mahoney is an award-winning expert on the consulting industry. After practising as a corporate, independent and internal consultant, Joe started his own firm, which he sold in 2008. Since 2003, Joe has been Professor of Consulting at Cardiff University and a consultant to the consulting industry. He has advised companies such as McKinsey & Co., IBM and Deloitte on growth, innovation and strategy, and helped numerous small firms grow towards a profitable sale. Joe has won awards for his research, writing and teaching about the consulting industry from the Chartered Management Institute, the Centre for Management Consulting Excellence, the British Academy of Management and the ESRC.

"A great refresh for the consulting industry that builds on Maister's epic on firm management. An important resource for anyone looking to start, scale and transition a services firm. Not just for partners but for anyone looking to build an ownership mentality at a firm."

— **Edward Beals,** *Founding Partner, Loft9; Partner, Sia Partners*

"Joe O'Mahoney's research into the successes and failures of those who have started and grown their own consultancy businesses is outstanding value to those on their own journey. Joe has captured the key lessons that consulting business leaders have drawn in growing and selling consultancies, and has included case studies that bring these lessons to life. Joe writes with great good humour that makes this book an easy read."

— **Calvert Markham,** *Ex-CEO & Founder, Elevation Learning (sold)*

"Prof. Joe O'Mahoney is the David Maister for growth."

— **Danco Dimkov,** *Founder & CEO BizzBee Solutions*

"This is the book I should have read twenty five-plus years ago when I set up my first consultancy. Like most consultants, I assumed my basic business knowledge would be sufficient. I can see now that it wasn't. Joe brings out so many pointers which will steer both the fledgling and established consultancy community. Essential reading."

— **John Oliver,** *OBE Ex-CEO Leyland Trucks*

"Prof. Joe O'Mahoney was able to superbly crystallize the essence of how to grow your consulting business via hands-on case studies and real life experience. I recommend the book to consultancies owners who have big aspirations."

— **Damien Duhamel,** *Founder & Ex-CEO, Solidiance*

"The book provides a fantastic guide to growing and preparing to sell your business, grounded in quality data and anecdotal experiences from the people who've lived it."

— **Julie Barber,** *Founder & CEO of Spark! Consulting*

"In this insightful, easy to digest book, Professor Joe O'Mahoney gathers insight from people who have been there and done it. In doing so, he teases out the remarkably similar themes and stages of the journey that anyone has tried, has experienced. I only wish I had read this when I was starting out. There are always blood, sweat and tears as you build a business, but reading this may have saved a few of each!"

— **Logan Naidu,** *CEO of Dartmouth Partners*

"A most impressive book, packed with useful ideas and tips about how to embark upon the process of preparing for and selling a Consulting business. I only wish I had access to it when I started out on my own journey of selling my company."

— **Nigel Povah,** *Founder & Ex-CEO of A&DC*

"This book is a must-read for all consultants, young and seasoned alike. The book contains a wealth of insights and analyses that will not only challenge your thinking and expand your views but also provide you with a roadmap toward building a successful and sustainable business."

— **Dr. Dorel Iosif,** *Founder & CEO of Lavaux Global*

"Essential reading for anyone who is looking to start, build or sell a consulting business. Joe has a deep understanding of how management consulting firms are grown for success."

— **Mark Palmer,** *CEO of Gobeyond Partners*

Growth

Building a Successful Consultancy in the
Digital Age

Joe O'Mahoney

Routledge
Taylor & Francis Group

LONDON AND NEW YORK

First published 2022
by Routledge
4 Park Square, Milton Park, Abingdon, Oxon OX14 4RN

and by Routledge
605 Third Avenue, New York, NY 10158

Routledge is an imprint of the Taylor & Francis Group, an informa business

© 2022 Joe O'Mahoney

The right of Joe O'Mahoney to be identified as author of this work has been asserted in accordance with sections 77 and 78 of the Copyright, Designs and Patents Act 1988.

All rights reserved. No part of this book may be reprinted or reproduced or utilised in any form or by any electronic, mechanical, or other means, now known or hereafter invented, including photocopying and recording, or in any information storage or retrieval system, without permission in writing from the publishers.

Trademark notice: Product or corporate names may be trademarks or registered trademarks, and are used only for identification and explanation without intent to infringe.

British Library Cataloguing-in-Publication Data
A catalogue record for this book is available from the British Library

Library of Congress Cataloging-in-Publication Data
A catalog record has been requested for this book

ISBN: 978-0-367-71083-5 (hbk)
ISBN: 978-0-367-71084-2 (pbk)
ISBN: 978-1-003-14921-7 (ebk)

DOI: 10.4324/9781003149217

Typeset in Goudy
by codeMantra

Contents

Acknowledgements

This is a book about how to successfully grow, and eventually exit, a consulting firm. This book would not have been possible without the 2000+ consultants and students I have taught about the consulting industry and the 700+ consultants and partners I've coached, advised or interviewed over the years. In particular, I have been privileged to be granted several non-executive director roles and learned much from each one.

More specifically, this study would have been impossible without the 72 founders who shared their journeys with me in very frank and open interviews and responded so generously to a survey and requests for further information. The text would also be much weaker were it not for the insights and comments from my network of experienced consultants and CEOs who volunteered to read and comment. Each chapter was picked over by at least two experts, which included Spencer Land, Rob Garner, Rob Wherrett, Nick Synott, David Shaw, David Powell, Gary Metcalfe, John Oliver, Adrian Rhodes, Ioannis Thanos, Julie Barber, Kartik Chawla, Dibyanjana Lodh Ray, Lone Anderson, Joe Wheatley, Justin Stirling, Carol Griffiths, Matthew Emerson, Varun Razdan, Jonathan Jewell, Richard Beevers, Dr. Dorel Iosif, Alistair Russell, Dr. Ehsan Derayati, Prasanna Amanan, Fredericka Sheppard and Cosette Reczek. Many thanks for your insights. I especially want to thank Steve Newton, CEO of Elixirr, who is always keen to point out when I'm overtheorising the simple truth that nothing beats client value and passionate leadership.

My publisher, Routledge, and editor, Rebecca Marsh, are also to be thanked for allowing me to write something that was neither an airport 'guru' text nor an academic tome, but something which, I hope, has the best of both worlds. You will be the judge, of course.

Thank you to Jane O'Mahoney (hello mum!) who proof-read the book and pointed out all my mistakes without laughing too much, and to Dr. David Frayne who helped me polish the draft manuscript. I should also acknowledge the two other Partners leading one of my firms, Consulting Mastered Ltd., from whom I have learned a huge amount about consulting: thank you Prof. Simon Haslam and Martin J. Williams.

As ever, my biggest thanks is to my wife, Dr. Hannah O'Mahoney. This book was written during the COVID-19 lockdowns with our two small sons, Alex and Felix, at home. During this time, Hannah not only continued her own job and cared for me and the boys, but also found time to do the coding of the interviews (a laborious but necessary job) and gave great advice on how to best analyse the data.

Preface

After leaving corporate consulting for academia in 2003, ex-colleagues, who often bumped up against partner grade or who simply wanted more control of their work, occasionally came to me for advice in helping them start and grow their new consulting firms. I was always a little embarrassed, for both myself as a 'Professor of Consulting' and for academia more generally, that 95% of the research on consulting is focused on large firms. As a result, there was no credible *evidence-based* advice for founders who wanted to *grow* (as opposed to simply start up) a consultancy. In the words of two researchers in the areas, Reihlen & Werr, 'it is surprising how little empirical research has been conducted in this field'.[1]

This project is my attempt to make amends for that absence of evidence, and also to pull together my experiences in a number of areas: as a corporate consultant, independent consultant, internal consultant and, since 2003, a consultant to the consulting industry and Professor of Consulting. This book is a combination of in-depth research on founders who grew and sold their consulting firms, my own experiences in a variety of consulting roles, knowledge gained through teaching and coaching consultants and 20-odd years of reading thousands of books and articles published about the consulting industry.

There are different paths to growth (and sale, should you wish it) and this book is not intended to prescribe one route for an ambitious founder. It should act instead as a resource to challenge, encourage and illuminate the reader based on the successes of others. Despite having launched four companies, sold one and researched hundreds more, I have become increasingly convinced that there is no golden formula. Luck plays a significant role in every story of success that is detailed here, but so too does bravery, tenacity and the humility to learn.

Due to limitations of space, I occasionally point the reader to the free resources available at www.joeomahoney.com. These are freely available tools and templates that I use with my growth clients or recorded talks that I have given for various institutions.

In the spirit of learning, I would be keen to hear from any reader who feels I've missed a crucial area or could improve something for the next edition. I hope this book is useful to you on your journey.

Joe O'Mahoney

Prof. Joe O'Mahoney, MA, MSc, PhD. FICMCI, FCIPD.

Professor of Consulting, Cardiff University

CEO, Consulting Mastered Ltd.

CEO, Consulting Pathway Ltd.

FICMCI, FCIPD.

Note

1   Reihlen, M., & Werr, A. (2015) Entrepreneurship and professional service firms: A literature review. In Joseph Broschak, Daniel Muzio, & Laura Empson, eds. *Oxford Handbook of Professional Service Firms*. Oxford University Press: Oxford, pp. 89–113.

1
Introduction

Why?

The purpose of this book

I originally thought this book was going to focus on how to grow and sell a consulting firm. However, when analysing the interviews and other data upon which it is based, I realised that growing and selling, although by no means easy, is not the major challenge. The challenge is doing this *well*. 'Well' means different things to different people, but here it means minimising the personal and business pains associated with growth, whilst maximising the value of the firm.

Whilst the interviewees for this book gave fantastic accounts of what they did to achieve their growth and eventual exit, the real lessons came when I asked, 'what do you wish you had done differently?'. Most pointed to things they should have done to grow faster, accrue value quicker or sell for a higher multiple. Others wished they had not worked so hard that their family and health were affected adversely. Out of the 70 or so interviewees for this book who actually sold their firms, perhaps only three or four did so without avoidable business or personal pain.

My point here is two-fold. First, it is not necessary to do everything in this book in order to grow and sell. Indeed, if you were doing the right thing (for example, cyber security or AI) at the right time, then it would actually be difficult *not* to grow, whether you followed these recommendations or not. However, if attention is paid to all sections of this book, you will maximise your chances of minimising your pains. Second, this book is as much about what successful founders did *not* do as much as what they did. With a few exceptions, I have no doubts that most of the interviewees would achieve more profit, quicker and with less pain, if they were to go back and do it again. This book will hopefully

DOI: 10.4324/9781003149217-1

enable new founders to learn from these experiences and avoid common pitfalls first time around.

A lack of evidence

Although small consultancies (1–20 people) represent around 97% of all firms in that sector, there is surprisingly little quality research done on the strategies and tactics linked with growing profitable consultancies. There are four reasons for this:

First, the sources of data. The few books that exist about growing small consulting firms are self-published 'best-sellers'[1] by consultants telling the story of how they did it. Even in the best case, where the consultant in question *was* actually successful (and knows, relatively, how successful), what worked for them in the past is unlikely to work for you in the future. Success is always tied to the local economic conditions in which consultants grow their practice. This means that without a rigorous examination of a variety of successful (and unsuccessful) consultancies in different locations and at different times, it is impossible to understand the common factors for success.

An interesting sub-set of the self-published 'gurus' are consultants who sell online consultancy to 'consultants'. I use the inverted commas because their advice is actually better targeted at coaches – if anyone. Any of you who are on LinkedIn may be inundated with offers from improbably young consultants offering **FREE!!!!** webinars promising **3 SECRET HACKS!!!** to earn **7 FIGURES A MONTH!!!** The difficulty with most (though not all) of these offers is that they are generally focused on creating a simple online sales funnel where a free **CHEAT SHEET!!!** or **EBOOK WORTH £150!!!** acts as click bait for an eventual hard sell 'strategy call'. While there may be a market for what is fundamentally social media hard-selling, sophisticated and sceptical clients tend to eschew promises of easy wins by unknown contacts in favour of high-trust relationships generally built on recommendations from acquaintances. As I will explore later, there is a place for funnels for some smaller consultancies, but as an exclusive route to clients, these are better left to nutrition coaches in California.

Second, it is much easier to write about how to be a good *consultant* (see Edgar Schein, David Fields, Richard Newton and many others) than it is to understand how to grow a good *consultancy*. Most consultants, and indeed most managers, could probably have a stab at the former, not least because the information is ubiquitous (how to present, how to sell and so on). However, growing a successful consultancy is rarer and requires knowledge of everything from understanding what qualitative measures investors in consulting firms use and how recessions change the shape of firms, to knowing what forms of intellectual property to prioritise and how to reach the balance between service personalisation and more codified forms of knowledge.

A third reason for the lack of evidence is that academics are not generally that interested in small consultancies and their successful growth. Big brands such as McKinsey & Co., Deloitte or Accenture not only look sexier on a research report or academic paper, but these firms also have the financial and human resources to engage and influence business academics and policy makers.[2] Sadly, most business academics are not particularly interested in such uncomplicated terms as 'profits' or 'sales', which lack the obfuscation often required to get published in top journals.[3] This is a shame, because the great thing about (most) academics is that they're not interested in selling you anything – they do research for the genuine love of knowledge (or because no one will employ them in the private sector – joking, joking).

As a result, most books in this area are not very useful for the ambitious practice owner, covering only the very basics. There are exceptions, such as *The Professional Service Firm* by Mark Scott and *Managing the Professional Service Firm* by the consulting guru David Maister, but these were primarily written about large consulting firms. More importantly, these books were penned when the consulting industry was relatively small, before most companies had websites and before Google, Twitter and Facebook existed. In 30 years the consulting world has transformed, and so too must our strategies for profitable growth.

Finally, and perhaps as a consequence of the points above, many founders avoid growth, pursuing a 'business as usual' strategy, remaining very small or taking on one or two people, whilst only a minority seek to grow, often with a view to selling the firm in the future.[4] In some ways, this avoidance is a pity, because many of the lessons for growth are also those for running a successful consultancy. It is not much harder to grow a consulting firm into a sellable asset than it is to run a successful small firm.

The world has changed

Although every week someone tells me that 'consultancy is dead' or that their business model will 'replace the stale advisory industry', the Professional Services business model has been relatively immune to disruption for 100 years. Most of the Big Four and the dominant strategy firms can trace their lineage back over a century. The primary assets of the firm are the same as always: valuable client relationships, specialist technical expertise and a strong brand. Whilst increasingly challenged, the basic business model is also still dominant: expert employees are hired out to clients for a price that equals their salary plus overheads and margins, and the profits are divided between the partners of the firm. The benefit of this model is its simplicity: so long as utilisation and project margins can be maintained, profit per partner is all but guaranteed. Yet the simplicity of the old model is also its downfall. This is because the growth in margins in this business model will only ever be linear: profit margins increase in direct proportion to headcount. Even worse, if (as is good practice) a firm wishes to maintain its leverage ratio (the number of fee earners for every partner), then after a certain size is reached, increases in consultants require increases in partners, thereby limiting additional profits for other partners.[5]

The digital revolution enables consultancies to break through this constraint. Most studies of 'digital' in consulting firms have focused on the services they sell, and it is true that digital offers clients huge value (even if they do not always deliver this in practice). Out of the 30 top consultancies listed in the *Financial Times*' 'Fastest Growing Companies',[6] only one is *not* focused on digital and 83% of consultancies see growing demand for their digital services.[7]

Yet, as with many bricks and mortar companies, the real impact for consultancies is in their internal operations. For example:

- **Digital separates expertise from people**, thus breaking the link between the employees and revenue. Increasingly, clients are paying recurring fees for access to knowledge assets such as software, apps, databases and multimedia resources. Once these are built, then – in the words of one founder I interviewed – 'they print profit because there are virtually no costs'.

- **Digital has vastly reduced marketing costs and improved targeting.** You can now ensure that your ads are only seen by your niche audience, paying only for potential clients that actually show an interest in your marketing. It is now possible to capture audiences of thousands of potential clients using 280 Tweeted characters. The decades-old advice that formal marketing should be saved until a firm has 500+ employees now looks particularly odd.[8]

- **Contractor marketplaces have collapsed the cost of administration.** Using Fiverr or Amazon Turk, you can build a website for £50, integrate eCommerce for £100 and find the email addresses of 100 leads for £20. Some would-be coaches repeat this process dozens of times just to find a promising niche.

- **Professional Service Automation (PSA) means that firms can spend less time and money on administration.** Used well, PSA systems such as Avaza will help increase project margins, increase day rates, reduce non-billable headcount and increase utilisation rates.

The speed of change is evident in how quickly previous consultancy guides have aged. One excellent 21st-century book, *How to Succeed as an Independent Consultant*,[9] contains a whole chapter on writing brochures, but only one paragraph on emails. The book's small section on IT focuses on modems, facsimile machines and tape drives. Alan Weiss' introductory book on consulting contains the phrase: 'you can't pay the mortgage with numbers of links, followers and friends'.[10] You might want to tell that to Vlad and Nikita who earn £240,000 for *every YouTube video* they make.[11] Or closer to home, Cardone, Vaynerchuk, Ramsey, Tracy, Forleo and countless other business advisors, who have become multimillionaires primarily from clicks and followers. This may not be traditional consulting, but the lines, as we shall see, are becoming blurred.

When Maister and Scott wrote their books, the global consulting industry was six times smaller than it is today and the primary focus of the authors was big strategy partnerships. It was reasonable for Maister to write 'few large consultancies have tapped into the power of the microcomputer' (p. 202). The consulting world and its clients were vastly different:

- The Big Four (then the Big Six) hadn't started doing consulting work in any significant form.

- Procurement departments bought only office supplies and hadn't started hammering down prices on professional services.

- Many clients were still relatively naïve in their use of consultants and there was little competition for their attention, thus little need for service differentiation and business development efforts – 'sales' was a dirty word back then.

- Founders of consulting firms were generally experienced (what Maister called 'grey hairs') ex-partners from large firms, and there were not that many of them. In contrast, the average age of my interviewees when they founded their firm was 40.

- Small firm marketing targeted its local vicinity and grew only as regional offices began to emerge.

- The 'grow to sell' business model was rare for consultancies. Maister, for example, argues the primary reason for firm growth is to meet the promotion ambitions of junior consultants rather than for founders to retire early (although it is debatable whether this was ever true).

Unsurprisingly then, many of the lessons that Maister and Scott provide are now out of date and there is little modern, evidence-based help for small consultancies that want to successfully grow their firms.

The consulting world has also changed in ways that are unconnected to digital. A few years ago, I interviewed the CEOs and managing partners of the top 20 consulting firms in the world and asked them about change in the profession. They all had the same worries: increased competition, the rise of procurement, more sophisticated clients and increasingly demanding graduate recruits, all meant that profit margins had been declining for some time. This, in turn, meant that utilisation levels and leverage ratios were up and investment in important things like innovation and training were down. Yet, when you ask clients what they most look for in a consulting firm, the #1 answer is 'innovation'![12] These pressures on the top firms are good news for smaller ones, whose size means they can provide a more tailored service, greater responsiveness and more access to senior partners. For this reason, the growth of smaller firms has trebled that of the larger ones in the last five years, as disillusioned and overworked experts leave the treadmill of the giants and seek to reap the benefits of their own hard (and often more interesting) work.

What and how?

What this book does

This book will help you grow a high value firm by explaining how the drivers of that value can be maximised (Figure 1.1). The second line of the figure shows how value is calculated by buyers or investors, and can also been seen as a proxy for a well-run, valuable firm for those not interested in selling. The base of the calculation is its earnings before interest, taxes, depreciation and amortization (EBITDA) over a period of three years and its forecast for the same period.[13] Yet it is important to remember that the quants aren't everything,

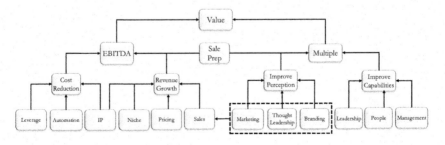

Figure 1.1 The value hierarchy.

or indeed *most* of the thing. The *multiple* paid of EBITDA has a more significant impact on the final valuation of the firm, and this is primarily assessed on qualitative factors that we will later delve into in some detail. Finally, the preparation for sale, discussed in Chapter 9, can do much to boost the final price paid for the firm.

In financial terms, this book aims to help small consultancies to grow revenues to the £5–10 million range (when founders typically begin to think about selling), to achieve EBITDA of over 20% and gross margin of over 50% and to grow at a steady and reasonably predictable rate. It is not necessary to do everything detailed in this book in order to grow or sell a firm. Some firms, for example, succeed without clear values and strong thought leadership because they have valuable assets (intellectual property and people) in massive demand with very limited supply (think Artificial Intelligence or Big Data). Valuable assets can prompt buyers to overlook the company's weaknesses. However, those few who achieved the best deals for the sale of the company were those who had (intentionally or otherwise) ticked most of the boxes in this book.

Not all CEOs/Managing Partners want to sell part or all of their company, of course. However, one of the key principles I follow in this book is that, even if you do not want to sell your firm (or do not know if you could), it is still worth starting off with a sale or investment as an explicit goal: whether you sell or not, having an exit vision as a guiding light will provide you and your senior team with more focus, direction and energy than simply 'seeing how it goes'. It will ensure that you actually do the strategic work that will make your life easier in the long term rather than chasing the short-term client wins. It will also prevent your firm being a result of happenstance.

My experience of advising firms on growth also suggests that deciding to sell later without having done the groundwork can be incredibly difficult. I concur with one M&A advisor who told me:

> we frequently get founders who are coming up to retirement come to us and ask us to sell their firms – which are often very profitable. It's quite heart-breaking when we tell them that the firm is worth nothing without them. At best, with these firms, it can take another two years and a lot of work to shape them into something that is sellable.

Founders who decide to sell later in the process will generally take much longer to get to the sale and their valuation is often much lower. They often find that buyers are interested only in one specific asset or service rather than the company as a whole. For every one of these firms that managed to salvage some sellable assets, there were dozens of similar ones where the founder endured all the pains of the labour of growth but none of its fruits. Throughout this book,

I build on the philosophy that it is better to design the company strategically as a valuable asset from the beginning and not let happenstance and luck or founder biases and blind-spots entirely dictate the growth strategy.

It is also important to remember that there are several options for exit. The biggest proportion of my interviewees and the market as a whole sell to strategic buyers (usually other consultancies), but a large proportion sell stakes in their firm to private equity (PE) and very few accept a management buy-out (which usually creates a lower price but maintains the culture)[14]. Only one of my samples, Elixirr, rejected offers from buyers, and instead floated on the AIM stock exchange.

Finally, it is also necessary to clarify what this book does not do. It is not focused on the soft skills of *being* a consultant and assumes the reader is familiar with things such as how to write a proposal and pitch an idea. For those without this kind of experience, there are already many excellent resources available.[15] Neither does this book cover the legalities of setting up a firm, nor try to provide the detailed, personalised advice that firms ought to seek a year or two before a sale (though see Chapter 9). I also want to stress that growing a consulting firm, especially for sale, can mean making considerable sacrifices for a decade or more of your life, and is especially challenging in the early years.

The evidence base

The evidence base of this book is significant and combines original research with my own professional experience. I have been, and continue to be, a consultant in a variety of contexts. I have coached countless small consultancies to achieve significant growth and taught over 2,000 international executives, partners and MBAs on different aspects of the consulting industry. As a Professor of Consulting, I have, since 2004, researched and written about the consulting industry, interviewing and surveying hundreds of partners, as well as analysing thousands of evidence-based reports, articles and books. Those publications (including a few of my own!) that are useful to this topic will be cited in this book, as will any online resources. Where useful, I have pointed the reader to additional free resources from my own firms, at www.joeomahoney.com and www.consultingmastered.com.

Most importantly, in preparation for this book, I interviewed 72 successful consultancy[16] owners, who had sold their practices in the period 2020–2021 and founded them post-2020. With the agreement of the interviewees, some of these are available at www.joeomahoney.com. The timeframe is important because the rise of digital, as we shall see, has transformed the landscapes of firm growth, investment and sales.[17] In addition, I interviewed 15 consultancy owners who had won independent awards (for example, Best Places to Work) or gained significant recognition (for example, FT fastest growing firm) and over 20 'unsuccessful' consultancy owners.[18] The latter are included because understanding what went wrong can be as important as understanding success, and helps both weed out bad practices and identify 'hygiene' factors (i.e. the things that all consultancies do which are necessary but insufficient for success). In addition, I interviewed three providers of PSA software and the CEOs of nine companies that purchased consulting firms (four PE and five consulting firms).[19] I also surveyed these and others to put some numbers behind the qualitative analysis.

To give an initial impression, the firms themselves were very different. All were consultancies, but had different services, sector specialisms, digital offerings and business models. As a result, their profiles were equally different. The averages are shown in Table 1.1 and the range of employees is shown in Figure 1.2.

Table 1.1 Averaged firm metrics (prior to sale)

# Employees	62	Years in business	12
% Associates	18%	EBITDA	28%
Staff turnover	15%	Savings in bank (business costs)	Four months
Revenue	£14 million	Average day rate	£720
Founder earnings	£119,000	Average partner rate	£1,950

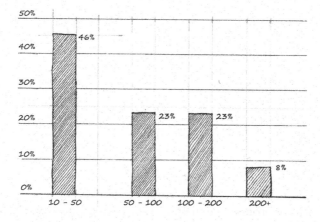

Figure 1.2 Number of employees of small consultancies prior to sale (my data).

If you are growing towards a sale, I would advise against comparing your figures with these too closely. Not only was the standard deviation high, but these were the figures just prior to sale. It would be akin to comparing your house right now to a house for sale that was expecting potential buyers to visit at any minute. Things tend to be cleaned and polished.

I should also stress here that these 'successful' consulting firms were by no means perfect. Most of those I interviewed said that they would do things differently if they had their time again, and almost all founders emphasised the role of luck in their achievements. Also, from my own perspective, all but one of the firms could have improved their final price and their profitability by making different choices: better pricing, more ambitious growth, greater use of employees instead of contractors, stronger emphasis on culture and better systems earlier were all things many of the firms could have done to effect better growth. You don't have to be perfect to be successful; you just need to be among the best among comparable, available firms at the right time.

The growth landscape

The growth of the small consultancy sector

Having outlined the purpose of this book, I spend a little time here outlining the context of small consultancies and their position in the wider economy.

The growth of small and medium-sized enterprises (SMEs) is fundamental to a healthy, vibrant economy. Indeed, as a McKinsey & Co. study argues, 'better understanding and improving the SME ecosystem [by] enabling the growth of SMEs' is a central part of solving the productivity gap in many countries'.[20] An important part of the growth ecosystem is small management consultancies, which represent around 97% of all consulting firms.[21] The growth of SME consultancies is, on average, 20% per annum – four times the rate of the largest consultancies – and their numbers are growing at around 10% a year (compared to negative growth of large consultancies due to consolidation).[22] It should also be emphasised that consultancy is primarily, still, a Western phenomenon, with around 70% of consulting revenue coming from just five countries (USA, Canada, UK, Germany, France). However, this is shifting quite rapidly as other countries develop and Westernise their markets.

An average of 2,000 consultancies are sold worldwide each year, which is less than 0.1% of the total market. If we assume that 40% of the 'sold' figure undertake other forms of profitable exit (for example, management buy-out [MBO]; retirement but continued ownership) and that it takes an average of 12 years to grow a consultancy to sale, then the approximate number of consultancies that are successfully grown for some form of earnings-based exit is around 1.5% of the total. This chimes well with the figure that 97% of consultancies have fewer than three people in them, perhaps leaving a remaining 1.5% that represent the big players that generally buy rather than sell.

The drivers of growth in the small consulting market are diverse. Large firms are less attractive places for experienced talent than they were 20 years ago. First, there is the pressure on fees. This has come from many sources: the extension of the procurement department from laptops and paperclips to professional services has put a damper on the quality and innovation of consulting projects, but also on prices.[23] Second, buyers are much more experienced and sophisticated now, and more likely to negotiate on scope and price. Finally, the increase in the number of consulting firms and the movement of large firms from specialists to generalists corresponds with an increase in competition. These factors have placed pressure on fees, especially at larger firms, and led to an erosion of profit margins and a slowing of pay increases (especially relative to the competitors for talent: banks and big technology firms).

The declining rates of profits in larger firms, combined with the recessions of 2000, 2008 and 2020–2021, mean that, in many firms, partners have not seen great returns on their investments and have occasionally had to reach into their own pockets to ensure the survival of their firms. One consequence of fee and margin pressure has been the commodification of consulting services in larger firms. Outside of the strategy giants, consulting firms can no longer (generally) rely on increasingly high day rates, and so their strategy has focused on maximising leverage by using younger (and thus cheaper) resources and IT to generate highly productised[24] services. One result of this has been the increase in utilisation rates (which has driven out some very talented but overworked employees) and another has been a decrease in personalised, innovative services upon which firms like McKinsey & Co. used to pride themselves.[25]

The culmination of these pressures is that many seniors wonder if there is an easier life running their own firm and pocketing some of the client fees that they see going to partners or shareholders. As utilisation hits 80%–90%, many rightly think that growing their own firm may not be much more work but with greater returns and job satisfaction. Even aside from those who left voluntarily, the redundancies associated with COVID-19 filled the start-up market with a cohort of skilled, ambitious consultants with decent client networks.

Yet, when starting new firms, founders, ex-consultants or otherwise are also impacted by socio-economic trends. Standardisation and increased competition means that there is a growing divide between more commodified 'known knowns' – things which clients could often do for themselves if they had time or resource (such as process work or social media) – and the 'known unknowns' – which clients know they need but have no expertise in (for example, M&A or big data analysis). Firms in the former group have become highly commodified and day rates have not moved significantly for a decade or so. Although there have been some recent moves to improve the procurement obstacles of small consultancies in some countries, larger clients feel big brands are a safer bet and often do not differentiate the impact of bureaucratic hoops on smaller firms. As a result, Knaup estimates that 45% of small management consulting firms fail within their first five years[26].

This said, the news is not all bad. First, a lot of larger consultancies that have lost their best people and don't have the time, resources or culture for cutting-edge innovation are now more likely to buy smaller firms to fill these gaps. Second, PE has shifted its attitudes to investing in professional services significantly over the last ten years, and the high margins and plentiful cash that good consultancies generate are now hotly contested. Third, the international spread of consulting means that many medium-sized firms that would have happily remained in their nation of origin are now being forced by client demands to grow quickly overseas. Buying a smaller firm in a target country is the quickest way of demonstrating international competence to growing clients. Fourth, it appears that clients have noticed the commodification of larger firms and are turning to smaller firms for innovation, creativity and sometimes just lower fees. Finally, as I detail throughout this book, digital has transformed the small firm's capacity to reduce costs, increase efficiency and offer value to clients.

A final trend worth noticing which has affected consultancies small and large is the slowly expanding international reach of the consulting industry. Fifteen years ago, 80% of consulting spend came from five large Western countries; that figure is now 70% and set to drop further as consulting expands out of the North American and Western European markets. As clients have expanded internationally, so too have consultancies. Fukuyama may have been wrong in his prediction that the world would converge towards liberal democratic capitalism, but consultancies have certainly found ways to adapt to Middle Eastern and Asian demands, and the liberalisation of these economies means that these markets are expanding at twice the rate of Western ones. As growth in Western markets slows, the eyes of consultancies based there are on foreign horizons.

S-curves and inflection points

In management theory, professional service firms are said to grow through a series of S-shaped stages from their founding through to billion-dollar multinationals. The S-shapes (Figure 1.3) are theorised because each stage of growth prompts new challenges which impact growth, causing the leaders to invest time and resources into structural (for example, governance, organisational, financial) solutions.[27] These, in turn, lead to a period of accelerated growth, which once again stalls when new problems are encountered.[28]

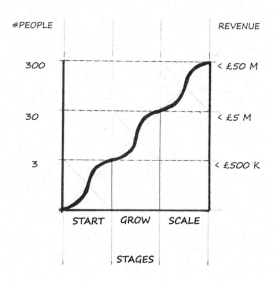

Figure 1.3 S-curve theory.

In practice, things are often different. Two-thirds of the founders I interviewed said they did not notice a plateauing of revenues due to reasons other than bad luck (for example, losing a large client) or recessions. The reasons for this are: first because successful founders tend to anticipate future challenges and take premeditated action to avoid issues, and second because Professional Service Firm automation software has reduced the bureaucracy needed for growth (I explore this further in Chapter 7). As founders can typically pay for this software by the user, the investment is gradual rather than focused on any specific growth point. Finally, it is also the case that many small firms that *might* have experienced a plateau ended up selling before they got to that point. Several founders explicitly told me that they did not like dealing with detailed systems, hierarchies or bureaucracy, and therefore sold before the firms ever required these kinds of investments.

The inflection point that *was* evident in many firms was less concerned with revenue and more to do with productivity. In the start-up phase, founders are doing everything and have no need for anything but the most basic planning systems. They are usually happy to burn the midnight oil in order to get clients that are happy to generate testimonials and referrals, and growth based on this and their own personal connections are often exponential. The next phase, the growth phase, is often when founders are pulled in different directions. One of the founders I coach told me (only yesterday):

> We're trying to generate sales for growth, but also know that we need to build the systems to support this....We're trying to get our new hires up to speed, but also trying to deliver. There just isn't enough time in the day.

Sadly, there are no easy answers to this, which is why the growth phase is the hardest phase to complete successfully. In addition, in the first two phases, many firms are still working out what their core services really should be. The final stage, when the key services are in place and there are some formal systems to delegate and manage work, is the scale phase, and it is here that things get a little easier for founders. If they have built the right engine, it is *generally* a matter of a steady hand on the wheel, sufficient fuel and an occasional service.[29]

This said, even when profits are not hit, there is still often a clear point where many report a fundamental change in the firm. This typically happens when the firm has grown to around 20–30 staff. After this point, things get a little complicated, and the informal communication and management systems that worked in the beginning begin to fall apart:

ANGREZ SARAN OF 8WORKS: 'we got to 20 people when sharing the administrative work across your leadership team of three or four people was really hard. We were being pulled into do quite tactical things, which just didn't make sense. So we made a conscious decision to actually outsource as much of it as possible and then bring in support. We enhanced our operations capability by bringing on an additional person'.

LOGAN NAIDU OF DARTMOUTH PARTNERS: 'we got stuck about 20 to 30 person mark for almost two years. I simply couldn't feed work to everyone at that size. We didn't have enough great salespeople. And we just didn't have any infrastructure'.

ANGIE OF VIRGO: 'we found ourselves at 30 people where it's the perfect size agent. You've got great mix of clients, a nice mix of people, but you can be in touch, and all over all events. You have to move into a different way of running the business after this'.

Those companies that successfully grew beyond this point did so by bringing in more formal, professional systems. PSA software, a new layer of management, formal training, roles, reporting and specialists in HR and finance, all helped ease the transition required by the increase in personnel. Yet consultants are also aware that this transition can mean a fundamental change in the *type* of firm. Moving from a fast-paced entrepreneurial firm to a steadier, process-driven company attracts a different type of recruit. By this stage, you may have exhausted the equity you are prepared to share, and this again changes the type of person you might be bringing on – perhaps more junior and incentivised by money rather than ownership. I explore this later in Chapters 7 and 8, but here it is sufficient to say that the more you can anticipate and prepare for this transition, the more smoothly it will go. The alternative is to exit before that point and leave the more formalised organisation to different leadership!

How long does it take from founding to sale?

Whilst the fastest route to sale I have seen is three years (a cloud data advisory firm), and two of the firms interviewed took five years, the average duration of those I've studied or been involved with is 12 years. The things that make a difference to speed are not surprising and in order of importance include:

- An early plan to sell within a fixed period of time with ambitious, early growth targets

- Mindset, hard work and a relentless focus on sales

- Moving to the right niche and pivoting fast when that niche is no longer ideal

- Luck

- Recruiting, onboarding, training and delegating to the right people

- Developing the right services

These are all explained in more detail in this book, but I should reiterate the role of luck here, at least in accelerating growth. Most of the successful consultancies I interviewed were lucky in some way, and many of them were happy to admit it. Luck manifests in many ways of course, but the most powerful lucky break is getting a large ongoing client early on – one that both drives and funds growth. Other forms of luck include leaving a large firm and being allowed to take your clients with you, finding the perfect partner early on or doing a form of consulting (service or sector) that happens to be in great demand after a few years.

Fast growth does however raise the issue of risk, ethics and stress. Concerning risk, typically, the faster the growth, the greater chance of failure, since not only do these fast-growing firms tend to borrow more, they may also neglect to take the time needed to put the infrastructure and processes in place to support the firm's expansion. If these are not addressed, the earn-out period for directors is longer and the multiple paid is lower, because buyers recognise those risks and seek to mitigate them.

Concerning ethics, many fast-growing firms decide to diversify into areas in which they do not have high levels of experience, possibly using juniors to do work for which they are not qualified, with a view that they can build competence as they go. This is a balance every founder must strike for themselves and their employees. Finally, concerning stress, the long hours that must be worked to achieve fast growth are, for many, too stressful to be sustained for long. Some (for example, Chris Gibson at Pen Partnership) deliberately opt for a slower growth trajectory so that they can achieve a more relaxed working environment and achieve higher quality deliverables with lower risk. As we see later, others who have grown and sold incredibly fast (three to five years) have acknowledged the personal stress that they experienced and the impact it had upon their families.

Growth challenges of ambitious consultancies

In this book I explore various challenges to growth and how they can be overcome. I felt it would be useful to bring together the most common obstacles here:

1. **A failure to fill the ever-expanding pipeline.** I deal with this in Chapter 6, but suffice to say that unless quality sales are made a central feature of the culture, systems, targets and competences of the firm, cash flow will cripple the firm when the first recession or big client loss occurs. A coherent marketing infrastructure with consistent, targeted content will pay dividends in the long run.

2. **A reluctance to systematise.** A common challenge is when an expanding firm outruns its processes. There comes a point when it is impossible to operate a firm with a mix of 'what is in the partners' heads' and a few spreadsheets. The consequence of not preparing for this shift is poor quality delivery, low utilisation and declining margins. I examine this in some detail in Chapter 7.

3. **A reluctance to pivot when the market shifts or gets saturated.** Sure, you're great at process-re-engineering, but so are 1,400 other consultancies and the day rates haven't shifted since 1993. How about learning a bit of Agile, Lean or Scrum? I provide some tactics for reframing and repositioning in Chapters 3 and 4.

4. **Not managing your knowledge sufficiently.** While I go into pricing in some detail in Chapter 5, the only sure-fire way to continuously increase your prices is to generate continuously higher value. You do this by better capturing, storing and sharing the experience and expertise that you and the market generate. If you do this and have confidence in yourself, you can, and should, price at the top of the market.

5. **A failure to manage costs.** Good consultants are expensive, so you need to make the most of them. Measuring utilisation, project margins and the cost of sales are crucial to ensuring you understand which clients, projects or teams involve weightier overheads. Processes which enable delegation will allow your lower paid staff to step up to the plate without diminishing quality. I cover cost management throughout this book.

6. **Ignoring culture.** Many of the more 'self-confident' partners may think culture is for 'sandal-wearing tofu-munchers' (as an old boss of mine put it). However, what they don't realise is that culture doesn't become irrelevant simply because you don't manage it. Instead, you can end up with a dysfunctional culture that will increase staff turnover and make your management and staffing costs higher. In Chapters 3 and 8, I show how culture is central to attracting and keeping great staff, but also minimising bureaucracy.

Exit

I go into some detail about exit strategies in Chapter 9, but a brief overview would be useful here. Founders are rightly proud of their past achievements, but buyers or investors care only for the future. Strategic buyers (usually larger consultancies) are a little fussier. A strategic buyer will want to see that your services are profitable but will usually be focused on how these can add synergies with their existing offerings – usually cross-selling or filling gaps. Sia Partners, for example, has bought several firms over the last five years in order to speed up their ability to offer their services internationally. To this end, it is useful, certainly in the two to three years before a sale, to think about specific firms that you might sell to and what gaps or synergies you might maximise to be most attractive to them.

PE buyers, which now account for around 40% of purchases, see your firm as a profit generating asset that (they hope) will generate (discounted) future returns in excess of the upfront price that they paid. It should be noted that PE generally focuses on larger valuations, and the 40% figure includes strategic purchases made by firms that are owned by PE. In practice, most sellers focus on strategic buyers because satisfying the needs of a strategic buyer is usually a pre-requisite to achieving the financial requirements of a PE buyer. In addition, another 2% of founders I've studied or supported simply wanted to keep their firm growing without selling control of the firm and a further 2% exited through an MBO. We discuss these in Chapter 9.

As we see later, there are nuanced differences in what strategic buyers, MBOs and PE look for, but these are not significant. At the front end, a strong, passionate team should be delivering relatively unique, high-margin consulting to great clients. At the back end, you need strong, improving systems and processes in all the major functions (governance, IP, marketing, sales, talent and leadership) in order to deliver this value. The rest of this book is dedicated to detailing how to achieve this.

Where do we go from here?

This book is structured around the major themes which increase the value of a firm. At the beginning of most chapters, I have a small section on what buyers and investors look for in that area. I urge you to read these even if you have no intention of selling your firm, as what buyers are looking for is simply a good consultancy[30] – although see Chapter 9 for exceptions. At the end of every chapter, I've detailed the main takeaways, as I realise that the busy entrepreneur may not have time to read this book in one sitting.

Takeaways

- There is a deficiency of evidence-based books on growing consulting firms

- The world has changed considerably since the guru of consulting, David Maister, stopped writing

- Digital has transformed the external markets for and internal capabilities of consultancies

- This book will help ambitious partners in small firms maximise their firm's value for investment or sale

- This book is based on 72 interviews with founders who sold their firms, a survey of 221 founders, 15 years' experience of coaching and advising small firms on growth and feedback from the 2,000 or so consultants, partners and MBAs I have taught and coached over the years.

Notes

1 For those of you uninitiated in the cynical methods of online publishing, see here for how to create a 'Number One Best-Seller' with a blank book. https://bit.ly/3rBnuMA.

2 O'Mahoney, J., & Sturdy, A. (2016) Power and the diffusion of management ideas: The case of McKinsey & Co. *Management Learning, 47*(3), 247–265.

3 If you doubt this, please glance at the *Journal of Organization Studies* or the *Academy of Management Review*, two of the top targets for management academics. They are generally unreadable.

4 SBA (2006) *The Small Business Economy for Data Year 2005*. Report prepared by the US Small Business Administration. Washington, DC: US Government Printing Office.

5 Thus when consulting firms buy others, they generally do not do so in order to add fee-earning capacity, but expertise, cross-selling, client access and intellectual property.

6 FT (2020) *Europe's Fastest Growing Companies*. London: *Financial Times Report*. (https://www.ft.com/reports/europes-fastest-growing-companies).

7 FEACO (2019) *Survey of the European MC market*. FEACO.com.

8 Scott, M. (1998) *The Professional Service Firm*. London: John Wiley, p. 49.

9 Holtz, H., & Zahn, D. (2004) *How to Succeed as an Independent Consultant*. London: John Wiley.

10 Weiss, A. (2019) *Getting Started in Consulting*. London: John Wiley.

11 Oh, and they're aged six and four. The videos are them playing with toys. And they've made £54 million so far.

12 O'Mahoney, J. (2013) Management innovation in the UK consulting industry. In: Haynes, K. & Grugulis, I. eds. *Managing Services: Challenges and Innovation*. Oxford: Oxford University Press, pp. 83–104.

13 Earnings before interest, taxes, depreciation and amortization is a more reliable estimate of the real profits generated by the firm because it excludes things (i.e. the 'ITDA') that vary depending on country, financing structure or investment decisions.

14 The US has a higher concentration of PE buyers compared to strategic buyers.

15 If you're not very experienced, visit www.consultingmastered.com for my course on running a successful solo consultancy or buy one of the dozens of books on getting started in consulting (I especially recommend Peter Block or David Fields).

16 Most interviewees founded management consultancies, but I also included research consultancies, IT and technology consultancies and financial consulting firms.

17 Some of my hardest clients are those who sold their own firms prior to 2000 and are seeking to do the same thing again. Now that investors have the option of funding software companies and platforms, which attract much higher multiples, the threshold for an 'investible' firm in any sector is much higher. Moreover, digital has completely transformed the effectiveness and costs of operations, sales and marketing.

18 Defined as generating profits for three years or more in the bottom 20% of all small consultancies.

19 Permission was sought in advance to use cited quotes and other information, and where this was not provided, I have kept the sources anonymous. If you wish to see longer excerpts from the interviews, these will be available at joeomahoney.com soon.

20 Albaz, A., Dondi, M., Rida, T., & Schubert, J. (2020) *Unlocking Growth in Small and Medium-Size Enterprise*. Article: McKinsey & Co.

21 IBISWORLD (2019) *Global Management Consultants Industry - Market Research Report*. London: IBIS.

22 MCA (2019) *UK Management Consulting Industry Report*. London: Management Consultancies Association.

23 O'Mahoney, J. (2011). Management Innovation in the UK Consulting Industry. Report for the Chartered Management Institute.

24 In consulting terms, a product is a more standardised, commodified version of a service. As discussed in Chapter 5, it maximises leverage and tends to generate more predictable, consistent results.

25 O'Mahoney, J. (2013) Management innovation in the UK consulting industry. In: Haynes, K. & Grugulis, I. eds. *Managing Services: Challenges and Innovation*. Oxford: Oxford University Press, pp. 83–104.

26 Knaup, A. E. (2005) Survival and longevity in the business employment dynamics data. *Monthly Labor Review*, 128, 50.

27 Phelps, R., Adams, R., & Bessant, J. (2007) Life cycles of growing organizations: A review with implications for knowledge and learning. *International Journal of Management Reviews*, 9(1), 1–30.

28 Despite S-curve theories of business growth being taught in most business schools, there is scant *empirical* evidence for this 'stage model'. As I have generally focused on successful firms, many of which sell before getting to an inflection point, my own evidence in this book is insufficient to test the hypothesis.

29 You can see why I get annoyed with all the internet advice on 'scaling' a firm! Unless you are a solo consultant or coach with primarily digital services, there is a lot of pain involved before you can get to the scaling phase.

30 Unfortunately, everyone exits, eventually.

2
Leading for growth

What are investors and acquirers looking for?

Let us begin with the question of what buyers of consulting firms look for in a leadership team. Greg Alexander, CEO of Capital 54, told me that with smaller firms he always bets on the people, not the service, because the latter is likely to change significantly. Elixirr founder, CEO, and occasional buyer of consultancies, Steve Newton, similarly told me 'I want passionate, committed people dedicated to delivering value for their clients'. For smaller firms, then, buyers and investors generally invest in the leadership team more than the assets of the firm.

Personal characteristics aside, buyers will also be concerned with the track record of the leadership team, and especially the CEO. Have they built successful firms before? Do they have leadership and management skills beyond simply being good consultants? Are they control freaks or can they delegate to responsible and empowered reports? Is there real leadership or are choices made by voting or committee?

The focus of buyers shifts as the organisation grows because value becomes more dependent on the intellectual property in the firm rather than individuals. Here, leadership is demonstrated less in the drive, motivation and achievements of individuals, and more in the processes which link the strategy and vision of the firm with the goals and key performance indicators (KPIs) that are cascaded through the organisation. This gradual shift from people to systems is one that is challenging for many founders, as eventually they must loosen their controls over what is happening. If a firm is highly dependent upon the relationships, expertise, knowledge and decision-making of partners, there is an obvious point of failure. With larger firms then, buyers want to see systems and processes which allow for high levels of delegation. As one buyer told me 'I ask myself, "if any of the leadership team were to leave immediately would

DOI: 10.4324/9781003149217-2

it significantly impact operations?" If the answer is yes, [the firm] won't get on the short-list'. My own experience indicates that this is truer of strategic buyers and less true of private equity investors, as the latter generally assumes the leadership team will be staying on for some time.

In most acquisitions, an earn-out period ensures the leadership team works for the buyer for two to three years, aiming to hit revenue and margin targets in exchange for the remainder of the purchase fee. If you are keen on minimising your earn-out, it is important to develop strong internal systems and processes which allow senior roles to be disassociated from the individuals who currently occupy them. This means the firm as a whole needs to move away from reliance on tacit knowledge – the advice, expertise and instincts held in the heads of seniors – to formal processes and systems – an internal form of intellectual property (which we examine in Chapter 5). This said, some strategic buyers have told me that they are only interested in firms where the founders are still passionate about the firm and want to stay on as part of the leadership team and achieve more with additional resources.

The risk for the buyer is not simply one of revenue, but also that they are recruiting several senior hires who can disrupt the culture and performance of the acquirer. Therefore, it should not be surprising that most buyers I interviewed not only emphasised a competent leadership team with a strong track record, but also a team that would 'fit' with the buyers' culture (I cover this in Chapter 8).

Buyers will also be concerned that the senior team are committed to making the sale work and not firing out their CVs as soon as they hear of the purchase (although PE are more concerned about this than strategic buyers). Therefore, a good spread of equity across key people will reassure buyers, especially if there will be an earn-out – some buyers talk about an ideal of 20% of the total equity distributed to people who are central to growth. Buyers will also look at the company culture and the churn of senior people in the firm to get an idea how motivated and committed employees are. Buyers generally interview key personnel in the firm as part of due diligence. Having a clear communication strategy and plan long before the sale is agreed is, therefore, important.

Finally, and especially with reference to private equity, investors will sometimes see your firm as one among many that they will be purchasing to develop a larger offering. If this is the case, they will be looking at leaders of acquisitions to see if any of them can 'step up' to lead the merger and operations of the larger entity. This is worth bearing in mind, if you *do* have experience of running larger firms or leading mergers, you may have considerable value to the buyer beyond your firm.

The founder mindset

Mindset traps

When Bain & Co. asked firms that were unsuccessful in their growth ambitions what went wrong, they found that 85% of senior executives blamed internal issues such as organisational complexity, a cultural aversion to risk, insufficient resources or lack of focus. Only 15% blamed the failure on external factors such as market conditions.[1] Their argument, in brief, is that young insurgent firms who are fast, innovative, passionate and energetic become mired in meetings, bureaucracy and risk-aversion. My own interviews with less successful consultancies confirm the hypothesis, but I would go further than Bain & Co. I argue that the biggest internal reason for failure involved the limits of the founder's mindset. Before getting onto what mindsets were common in *successful* firms, I here outline five common 'mindset traps' that often trip up founders.

The Great Consultant trap

The 'Great Consultant' believes that because they were a successful consultant in a large firm, they will easily be a successful CEO of their own firm. This is not always a conscious thought, but often manifests itself in a certain over-confidence about one's capabilities, or an aversion to engaging in those activities to which one is not adept (typically building internal processes). At least once a month I am approached by a partner or founder who believes their firm is ready for sale simply because it is making high profit margins. In the majority of these calls it becomes clear the firm is a collection of individuals who are good at selling and delivering, but where there is minimal value in the firm itself. On the rare occasions buyers consider these purchases, they frame it as buying a team rather than a business, and on a much lower multiple with an earn-out period of up to five years.

The Bureaucratic trap

The Bureaucratic trap happens when the firm grows to a size (often 35+) where the early entrepreneurial and aggressive focus on sales starts to become a bureaucratic mindset. The key distinction here is between forward-looking management and backward-looking reporting. The vision of the firm becomes lost in an avalanche of reporting, box-ticking and report writing. The voices of managers get louder and the voices of those making the sales get crowded out.

Whilst systems and processes become crucial as the firm grows, some firms seem intent on mirroring the founder's experience at much larger companies: the CEO often thinks that 'this is normal' because that is what they did at their previous Big Four company. I can only stress that excessive bureaucracy leads to death by a thousand cuts: meetings expand, documents multiply and there are simply too many data points reported.

I am occasionally asked to observe board meetings where there will be ten or more people present, all of whom want to talk. It often becomes evident that board meetings have turned into a reporting exercise where a dozen or so metrics are pored over. Often, no one talks about clients or margins, new opportunities or the pipeline. What typically happens here is that bills go up due to administration and revenues go down due to the shift of focus away from growth. If the issue isn't addressed directly and dramatically, the firm is likely to fold in on the weight of operating costs. When I meet founders who are in the bureaucracy trap, I ask them if their younger self would join the firm that they have now created (a question I borrowed from Bain's James Allen). The answer is usually 'no' because the firm has lost its vigour. This is not to argue that systems and processes are redundant, but their development does need to match the size of the firm and should always be driven by the goal of future sales and growth rather than past reporting and bureaucracy. Think lean and agile rather than public sector.

The Genius trap

In his book *Outliers*, Malcolm Gladwell showed that genius, at the wrong time and in the wrong place, dies a sad death. I would extend this argument to argue that super-bright people rarely make the best business entrepreneurs.

I was once asked to help a large IT/consulting firm with their innovation management. The firm spent around £10 billion on innovation every year and had employed several Nobel Prize winners on their technology teams, so my hopes obviously weren't high that I could add anything. Yet, on meeting the geniuses (and I use the term literally) it was clear that they weren't in the slightest bit interested in the firm or how they might contribute to its profitability by creating products that would add value to clients. Instead, they focused on creating technically astounding breakthroughs that might lead to top academic papers or even a Nobel Prize. When I got them together with the consultants who wanted the brainboxes to build things to solve client problems, the geniuses glazed over. I was reminded of the discos that my all-boys school arranged with the local girls school: lots of staring at the floor and nervous sweating.

Whilst there are exceptions, super-bright people are generally too interested in solving complex, often abstract, problems than the more mundane but crucial activities needed to grow a successful firm. As I detail later, this *does not* mean they should not start consultancies, but that they should be aware of their weaknesses and seek to partner with (and empower!) people who complement them.

The Super-Hero trap

The Super-Hero trap is created by a culture which turns specific employees (usually partners but often others) into legendary superheroes, who won THAT contract by flying in from Ulan Bator and not sleeping for three days. The trouble with such legends – even if true – is that they encourage a dependency on big personalities rather than systems and processes. What is worse is that these personalities are the very ones most likely to leave. In addition, these 'superheroes' often develop excessive sway in decision-making rather than focusing on what they are good at (usually sales). Greg Alexander, founder of SBI and now an investor in small consultancies, told me:

> founders who have grown a firm often become 'heroes', their employees love them, clients want to see them, and they often believe the firm can't run without them. This is exactly the opposite of what should happen. Eventually, they need to become unnecessary. Actually, they are often the wrong person to grow the firm beyond say the 100 employee mark. They are often entrepreneurs not process people.

The security trap

There is a final mindset for which I'm unsure there is a cure. The 'Security' trap involves a failure of founders to take sufficient risks in the early phases of growth. This is understandable, but in a cash-rich business that has virtually no capital expenditure, and where the average growth rate of the whole consulting market averages 7% per annum, the business risk is relatively low.

A firm I interviewed some time ago was what would now be called a cybersecurity strategy firm, started in the mid-1990s, with a focus on protecting digital assets. Everything about this firm screamed growth: they had an outstanding reputation for quality, years of experience and strong people. However, the founder has an aversion to risk born out of his own upbringing and has never wanted to recruit people, to borrow or take on projects outside of the company's core offering. The company isn't unsuccessful and has a handful of consultants (mostly family members) and a decent revenue base, but even if it had expanded at the market growth rate (let alone the cybersecurity growth rate!), they could have had revenues of £50+ million. What is more, they could have potentially sold for nearly double that and be drinking Pimm's on a yacht somewhere hot. To be clear, it was not a lifestyle choice, but an aversion to risk that determined their position.

I would also argue that aversion to risk is a significant drawback when it comes to intellectual property. Many solo consultants and founders I've coached and interviewed have often held back on sharing their expert knowledge or methods with potential clients for fear, in the words of one, that 'the client will just steal my ideas and do it themselves'. This means that their videos, publications and blogs are often devoid of depth, and even their conversations or pitches with clients are purposefully coy. Such attitudes assume that expert knowledge is a scarce commodity, but this overlooks the fact that pretty much any management challenge is now the subject of tomes of publicly available research, articles, videos and books. If anything, there is *too much* knowledge available. What is actually rare and valuable is the bespoke tailoring and implementation of expert knowledge and the brand value that comes with doing this consistently well. When you limit the display of your knowledge and expertise, you may simply be limiting your reputation as an expert (a problem I explore further in Chapter 6).

So, now we know which mindsets are dangers to the consulting entrepreneur and which ones are crucial to success? There appear to be three mindsets that were important to the success of my interviewees, but that remain a challenge for many founders.

A humble mindset

Let's face it, humility is not a character trait associated with consultancy. The bright young Oxbridge graduate snapped up by Boston Consulting Group and getting the attention of multinational boards at the age of 26 is not going to lack in confidence. However, after ten years honing their craft, becoming a world expert in a niche and effecting change in dozens of companies, it is easy for confidence to spill into… ahem… 'over-confidence'.

According to Equiteq founder, Paul Collins, the biggest challenge new founders have is shifting from the mindset of *doing* consulting to a business owner mindset. In our interview, he argued many founders who come from large consultancies are confident experts that struggle with being a novice in many areas. Damien Duhamel from Solidiance emphasises that importance of humility in adjusting one's mindset here:

> Small firms often say that they beat McKinsey in winning a bid. You did not beat McKinsey, you were just cheaper! It's important to be humble here –

we know that we are not a Rolls Royce, we are, say, an Audi. If you want expensive luxury then go for Rolls Royce, there is a market for all types but it is important to know who you are.

A common manifestation of the wrong mindset is a complete misconception of the firm's market positioning: who the competitors are, the quality of the people and service and what realistic pricing looks like. People without a humble mindset rarely let the facts about these things get in the way of their opinions.

Corporate consultants, whilst often working in a team, are often solitary and competitive creatures. Sadly, in many firms this gets worse the closer one gets to partner, where there is a greater incentive to hoard information, clients and good employees. A successful leader will need to manage this to avoid the hoarding of power. Crucially, this doesn't mean that communal decision-making is efficient. It isn't, and the ambitious founder should avoid this. However, successful growth usually involves:

- Delegating decision-making to the lowest possible level.
- Allowing subordinates to flourish by encouraging them to experiment and make mistakes.
- Having a CEO who focuses on orchestrating rather than looking over shoulders.[2]
- Sharing equity so the senior team is motivated to make a sale successful.

In addition to enabling a devolved, empowered workforce, humility also enables learning. An exploratory study of the relationship between humility and knowledge sharing found that 'humble inquiry and response can promote the creation of strong…relationships in a knowledge sharing process'.[3]

To develop this point, Mark Long, founder of Ignite, told me:

you must tell your students that it is a privilege to be asked into a client to help them through a stage of difficulty. If you ever lose that sense of humility, and develop the sense of arrogance that some consultants have, you will stop learning, and alienate clients.

For those struggling with humility, often the last to realise, it is worth reading *No Filter*,[4] an excellent book about the hubris of Silicon Valley, or *The Smartest Guys in the Room*,[5] about the rise and fall of Enron. Both show how near-genius insights by entrepreneurs led to great businesses being built, but that subsequent pride and arrogance led to failure. In the former case, founders such as Zuckerberg or Systrom created highly successful products but their single mindedness (Zuckerberg would end his meetings with a shout of 'Domination!') ultimately led to failure and lost opportunities. In the latter case, the arrogance and elitism built purposefully into the culture of Enron by the leaders lent itself to a disregard of both ethics and the law. As the Greeks used to say *Metron ariston*, everything in moderation: a balance between humility and confidence is perhaps ideal.

An entrepreneurial mindset

It is not surprising that entrepreneurialism is crucial to starting and growing a successful consultancy. In my interviews with consultancies that wanted to grow but failed to achieve this, however, the most common barrier to the entrepreneurial mindset was an aversion to risk. Employing people, borrowing money and investing in assets are inherently risky, but perhaps not as risky as many think. The small and medium-sized consulting market has grown over 15% a year for the last ten years (COVID-19 excepted), the cost of debt is at an all-time low and the costs of growing a consultancy are tiny compared to say a manufacturing firm (I know, I've tried both!). In this context, if you are providing a quality service in a high-demand market, a more relaxed attitude to risk is appropriate for fast growth.

Entrepreneurialism is less about creativity and innovation than it is about persistence, hard work and resilience. Mark Long, founder of Ignite, told me, 'sales is everything in our world. Having people who can hustle and find work is crucial'. He then reflected on the times he used to buy a pass to the first class lounge in airports so that he could intersperse his work with chatting to senior decision-makers – a strategy that he assures me paid off. Steve Newton, founder of Elixirr, talked on a similar theme, saying, 'I've hired a lot of senior people who want to sit in a room creating a proposition. I tell them to get out and talk to the client...Delivery is sales and sales is delivery'.

The entrepreneurial mindset focuses on front-line action (the client), heavy bets on rapid action (innovation) and a minimisation of costs (lean). It has a bias to action, a hatred of bureaucracy and a continuous bias towards change (see the Elixirr case for an example). Here, firms experiment a lot and then bet heavy on a few opportunities. The entrepreneurial mindset must infect the firm: they will need to recruit risk-takers over bureaucrats and encourage innovation in their culture, reward structures and HR processes.

All this said, entrepreneurialism needs to be in balance. Risk-taking and change will maximise growth, but as I detail in Chapter 7, growth is unsustainable without building processes, systems and structures. Often, entrepreneurial leaders will partner with or recruit a person with this attention to detail. For the same reason, the entrepreneur is rarely the person needed to grow the firm beyond the 100-employee mark where growth should be more dependent on systems than on individuals. When a firm has been bought, entrepreneurs often get uncomfortable working within the constraints of the buyer, so it is important to be realistic about this in the negotiations. It is better to leave early than fall out with the new owners. I discuss this further in Chapter 8.

The boss mindset

A common theme in this book, and the interviews which inform it, is the ability to shift from working as an employee to working as a boss of the firm. As detailed above, many founders are experienced and ambitious corporate consultants who strike out by themselves but have never had to run a company. The shift from working *on* the company rather than *for* the company requires a commitment to strategy, processes, planning, leadership and communication, which doesn't come naturally for many.

Interestingly, the boss mindset can also be a trap when the firm grows past 30 employees. As with all start-ups, founders are proud of their achievements, which are down, in no small part, to their own shouldering of most of the tasks. Even when in a small partnership, they are likely to have detailed involvement with every 'function' that a traditional firm performs. As we will see later, the trap comes when the firm grows too big for one person to capture and communicate all management information and make all important decisions. This is, after all, why larger firms have boards of directors. Mark Long, for example, admits that he 'struggled with this for some time'.

In summary, there is an interesting paradox at the heart of the founder's mindset. You need to be confident enough and have sufficient self-belief to take risks, lead a team and to 'go large' (as Angie Willies, founder of The Difference Collective, put it). At the same time, you need to be humble enough to accept the limits of your experience, to devolve power and decision-making to others.

Equiteq has helped over 200 highly successful consultancies through the selling process, and Paul Collins, the founder and CEO, has been involved in most of these deals. When I asked Paul what the biggest challenge to growing firms is, he replied:

> the biggest problem is founders working in the business too much and not on the business enough. The founder must spend less time on clients and staff and more time on the growth strategy. The day-to-day issues need to be delegated through the structure whilst you focus on growth.

Growing a successful consulting firm is, in part, about the consulting itself: your specialism, market, clients and projects. Yet, it is equally about building the business: the strategies, plans, processes, templates, guides, databases and technologies that enable consultants to function effectively. I have seen many able, expert consultants start businesses that were ultimately unsustainable. Typically, their early growth collapsed back in on itself when the business systems and processes could not support the growth. This leads to bad work, unhappy clients, high turnover and fewer barriers to entry for competitors.

Leadership and partners

Founder leadership

Successful leadership is concerned with establishing, communicating and inspiring a realistic and specific vision of growth. The *fastest* growing consultancies I encountered had visionary founders who were bordering on the obsessive about driving growth. I'm not saying this is a healthy thing, I'm just letting you know.

Whilst it is trendy to talk about leadership from behind,[6] for entrepreneurs such luxury is unworkable. Growing companies need vision and leadership from the front in order to establish, communicate and reinforce strategy, culture and direction. New firms often require 'work beyond contract' (i.e. not 9–5 clock-watchers) that is unlikely to be inspired in non-shareholders. You have to sell the vision. The work of actually leading, in addition to strategy setting, should evolve into a full-time job. This means the leader slowly delegating operational responsibilities and focusing on selling the firm rather than selling the services.

Leadership of the senior team therefore often relies upon the team's respect for the ability of the leader (both personal traits and market success), frequently supported by conversations, alliances and negotiations. Concerning personal traits, the section on mindset above provides some insights, but I would also add three other traits that I have witnessed in highly successful consultancy leaders over the last 25 years. These can provide a useful basis for both your employee surveys and some points for reflection in your development work.

- Integrity: The best leaders project high levels of integrity. In the consulting world, this is crucial because it leads to the trust necessary for client and consultant relationships. These will help generate the 'beyond contract' work that is crucial for a successful, growing consultancy. This is also crucial when the firm is being sold and the employees need to trust that they will still have the same type of job and support as before.

- Reassurance: Many consultants are insecure over-achievers who desire reassurance at a fundamental level. Some larger firms explicitly play upon this, which creates high levels of stress and turnover. If you wish to avoid this as a leader, then reassure your team and reward them with praise as well as money. During growth, reassurance generally means communicating with and involving the team regarding the direction and values of the firm.

- Persuasion: Sometimes, there will be doubts and concerns regardless of how good and reassuring you are, and it is here that the skill of persuasion comes in. If this is a weakness, I recommend Kolenda's *Methods of Persuasion* and Cialdini's *Influence*. Both are great books on the psychology of persuasion. They will also enhance your business development skills.

A final point to be made here is that some firms occasionally bring in a new CEO before the sale is done. The reasons for doing this, other than personal reasons, are usually either that the founder is highly entrepreneurial and doesn't enjoy the formality than ensues once a firm grows above 30 or so employees, or has little experience in preparing firms for sale. Sometimes it is done so that the founder can avoid the earn-out period. Other times, there is an increasing gulf between the day-to-day management of the firm and the more innovative 'moonshots' that companies need to take to stay ahead of the curve, so the CEO role is split into Executive Chair and CEO. Speaking personally, in all of the companies I have founded, I have tended to hand over to another CEO

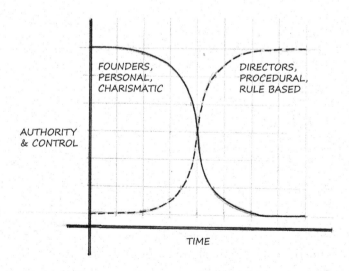

Figure 2.1 The shift in authority and control in a growing firm.

once growth is driven more by processes and systems (my Achilles' heels) and less by entrepreneurialism and motivation (my strengths). Respecting these divergences is one of the top reasons start-up CEOs consider hiring a growth-stage CEO.

Partners and leaders

The quality of the leadership team is ranked joint first (with profit growth and market proposition) as the most important factor in buyers' minds when considering a purchase,[7] so it is important to get it right. Leadership in a growing firm isn't just about the founder(s). Amancio Torres, who sold ShiftIn in 2017, told me:

> the first thing you must tell your readers is not to do it alone. Don't even do it with two of you. Get two or three partners early on. Solo works in some businesses but it doesn't in consulting.

Only one of the 72 founder interviewees for this book achieved a sale without a partnership, and that founder regretted the decision. The benefits of finding a good partner are:

- Overcoming loneliness: being an entrepreneur is a tough journey, and even the most understanding spouse or significant other may not provide you with the empathy and support that you need.
- Synergising skills: you are likely to have weaknesses that hamper your efforts. A well-chosen partner or two can fill the gaps and provide a more rounded offering.
- Better decisions: two heads are usually better than one. Having someone bright to bounce ideas off of can lead to better decisions (although be mindful of group-think).
- Networks: double the partners can mean double the network which can mean double the sales.
- Economies of scale: you don't both need an accountant, a website, a LinkedIn presence and a lawyer. Splitting the administrative burden frees you up to spend more time billing.
- Risk: with several partners, you might end up putting less money into the company, which means the investment is more feasible and the risk is lower.
- Time: with one or more partners, there is more scope for you to spend less time in the office. The shared CEO role in Virgo meant they had more time to do things they loved. Either way, a partnership often means a more civilised existence.

The downside of partnerships, other than sharing the rewards, is that relationships can turn sour. This can be messy and expensive, with lawyers and accountants being involved, low levels of performance, a loss of clients and acrimonious relations. When founders were asked what their biggest regrets were in growing a firm, 'partnering with the wrong person' was ranked top (with 'not taking more risks'). I will explore how to avoid this in Chapter 8, but part of it undoubtedly comes down to luck. We can consider the pairing of Angie Wiles and Sarah Mathew, the co-founders of Virgo Health, whose story is told in detail at the end of this chapter.

Yet, there is a fundamental conflict at the heart of growing consulting firms. Partners and senior consultants often want autonomy, but also realise that some controls are needed for strategy and strategy implementation to work.[8] The tension is further complicated by the fact that senior partners can both ignore the CEO/MD and sometimes have enough shares between them to vote to remove them. Leadership of partners, therefore, often needs to be based on the traits mentioned above: integrity, reassurance and persuasion. If you end up with many partners, it is important to evolve into a position where everyone is clear on their decision-making role in the firm. For some, this may realistically mean having no senior role at all.

Sadly, many growing firms do not manage this evolution well, because they put off the frank discussions needed about how decision-making will change as the firm grows. Two problems abound. First, in most newer consultancies, a handful of partners take on leadership roles between them – discussing strategy, taking the initiative on the different challenges that emerge and managing the co-ordination of an increasingly complex firm. It is easy for this situation to become entrenched and results in partners leading things for which they have no skill or desire. Partnerships in larger firms often confuse an optimal allocation of roles and responsibilities with ownership. In larger firms, partners should focus only on what they are good at. If that is just delivery, then let them deliver.

Second, as firms get larger, the number of partners typically increases, and it is often automatically assumed that partners should be on the leadership team. Typical problems emerge quickly:

- There is no one leading important but unglamorous processes such as thought leadership, creation or process development.
- There are too many partners 'leading' more glamorous processes such as the sales strategy.
- A handful of people don't lead anything at all, but still want their voices heard.
- A handful of people, who are often great at delivery or sales, really have no competence at strategy or leadership, and at best, muddy the waters.

Later in Chapter 7, I will discuss the governance structures that prevent such confusion, but it is sufficient to say here that as the firm grows above 20–30 or so employees, one person should have moved into a more or less full-time CEO position, partners should be clear on their responsibilities, the firm should focus on establishing a leadership team based upon necessary competence rather than partnership coincidence and processes and metrics should be in place to encourage as much delegation as possible.

The other type of partner

Paul Collins is the founder of WCI Consulting, which grew to £100 million in sales and 350 staff before its sale. He is also the founder of Equiteq. Paul is in semi-retirement now and spends much of the year fishing. For a man who has, and has done, 'it all', it is sobering to hear his reflection:

> I've had divorces, I've had family splits and all sorts of things that I'm not proud of...I would have done things differently from the work-life balance point of view. I now know what to do, but it's a bit late now.

No person is an island, and whilst you may be happy to spend vast amounts of time building a profitable business, every hour you spend on it is an hour away from your loved ones that you will not get back. The idea for many is that this will be repaid with dividends when the firm sells, and of course, the road to the top in any industry requires sacrifices, including consulting at large corporates.

Even Dom Moorhouse, who managed to launch and sell his firm within five years (with three children under six!) says:

> I nearly paid [for the over-work and] I just about got away with it. I wouldn't like to say how close it was but certainly if I had pushed the same focused agenda for another few years, I wouldn't deserve to be married or to have children that know me as a father.[9]

Dom's partner Roz also writes:

> I had to work harder and make more sacrifices than I could have imagined.... Our family suffered.... Dom was not there enough and I, and our children, suffered as a result. For a lot of the time, I did the work of two parents. Indeed, I often saw myself as a single parent as, for much of the time, it felt like I bore the responsibility for our children alone.... even when he was with us, his mind was often elsewhere.

Roz argues that, in the end, it was worth the sacrifice, but suggests a few tips for keeping going during the tough times:

- Arrange periods when your phone is turned off (such as Sunday evenings).
- Have a regular date just for the two of you.
- Make sure your partner can have time to themselves.

Not everyone is so understanding; so it is a good idea to have a frank conversation with your loved ones about what you will be doing, for how long and what the potential rewards are. You will be relying on them more than you think. It is also worth being clear with yourself why you are doing this and what you would be doing otherwise. It could be worth remembering that if you were working for a corporate consultancy instead, you would probably be working similar hours, but without the likelihood of a big pay day and the personal satisfaction at the end.

Takeaways

- Buyers are looking for a strong leadership team, with a history of success both in and out of the firm.
- Eventually, the CEO should seek to remove themselves from the minutiae of the firm and focus on selling the firm, not the services. A short earn-out is based on the leadership team shifting competences from individuals to systems. The Boss Mindset will help here.
- The Great Consultant Trap is when founders assume that great consulting delivery equals great consulting leadership. It doesn't. The Humble Mindset is a cure for this.
- The Bureaucratic Trap is when founders, especially from large firms, assume that detailed reporting on past events and large meetings are the foundation of a good firm. They are not. Focusing on the Entrepreneurial Mindset can improve things.
- The Genius Trap is when a very bright founder thinks that their brilliance is an adequate substitute for asking clients what they want and listening to feedback. The Humble Mindset can help here.
- The Super-Hero Trap is when a successful founder feels they can't let go of the reins because the firm simply wouldn't survive without them. Again, the Humble Mindset might improve things.
- The Security Trap is the inability to take reasonable risks in the pursuit of growth. The Entrepreneurial Mindset can help here.

- Few successful consultancies are grown with one owner. Find a partner who shares your passion and ameliorates your weaknesses, but be slow in your courtship.
- As you grow, the leadership model must change. Joint decision-making must give way to specialisation; personal command and control must give way to culture and rules; the drive from superheroes must give way to a systematised process for growth; partners as leaders must give way to leadership based upon competencies and experience.

Case study: Virgo Health

Although Angie Wiles and Sarah Mathew travelled via different routes, they both found themselves being promoted to lead medium-sized healthcare communications consultancies. Angie came up through the agency route and Sarah by working for large pharmaceutical companies. Sarah takes time to remind me, 'Angie was my arch-rival…In the Communiqué Awards Consultancy of the Year, I'd won it with my agency three times, and she'd won it twice'. Yet, despite the rivalry, the pair shared enough panels, conferences and advisory committees to know that they had 'similar values, and a similar work ethic'. Indeed, the eventual name of their company, Virgo Health, pointed to the shared characteristics of their star sign: practical, hard-working perfectionists.

Shortly after the birth of Sarah's first child, Angie visited Sarah to put the case for them both going alone. Together, they had worked for almost all the major pharmaceutical companies, had strong reputations and felt that an offering which combined the client attention of the smaller firms with the expertise of the larger companies would create an attractive niche for clients. Yet the decision to go it alone was not without risk: both women had very young children and mortgages, and were the major breadwinners in their households. In the end, the drive to create something different and to be their own bosses won out. As Sarah told me:

> We wanted to work in a way where you got up in the morning, and you thought "Yeah, I really want to go and do that", so it was worth it, psychologically and emotionally, to leave your kids with someone you were paying to look after them.

Moreover, after the initial reaction of one very senior PR leader ('Girls, it will never work'), they were keen to prove him wrong. So, in July 2003, Virgo Health was born.

The vision of the new firm was very much built around their shared values, and in reaction to what they had recently experienced: both of their firms had been bought by a much larger consultancy, which meant they felt short-term pressure on financials was negatively affecting the culture at the larger firm. Angie reflected: 'These firms had really strong reputations and cultures – they were dynamic, and maverick and brave – and [the buyer] squashed this and made people work harder for longer for less'. Sarah agreed: '[the buyer] effectively put short term quarterly reporting ahead of people'. The tagline, 'Communications Without Compromise' was intended to be more than empty rhetoric.

The duo wrote a five-year plan, with assumptions about the numbers of projects, clients, employees, day rates, costs and revenues. The plan assumed a 50% success rate with pitches. In terms of growth, the pair wanted to grow rapidly and professionally, so initially sought external funding. However, rapid interest from banks and investors gave them the confidence to fund their own growth instead. The money went on building the foundations of a growth infrastructure: quality HR advice, 'fantastic' PA support, a 12-person office, Professional Services Automation software, and strong marketing and branding. Sarah reflects: 'Some people start out small and think small, but we always intended to think big and aim high.' For clients who might otherwise have thought the duo could not cope with larger projects, this investment stressed their commitment to both growth and quality.

Fortunately, as Sarah recalls with a smile, 'We did 10 pitches between July and December 2003, within our first six months of setting up, and we won all 10'. In addition, they got to announce their launch at an industry awards ceremony in front of 1,200 potential clients and employees. As a result, their pipeline became so full that they stopped pitching for eight months from January 2004. Indeed, Angie tells me: 'in the industry we were known as the consultancy with a waiting list' – something that would not have done their reputation any harm. This demand also meant that they could be choosy about who they worked with. They purposefully turned down client work that did not sit well with the agency proposition or capacity, and their five-year plan was achieved in three. Yet, despite the demand for their services and their commitment to growth, having a partnership meant that neither had to do the crazy hours of many of those I have interviewed. Sarah recalls:

> We would go to work, because remote working wasn't the way that it is now, and we were able to keep reasonable hours, and we would encourage all of our team to do exactly the same. Then we'd both go

home to sort the kids out and carry on working in the evenings if we needed to.

Growth did however bring new challenges. First, the growing firm, led by two self-professed perfectionists (or 'control freaks', as Angie says), increasingly required its founders to step back from the minutiae. This required some pressure from their new recruits. 'You have to step back' Angie said, 'not be the megalomaniac …give people the accountability, opportunity, and reward and recognition to run their own show'. Second, the shared Chief Executive role had to evolve so that the founders could have different areas of focus, coming together to make the big decisions. Finally, both founders felt that their growth had hit a 'sweet spot' at around 30 employees, where it was easy to keep in touch with the team personally and maintain strong client relationships. There was considerable temptation to stay at that size, but Angie argues that if things stay still, 'people get demotivated and creativity drops'. By the time it was sold, nine years after its founding, Virgo Health had almost 70 employees. As a wonderful piece of poetic justice, the company led by the man who had dismissed their plans early on, came to them looking to see if they would sell. He was turned down.

In terms of lessons learned or regrets, Angie and Sarah have very few. They both speak fondly of Virgo Health, yet have both moved on to new pastures. After experiencing some 'miraculous' transition coaching after the sale, Sarah was so impressed with its effects that she flew out to the US to learn the method. This now informs her blended coaching/consulting approach in The Vibrant Company. Angie, meanwhile, has launched a virtual communications consultancy. The Difference Collective has over 100 expert healthcare communications consultants and allows her to avoid the worry and responsibility of having dozens of employees: 'Virgo became a monster…it was a lovely purple monster, but it needed constant feeding… I wanted to recreate Virgo in its heyday, when we were firing on all cylinders, smashing it out the park with a happy vibrant team'.

Notes

1 Zook, C., & Allen, J. (2016) *The Founder's Mentality*. Cambridge, MA: Harvard Business Review Press.
2 Wallin, J. (2006) *Business Orchestration: Strategic Leadership in the Era of Digital Convergence*. London: John Wiley.

3 Anand, A., Walsh, I., & Moffett, S. (2019) Does humility facilitate knowledge sharing? Investigating the role of humble knowledge inquiry and response. *Journal of Knowledge Management*, 23(6), 1218–1244: 30.
4 Frier, S. (2020) *No Filter: The Inside Story of Instagram*. London: Simon & Schuster.
5 Elkind, P., & McLean, B. (2004) *The Smartest Guys in the Room*. New York: Penguin.
6 For example, Hill, L. (2010) Leading from Behind. *Harvard Business Review*, May 5.
7 Equiteq (2018) *The Knowledge Economy Global Buyers Report*.
8 See, Empson, L. (2020) Ambiguous authority and hidden hierarchy: Collective leadership in an elite professional service firm. *Leadership*, 16(1), 62–86.
9 Moorhouse, D. (2012) *The Five Year Entrepreneur*. Self-published, p. 44.

3
Strategy and planning for growth

What are investors and acquirers looking for?

Buyers ideally want strategies that produce sustained, growing revenues for at least three years and projections of the same for a subsequent three years. Ideally, past growth will be smooth as this reassures buyers about the predictability of future revenue. Generally, revenue *growth* is more important to buyers than absolute revenues or even margins because the former indicates a growing market and safe management. A firm with zero growth can still sell, but will generally attract half the price of a firm with revenues growing at 30% a year. A minimum of 20% EDITDA growth for the previous three years is usually sufficient to drive a good price (see Table 3.1). Double the number of buyers would reject a firm because of low growth compared to low profits (Equiteq 2014), and for every 10% increase in annual EBITDA growth the multiple goes up approximately by a factor of one.

When growth drops or even reverses during a sales negotiation, buyers often pull out or want to renegotiate. The multiples in Table 3.1 are averages and it should be stressed they can be as high as 30, depending on the niche and

Table 3.1 EBITDA growth and valuation multiples[1]

EBITDA growth (p.a.)	Strategic buyers	Private equity
No growth	5.9×	6.1×
10%–20%	7.9×	7.6×
20%–30%	9.3×	8.5×
30%+	10.5×	9.2×

DOI: 10.4324/9781003149217-3

intellectual property (IP). In terms of the minimums, according to Equiteq (2017), buyers get concerned by EBITDA lower than 14%. However, this is mediated by the strategic positioning of the firm and the economic climate. I am generalising somewhat here, but typically 50% of revenue will be spent on the delivery of services, 30% on overheads (cost of sales and administration), leaving 20% for EBITDA. Firm owners might be wise to consider investing any EBITDA above 20%–25% into growing revenues.

In terms of strategy, founders with the intention to sell often forget that strategic buyers are generally more interested in filling a *specific* gap in their offering than the revenues or profits of the target firm. The latter are important of course, but more as an indicator that the target's offering is sound and less as an investment opportunity. This is why, when valuing firms, M&A specialists tend to have more qualitative than quantitative indicators.

The gap that strategic ('trade') buyers seek to fill is often quite specific. Examples might include a digital maturity benchmarking service to generate leads for a digital transformation firm; a strategy boutique for distributors to extend the reach of a strategy firm focused on food retail; or an Asian supply chain consultancy to follow the international clients of a similar European firm. Generally, there is a specific gap in the buyers' services, sectors or geographies that the acquisition will fill – most commonly a service which can be cross-sold to the buyer's existing clients. Private equity buyers are less bothered about a specific gap and more interested in a machine that will continue to generate high-margin, relatively predicable growth. To a great extent, your ability to achieve this will be dependent on delivering the right kind of services (high-margin, protected and leveraged) with the right clients (large, repeat business, multinationals, ideally with board-level clients).

Aside from the strategy itself, buyers appreciate a solid strategy *system*. Timetabled, structured and quality processes for competitor analyses, growth plans and strategy formulation will be looked upon positively as well as having a real benefit for your strategising. It is also important to remember that strategy is not just a process; it is also manifested in the assets of the firm which provide competitive advantage. Examples include a business model which maximises innovation (see Elixirr), a culture which attracts and keeps rare talent (see Exellys) or a brand which delivers superior margins (see Water Street Partners). Before unpacking this rather daunting list, let's provide some context to strategy in small consulting firms.

Your strategy

The strategic advantage of small firms

Whilst it is easy to focus on the drawbacks of competing with bigger brands, virtually all small professional service firms have some advantages over larger competitors. They have a lower cost base, because they generally do not need riverside offices in major cities to impress clients. Unlike large firms, which have to be manoeuvred like an ocean tanker, small firms are also more agile, able to change their value proposition and marketing almost overnight. Small firms can also offer a greater level of independent decision-making compared to listed companies which generally results in more focus on high-quality delivery and less focus on sales at any cost. As one founder told me:

> When I was at KPMG, it was constantly about upselling and cross-selling. It's nice to be able to focus simply on what the client needs, and that is one reason why we have been so successful.

Finally, and as a consequence of the previous point, smaller firms can also pursue a business model that does not depend upon leveraging young graduates. Although this is certainly an approach that smaller firms can take, many (for example, Evolution Partners) choose to focus on highly experienced hires, supported by IP that provides additional value. When reading the sections below, it is worth remembering these advantages and making the most of them. During the COVID-19 pandemic, it amazed me how many small firms failed to pivot their offerings quickly enough to make up for lost business elsewhere.

Defining strategy: digging your moat

The term 'strategy' is often misunderstood as defining the point that the firm wishes to get to. If only it were that simple! In reality, firms are constrained by their resources, environment and competitors, and must usually make do with the limited choices open to them in order to create a ongoing revenue streams. The closest definition to this I have seen is that strategy is a set of *self-reinforcing choices that provide sustainable competitive advantage*.[2] The key phrase here is *self-reinforcing*. The options that are available to the small firm must be mutually supportive, so they generate a virtuous cycle by which strengths and uniqueness are continuously improved. This is why there can be different successful strategies in the same market. In the dining market, a successful company can be a Michelin-starred restaurant, a chain of burger vans or a

McDonald's franchisee, and each will have wildly differing strategies. In the consulting world, David Maister noticed something similar over 30 years ago: different leverage ratios had implications for the ways in which different aspects of the firm such as recruitment, promotion, training and delivery reinforced each other.

A good strategy will provide your firm with a competitive advantage – a 'moat' against the competition. From the successful firms I have researched, this might be innovation, service performance, client satisfaction, cost, IP, service performance or even the network/relationships the firm has. Whatever it is, it is important that all your capabilities work together to make this advantage as great as possible.

In my teaching and coaching, I have generally used the questions 'Why?', 'What?' and 'How?' to identify the main self-reinforcing components of a consulting firm's strategy,[3] and I flesh these out in more detail in the next sections.

Why?

What is your why?

Being clear on *why* you want to grow a consultancy is crucial if the next few years' hard work is going to be worthwhile. What are your life goals? How does growing a consultancy fit into these? My interviewees tended to give three overlapping answers to these questions, with a different emphasis for each founder:

- **Creative freedom**: entrepreneurs want to create new (successful!) things, think for themselves and have confidence in their ability to do things better outside bureaucratic company structures. Many of the founders were serial entrepreneurs who constantly wanted to do things differently.
- **Financial ambition**: whilst few admitted founding the company for purely financial reasons (there was one exception) it is important to be realistic about the financial gains. After advisory fees, limited success in the earn-out, sharing the cheque with others and tax, an average sale will net the average founder around £1.5 million. Since, on average, it takes 12 years to sell a firm and another two to three for an earn-out, this equates to around £100,000 for each year[4] on top of the founder's salary. This is considerable, but a fraction of what a Partner at a Big Four firm would earn annually (typically around £800k).

- **Workplace values**: many founders were prompted to start their own firms after leaving firms that were unpleasant to work in. As one founder told me, 'we felt that if you're going to work somewhere for the next twenty years you may as well make it as pleasant as possible'. Others stressed being able to deliver quality projects for clients without the pressure of 'upsell'.

It is well worth writing down your 'why' and sticking it near your workstation because this will impact your choices at every stage. What will your exit strategy be and, if selling, your target price? What role will you occupy in the firm? What will the culture of your firm be, and will you choose to grow beyond the 'sweet spot' when systems and processes begin to take the place of interpersonal relationships? The 'why' will influence all of these choices, and it is to these questions that we now turn.

What is your firm's why?

Given the cost of attracting clients and employees, loyalty is crucial to the small consulting firm. The companies that really excel in driving loyalty, those that inspire customer tattoos and employees who would work for nothing – from Harley Davidson to Apple, Disney, Google and Lego – are those who start with the *why* and not with the *what*.

The 'What?' refers to the facts and features: What do you want to achieve? What income are you aiming at? What growth rate do you need? What are your services? What features do they have? These are necessary questions, but are secondary to, and follow from, the 'why?' question.

Fortunately, there's a slew of evidence showing that buyers and employees generally choose on the basis of emotion and then retroactively justify on the basis of logic. This is why your 'Why?' is so important. The 'Why?' questions concern the emotions: Why do you get out of bed in the morning? Why should anyone care? Why would an employee work for you? Why would I give you my trust? It is much deeper than what you do; it's about what you believe and how you make people feel.

Consider the emotional quality of successful campaigns:

- BMW: Designed for Driving **Pleasure**
- General Electric: **Imagination** at Work
- Disneyland: The **Happiest** Place on Earth
- Samsung: **Do** What You Can't
- Apple: Here's to the **Crazy** Ones, Think **Different**

When the meaningful and ambitious *why* of such slogans is actively translated into company culture, practices, values and marketing (which, to be frank, is rarely the case) it can create an emotional and instinctive bond between the company, its employees and its clients.

This is crucial for you because as a small growing company, you don't have a brand name that is going to inspire loyalty. As Steve Newton, founder of Elixirr said to me, 'one of the steepest learning curves to overcome….is that you're without the power of a calling card'. Yet even though his firm, Elixirr, hires around seven graduates a year and employs only 130 staff, each year they get over 1,000 applications from Oxford and Cambridge – many of whom would choose Elixirr above McKinsey, Bain or Deloitte. A primary reason for this is their culture.

Culture, values and purpose

In my view, creating and articulating a strong culture can benefit a firm as much as any financial, marketing or pricing strategy. The most successful firms I interviewed not only had strong cultures but were great at communicating cultural values in their messaging, brand and marketing. Elixirr's culture emphasises innovation. Solidiance was more aggressive – 'We fight to win', 'We punch above our weight', 'We like rough industries' – whilst Secure State emphasised a fun and a laid back approach. Others focused on being practical and hands-on, being the best in the market, the smartest in the room, the most ambitious for the client or on being honest and frank.

As we discuss in Chapter 8, culture is *especially* important for the small firm. You need to give great consultants a compelling reason to work for you rather than going to a well-known firm or starting up by themselves. In addition, a strong culture means that people know how to behave without detailed rules and prescriptions: this is especially important when the firm scales and the risk of bureaucracy stifling innovation increases.

A great culture, as we discuss later, distinguishes your firm from the vanilla cultures of larger firms. If you examine the espoused values of the large firms, they are loosely the same (integrity, teamwork, diversity, blah blah). This is because they need to play safe and appeal to the mass market. You don't have this problem, and in fact, if you try to compete with vanilla, you're likely to fail. For this reason, it is worth having an honest, frank discussion about what your values are and the type of culture you will create. I emphasise honesty here, because if you are inauthentic you will get found out, and those that find you out will sometimes post their findings all over the internet. There is no point saying you have a culture which values work-life balance if your high-leverage business model means that juniors are hammered or saying that ethics is fundamental to the company if you do PR for the coal industry. Clients and employees can sniff out disingenuous firms, and you are likely to lose both.

In addition to honesty, there are other basic principles when thinking about the values you prize:

- Don't have a long list. Five is better than ten and three is better than five.
- Think about what you *don't* want on the list.
- Focus on what makes you unique.
- Think about what clients you *love* working with (and those you don't).
- Think about what type of people you want with you (and those you don't!).
- Don't be vanilla.

Again, to embed your values into the firm's culture, they need to be consistently and universally demonstrated by leadership and woven into all aspects of the firm, from recruitment and promotion to client selection and branding. Values also need to be reinforced by the traditions of the firm and the competences it prizes as well as the symbols and artefacts of the culture. However, nothing is more important than *behaviour*. Let me illustrate this with an old story.

In 1966[5] researchers put five monkeys in a cage with a ladder leading to some bananas hanging at the top of the cage. Every time a monkey climbed the ladder, the whole troupe was sprayed with cold water. Eventually, no monkeys bothered climbing to get the bananas. When the experimenter replaced an original monkey with a new one, the new one tried to climb the ladder but was jumped on by the other monkeys. Eventually, the new monkey knew not to try. One by one, each original monkey was substituted with a new monkey and the cycle of climbing, icy showers and learning was repeated each time. Eventually, there were five monkeys in the cage who had never been sprayed with water but who refused to climb the ladder. None of them knew why. The lesson is that consistent behaviour creates norms, and you are one of the first monkeys (in the nicest possible way).

It is worth taking time out to think about your value proposition, culture and values, and ideally get in an external expert to help you both define this and structure the messaging and branding around this. I have put the presentation I use with my own clients at www.joeomahoney.com that will help you with this.

What?

Analysing the market

One thing that often surprises me is how few consultancies, small or large, really take time to understand the value drivers of the client: what does success really look like for the client? What metrics are reviewed most commonly? What would a dream consulting project look like for them? In my experience, most consultants are understandably so focused on the project in hand that they often miss out on a potentially bigger, more impactful and profitable project just around the corner.

I can give you the example of a coaching session I held with a very bright polymath, who had been doing strategy innovation consulting for 15 years but had consistently failed to grow his firm. 'Whenever I get a project, the clients are blown away', he told me. 'My work is out of the field innovative and really works, but the services just don't sell'. I asked him why he was selling those services and not something easier. His answer was 'because it works'. When I asked if he'd ever followed up on his failures, he became very dismissive of clients that could not see his value: 'They're just not that bright. They're risk averse and would rather go with a brand rather than something that actually works brilliantly'. Whether he is right or wrong does not really matter from a sales standpoint! Understanding what clients want and the market trends which affect their wants is crucial if you want to sell.

Here are some questions you can ask yourself when researching a niche or service. By researching, I mean talking to potential and actual clients, and also those who once turned down your proposals:

- What are the current and future big challenges or opportunities of your potential clients?
- Of these, which are CXOs aware of and which do they need help with?
- Of these, which require specialist knowledge, skills or methods that you have or can develop?
- Of these, which will clients seek to solve or exploit with high-margin projects?

In order to research these questions, you might also undertake the following (depending on your budget and maturity):

- Read *Harvard Business Review*, *Sloan Management Review* and *McKinsey Quarterly* for the key trends affecting your potential clients.
- Fund external research (or an MBA dissertation) to do a market analysis.

It is important to recognise two things about the answers to questions about your niche. First, what clients really want changes over time. Clients used to pay a lot of money for transcription services for example, but not so much anymore. Second, wording changes. Consultancies used to charge a lot of money for process engineering. They still do, but it now falls under the umbrella of 'digital transformation'. Like skirt lengths and flares, client and consulting messaging are influenced by trends and fashions. Ignore these shifts at your peril.

Analysing the competition

For a *small* consulting firm, competition is not the end of the world. It shows there is client demand, and it can make you raise your game. Indeed, it is possible to be a successful firm without existing in a unique niche because the consulting market is so huge, often geographically tied and often poorly marketed. Clients never know every firm that can offer a service.

Yet, there is an important caveat for the *growing* firm. This is that there is competition and *competition*. It is fine to have firms that solve the same problems as you, but having firms that solve the same problem, in the same way and in the same sector and region as you, *is* an issue. As a firm grows and needs more clients, it will increasingly find that it bumps against competitors. If the firm is not differentiated enough, this can lead to a low price ceiling as clients play similar firms off against each other. Worse, you may find that to grow any further, you need to take business away from similar consultancies, and low pricing is the most effective way of doing this if you are not differentiated. The best way to assess your differentiation is to speak to current, past and potential clients. As someone that spent a few years buying consulting services in the private sector, it amazed me how similar most proposals tended to be.

For this reason, doing research on the competition is crucial. Firms that do frequent research grow 12 times faster than those that do none, and are twice as profitable.[6] Of course, there is the possibility of reverse causality (i.e. those that are more successful can afford to do more research), but in my experience many firms over-estimate their knowledge of client markets and competitors. Research has shown that there is only a 25% overlap between who clients and consultants think the competitors are.[7] This means that it is worth asking clients (and associates) who *they* think the competition are, and also keeping an eye on any press releases – or, in the public sector, tender awards – so you know who you're really competing against.

Competitor assessment should be done as part of your annual strategy review, but also when there are significant changes internally or in the market.[8] Information on market shifts should be incorporated with feedback from your clients into continuous improvements as well as more radical changes to your pricing, marketing and service development (all explored later in this book).

In terms of practical advice here, I suggest the following:

1. Develop a prioritised list of your competitors in the eyes of your clients, associates and team. Clients are crucial here, as is their view of your Unique Value Proposition (UVP). You might want to map the competitors on a 4×4 in terms of size and the number of services/markets where they compete. We are consultants after all.
2. Once you have a list of competitors, do a detailed analysis of their services, website and how they do marketing (for example, using sites such as SimilarWeb and SpyFu). This should elicit competitors' paid advertising, key words and social media posts, which will tell you their marketing priorities.
3. For the top 20% of competitors undertake a more detailed qualitative analysis of their website summarising services, markets, UVP, expertise, business model, thought leadership and digital assets.
4. For top 5% of competitors pay an external market research firm (or MBA student) to do a very detailed analysis of pricing, response time, sales process and other 'client experience' measures.
5. Use (2), (3) and (4) to inform your strategy and marketing, both in terms of differentiation (what you can do that is unique) but also imitation (what existing ideas in the market can complement your offering).

As you grow you will find that your competitive landscape changes, as does your ability to compete. As a small firm, there will be many projects that you cannot bid for because of your size or because you cannot afford the time to invest in the selection process. Yet, growth also means that you are competing against the bigger brands and the economies of scale and scope they have built into their systems. Being clear on your differentiation from these brands is crucial both in terms of what you *do* and what you *don't do*.

What is your niche?

It's an easy thing to say 'sell what your clients want to buy', but you would be surprised at how many capable consultants do the opposite. Paul Collins, founder of Equiteq, told me:

> Consultants tell me 'I'm really passionate about JIT and lean'. But then wonder why they're getting 500 quid a day and have no demand. You have to morph your subject matter, change your skill set and sell something that is unique.

The 'what' of strategy for consultancies concerns three questions: what is your niche? What is your business model? What is your UVP? We deal with the first of these now and the others later in the chapter.

It has long been known that targeting a specific niche provides a firm with several advantages. As Carman and Lageard wrote back in 1980,[9] 'the service firm should not overuse its delivery system and its image by attempting to serve the needs of too many segments'. The first reason is that a niche provides you with competitive advantage in your marketing. An automotive buyer who needs a specialist in supply chain management is more likely to buy from an automotive supply chain consultancy rather than a general supply chain consultancy, because they will perceive them to be more focused on the client's needs. The second is that niche services can attract higher prices. As expertise becomes more specialist, it becomes more valuable. This is why Nurofen Migraine Pain

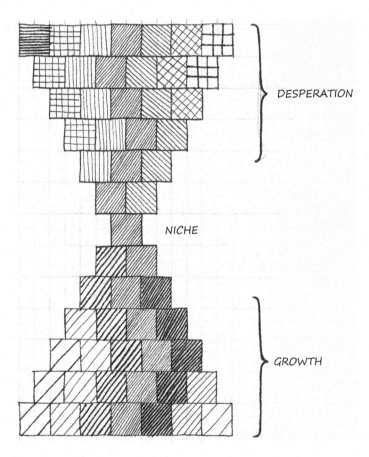

Figure 3.1 From desperation to growth.

or Nurofen Back Pain products sold at nearly twice the price of their standard 'painkiller' product, despite being exactly the same thing.

Third, niches can also act as a barrier to the entry of competitors. Solidiance CEO and Founder Damien Duhamel says that 'we love doing work that is dirty, dusty or rusty because few others want to do it'. They specifically chose business-to-business (B2B) consulting in the engineering sector because it was more difficult for people to gain in-depth knowledge about that: 'if you are doing consulting about selling ice-cream to customers then everyone can understand that market. But if you're doing concrete pipes and drill bits between companies, it's a lot harder to understand'. Finally, the most important reason for developing a niche is that it allows you to accumulate expertise more quickly than if you are spread over several sectors or services. This, in turn, allows you to charge higher prices.

Thus, while growing consultancies rarely start or end with a niche, they do often focus down on a niche before growing sustainably. Typically, an hourglass shape forms over time (Figure 3.1): initially a firm will often (though not always) needs to say yes to things that are outside their core focus, because there isn't enough business, and they might be experimenting with the market's responses. This is the start-up phase. As time goes on, repeat business and a growing reputation allows the firm to specialise more, and thus accumulate and codify the expertise necessary for leverage to occur. As Roger Carlile, founder of Ankura, told me, 'you've got to get smaller in order to get bigger'. This is the basis for the growth phase. Once a high-value, high-growth niche has been defined, the scale phase sells that niche heavily and then develops offerings strategically (i.e. the same service in adjacent markets or adjacent services in the same market). This doesn't mean that you need to focus on one single service. Complementary services that allow cross-selling, follow-on sales, or

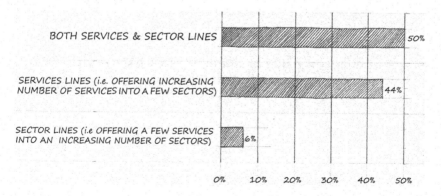

Figure 3.2 How the sample consultancies grew (service vs. sector).

protect against cyclical demand make total sense, even for a small firm. More on this later.

In terms of identifying *what* niche (or niches) a firm should focus on, the usual advice for small firms is to look at the overlap of what one loves doing, is great at doing and can get paid well for doing. I can only give advice on the latter here. Niches have ten different variables, which we discuss throughout this book. These are:

1. Service offering
2. Sector specialism
3. Market focus
4. Buyer role
5. Client/project size
6. Geography
7. Business model
8. Culture and values
9. Pricing model
10. Method/approach

Areas which are traditionally the highest paying for consulting work are listed in Table 3.2, but these change and are highly dependent on the country and the economic cycle. For example, a US list would include healthcare, but a UK list would not. Another caveat is that it is possible to carve out a profitable niche in pretty much any *sector*. I have seen highly profitable consultancies that specialise in, for example, public sector digital transformation or higher education strategy work. The same is not true for the *service* offered: it is extremely difficult to make high margins doing process or standard HR work, though there are some exceptions. Later in Chapter 5, I argue that the logic of moving into new markets and services is as important as the initial niche in which the firm begins.

Table 3.2 The highest paid consulting sectors and services

Sectors	Services
Banking and Finance	Strategy
Energy	Finance
Technology	Mergers and Acquisitions
Pharma and Biotech	Digital and Technology

It will also help growth if your firm, initially at least, focuses on one (ideally CXO) target buyer role. Research by Hinge[10] found that high-growth consulting firms were 55% more likely to specialise in serving a specific role in client firms.

In terms of focus, many advisors argue that it is better to be in the painkiller business than the vitamin business. In other words, clients will pay more to move away from pain than they will to move towards future benefits. Personally, I haven't seen much evidence to support this. Clients pay well for advice on innovation, strategy and M&A and less well for cost-reduction services; I think that marketing a sense of hope and possibility is actually more attractive to many clients than talking about specific pain points.

The other market feature worth noting is that, in my experience, there is an increasing gap between the pricing of high-value work (important work that clients cannot do for themselves) and low-value work (discretionary work that clients could do, but don't have the people to do it). As I emphasise in the next section, this is one of many good reasons for taking a high-quality/high-cost niche positioning rather than the opposite. This is a trend that I feel the growth of AI-based services will exacerbate.

Before we get off the subject of niches, I want to finally stress that the niche of your firm is also highly relevant to the multiple of EBITDA that you will be paid (covered in Chapter 9). For investors, the *category* of your firm is important. For example a training firm will attract a typical multiple of 5–6 times EBITDA, a consultancy will attract 7–10, whilst a software firm will attract a multiple of 10–20. As Greg Alexander of Capital 54 told me, his firm was initially categorised as a training firm and he worked hard to get it marketed and positioned as a consultancy in the minds of buyers.

Compete on quality not cost

Sarah Matthew, founder of Virgo Health, told me of her philosophy when she first started out: 'we were determined that you focus on doing the best job you can possibly do and looking after your team and everything else follows'. This sentiment was echoed by the majority of my interviewees – the importance of focusing entirely on quality in the pursuit of growth. To this end, a statement from 40 years ago that 'a low-cost strategy is not a viable one for the Professional Service Firm'[11] is still valid today, though with some caveats. With few exceptions, all consultancies should seek to compete on the quality and the perceived quality of their work, except when the consultancy has a cost advantage over its competitors. When a smaller consultancy competes on prices, several bad things happen.

First, and most obviously, margins are lower. This hits partners in their pockets, but also means there is virtually no cash flow for growth, training, decent salaries or investment in company assets. Second, low-cost services tend to be the lowest skilled and the most commodified of offerings, and thus not only suffer from low transaction costs (clients can easily swap one provider with another) but are also most likely to be replaced with internal, automated or outsourced alternatives. The race to the bottom is not simply between low-value consultancies. Third, successful bids will suffer from a variant to winners' curse: underbidding for work that is likely to result in poor quality delivery and reputational damage, if not disputed fees. Finally, working with low-cost consultants on highly commodified projects and worrying about cash flow is unlikely to be the reason you gave up a comfortable job with a pension.

Now, high quality doesn't necessarily mean highest price (that is usually reserved for McKinsey & Co.), but there are exceptions to doing high-cost work. For the very new consultancy, with no clients in hand, it may be worth doing a few selected low-cost engagements[12] to get experience and testimonials, but this does not mean delivering low quality! Additionally, if you are venturing into a new, promising client or service area, expect to develop useful IP and skills from low-cost engagements. Low-balling can even be a strategic way of potentially influencing a larger purchase down the line.[13] Additionally, you can compete on cost if your own costs are lower than the competition, if you have particularly efficient leverage, if your standardised work is done in a low-cost country or your use of technology decreases operational costs. Even then, you might ask if low-cost work is really what you want to spend your time doing.

While we're on the topic of quality, it is also worth stating something that few founders like to admit: that quality of delivery often diminishes at two points. This can first happen when work is no longer delivered exclusively by the partners, and second, when partners stop directly reviewing the deliverables. As we discuss later, this is where productisation/commodification and culture are essential, but even with these in place, it is likely that the sheer effort that start-up founders put in, in order to delight every client, is unlikely to be replicated by salaried staff. This said (another heresy coming) a drop in quality is not *necessarily* a bad thing in a growing firm if that quality was achieved by unsustainable utilisation rates. In pursuit of more leveraged, commodified services, a growing firm may need to sacrifice quality achieved through over-work for more predictable, systematic methods and outcomes.

Your Unique Value Proposition

"We have great clients, and we have great consultants. Sure. Who's gonna say we have crap clients and consultants?". Paul Collins has seen hundreds of firms sell and seen many fail. Most small consulting firms will tell you that they have great people. If they only have one person, the solo practitioner, they will generally tell you how great they are. You may read about the founder's dog or scuba diving qualifications but, do excuse my bluntness – *no one cares*. The time-pressed potential client certainly doesn't care and won't understand why you are telling them. Slightly better are the consultancies that tell you what they do – the services they provide and their features. The trouble is that the 'so what?' question still remains unanswered because you haven't told the client what the service means for them. If car manufacturers sold their cars through descriptions of what service is provided, the ad copy would generally read 'gets you from A to B'.

What is important to stress is what the service will do *for* clients. What value and benefits will they receive? This is as much about delivery and client perceptions of your value as what services actually do. This is your value proposition. If your value proposition is not at least relatively unique, you are more likely to end up competing on price, which can mean a death spiral of deteriorating quality and prices.

There are very diverse and often conflicting understandings of value propositions. My definition is more abstract than the specific services that are offered and encompasses the entire purpose, culture and personality of the firms:

Why should clients select your firm?

At a superficial level, this is about the 'elevator pitch' and the strapline that is usually mentioned when discussing value. These are important, not necessarily because they will win you clients, but because they provide a clear, short vision of why clients would select your firm rather than the competition (Figure 3.3).

At a deeper level, your UVP will reflect the convergence of your culture, brand, leadership style, services marketing and people. Your value proposition is not set in stone and may shift in response to major changes such as recessions, changes in corporate form, expansion or simply in response to significant market changes. Ironically, your UVP also does not have to be unique. It simply needs to be rare enough that most of your clients won't encounter the same statement. The UVP is 'the tip of the spear': the information clients need to know why your firm is different.

It should be stressed that developing a serious UVP necessarily limits your market. It means that you are no longer vanilla. You are cookie dough gelato, and some people won't like it. Since you are not competing with everyone, you should embrace this as a good thing. You are now more exclusive and expensive. You know who your clients and potential employees are and understand

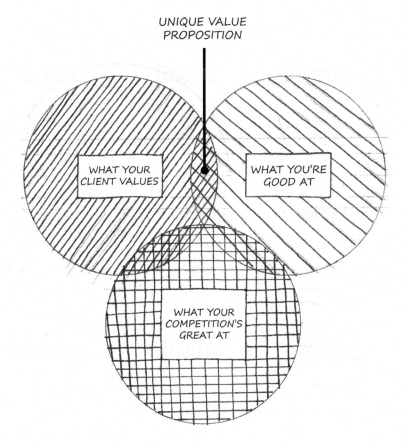

UNIQUE VALUE
PROPOSITION

WHAT YOUR
CLIENT VALUES

WHAT YOU'RE
GOOD AT

WHAT YOUR
COMPETITION'S
GREAT AT

Figure 3.3 Your unique value proposition.

the value you bring them. For this reason, as we shall see, it is important to know what you won't do, who you won't work with and who you won't employ (no matter how 'good' they are).

It's up to you how you define your UVP, but I personally like the version that provides a strapline followed by a sentence or two of description:

> *Prof. Joe O'Mahoney helps small consultancies grow faster and better. His trusted, research-based method for growth helps your firm learn from the mistakes and successes from over 100 successful consultancies: maximising margins and revenue whilst decreasing risk and worry.*

Breaking this down, we can see that UVP answers:

• What do you do brilliantly and (relatively) uniquely for your clients?
• How do you do it differently from others?
• What benefits will the client gain?

Figure 3.4 emphasises that the value proposition of a very small firm will bring together the benefits of the firm's services with its strategy and branding. However, it should be stressed that the value of each service is not the same as the value proposition as a whole. As we can see in the examples above, the value proposition is more general, aspirational and market-driven than the details of what your services achieve. This is important because it allows you to shift the value proposition by tailoring the language to suit the current market: from process re-engineering to digital transformation; from quality improvement to Agile; from downsizing to rightsizing.

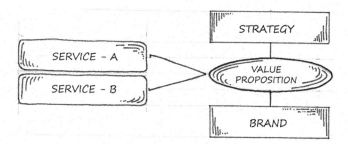

Figure 3.4 Early value propositions.

When the firm is small, its value proposition will be virtually the same as its services. However, as the firm grows, it is likely to develop many more services grouped around more than one value proposition (see Figure 3.5). It is worth noting that not all services map to all propositions, although it is likely that all your value propositions will be related (in order to maximise cross-selling and consultant synergies). Note also that an increasing number of value propositions should be represented by your overarching *strategic* value proposition, which is, in turn, driven by your strategy, and influences your brand and marketing efforts.

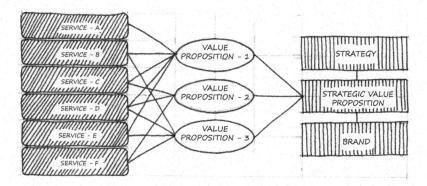

Figure 3.5 Later value propositions.

Here are some examples of a strategic value proposition from the firms I have studied or coached:

- Quick Release: 'Solving your product data challenges today, and future-proofing your tomorrow'.
- Dartmouth Recruitment Consultants: 'Recruiting excellence from class-room to boardroom'.
- Ducker Frontier: 'We deliver the insights you need to capture growth and mitigate risk'.

Visit their websites and each has a short paragraph underneath, expanding on the value that is delivered to the client, how it is achieved and what makes the firm different. The potential client is left in no doubt about the benefits of working with the firm and what sets it apart from the competition.

If you would like access to a workshop presentation on developing your UVP, I have one at joeomahoney.com that is freely available.

Leverage

Leverage refers to the ratio of consultants to partners. David Maister saw it as central to the strategy of the large professional service firm. Whilst leverage is still important, especially to larger firms, it is less important now than when Maister was writing, for a few reasons. First, the increased levels of digital technology and the growing use of off-shore centres of expertise mean that the value of teams is based less on the people visible on the project and more on other assets. Second, consulting firms, and to a less extent, clients, are increasingly fond of value-based pricing. Whilst this does not mean that team costs do not need to be tightly managed, it *does* mean that many consultancies are rightly focused on the value they deliver for clients rather than the cost of the resources that deliver this value. Strategically, as we discussed above, it is better to be best rather than cheapest in class. Third, clients themselves are sick of being charged a fortune for 23-year-old MBA graduates with no work experience, and are not afraid to make experience a criteria in their procurement exercises. Finally, service models are changing as consultancy business models change. Joint-ventures, equity investments, shared IP development, expert panels, associate teams, and many other variations on the traditional model mean that a simple ratio of juniors to partners often seems an out-moded method of measurement.

Still, leverage is far from dead. In large firms, some service lines are still heavily dependent on large teams which generate profit per partner in part through their leverage ratios. Yet, a precise leverage ratio is difficult to establish and

Table 3.3 A simple dichotomy of leverage strategies

	Low leverage	High leverage
Service	High-quality, bespoke services usually for strategy or innovation projects. Outcomes tend to be open and hard to measure. Task complexity tends to be higher.	Standardised, repeatable services usually aimed at implementation or operational projects. Outcomes tend to be more specific and often measurable. Task complexity tends to be lower.
Finances	High day rate, high-margin work, but for shorter projects. Costs are higher due to high salaries.	Lower day rate, lower margin work, but for longer projects. Costs are lower due to lower salaries, but can be nudged upwards through investments in IT.
Knowledge management	Knowledge is generally passed though person-to-person relationships. Interpersonal networks are important.	Knowledge is embedded in IP which forms a great part of the standard operating procedure of these companies. IT systems are important for this to be effective.
Employees	The 'brand' of the company and the people within it are important. Top influencers, MBAs, client names and awards signal quality in the market. Focus on expertise, innovation and brilliance. Utilisation rates tend to be lower. Employees tend to demand and be given higher levels of autonomy.	Employees must be able to follow standardised processes. Graduates are not uncommon here, though unlikely from top-flight MBA courses. Utilisation rates tend to be higher. Employees tend to have less autonomy, even up to the middle management level.
Training	Partners are central to mentoring and developing employees on a one-to-one basis. High investment in talent development.	People are trained on the process, usually through IT systems or in groups. Lower investment in talent development.

perhaps a distraction in firms which are either too small to have mature services and more than a handful of teams. I would argue, however, that having a clear idea of what type of firm you *will become* is a crucial part of your strategy and will influence your decisions on who to hire and how to manage. This remains the case even if you don't have enough employees to have a stable leverage ratio!

Whilst most firms fall somewhere between the extremes, it is useful to look at the two opposing strategies for leverage strategies presented in Table 3.3. A low leverage firm such as Water Street Partners demands very high fees per consultant, generally for short-term, high-end strategy and M&A work. As their fees are high, they need to provide, and signal, the highest quality consultants possible: consultant CVs tend to be outstanding and will include well-known markers of quality education and employment, but a higher salary will be needed to attract this talent.

The type of work in high-leverage firms tends to be relatively tailored, high value and innovative. There is, after all, no point paying a fortune for talent who will learn by reading a manual! Skill development, therefore, is at a premium, and tends to be done through partner mentoring rather than outsourced training courses.

Firms with higher leverage ratios on the other hand tend to work on relatively standardised projects (e.g. implementation) where juniors do not need high levels of senior interaction to do their job well. To some extent, the job can be done by following instructions. This type of work is more standardised and commodified, with lower day rates, but projects tend to be larger (albeit with lower margins). The higher numbers of reports per senior mean that significant development time with partners is generally substituted with standardised training programmes delivered by HR or third parties. In terms of talent, astounding CVs which justify astounding fees are not necessary, and creativity is much less valued than someone who can simply follow instructions. This is not to say that their hires do not need to be bright, but with strengths in process rather than innovation.

For firms that rely upon the leveraged model, managing the mix is crucial, especially once they move beyond the 25–35 employee threshold. Before this, partners can often directly mix and manage across the organisation and rely on personal stewardship rather than IP to manage delegation. Beyond this point, however, leverage becomes increasingly important, both in minimising costs and for providing a guide for strategic decision-making in the group. Managing leverage in the project or proposition is still very important if costs are to be controlled and quality is to be maintained. Figure 3.6 shows that if leverage is high on what should be a low leverage project, then quality will suffer. Figure 3.7 shows that if things are the other way around, then profit margins will suffer.[14]

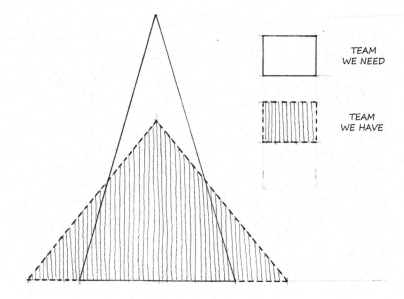

TEAM
WE NEED

TEAM
WE HAVE

Figure 3.6 Too few skills: quality will suffer.

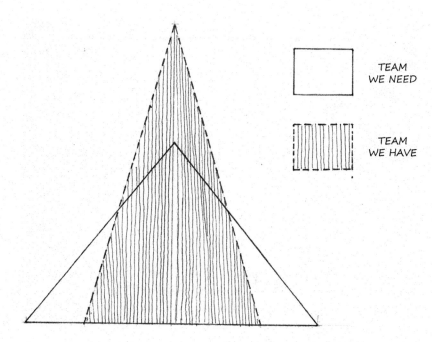

TEAM
WE NEED

TEAM
WE HAVE

Figure 3.7 Too many skills: wage bill is too high.

In medium-sized firms, managing leverage effectively on the project, and the firm as a whole, is a skill that managers should be taught about and actively reflect on, post-project with reference to the project margins achieved.

Utilisation

Utilisation refers to the percentage of billable time for any consultant. It is a strategic as well as an operational metric. High-leverage firms tend to have high utilisation rates because the work is more commodified and there is less need for employee development and tailoring of services (see Table 3.3 above). Whilst I have anecdotal evidence that utilisation rates over 85% tend to lead to higher levels of turnover, it should also be noted that slight increases in utilisation, especially for juniors, can also have a tremendous impact on margins. In an average firm, which breaks even at 50% utilisation, a 15 percentage point increase on this will allow them to make 20% margins. For this reason, measuring and managing utilisation is crucial (Figure 3.8) so you have a clear view of who is under-utilised, and who may be feeling the stress of being over-utilised.

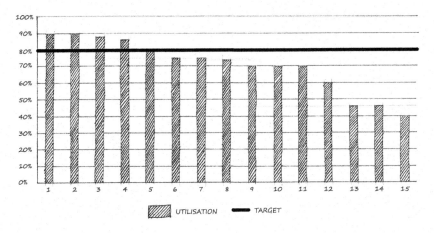

Figure 3.8 Target utilisation tracking.

As detailed above, utilisation must fit with the firm strategy: lower leverage firms tend to provide consultants with more time for IP development, research and training (Figure 3.9). Even in these firms, however, utilisation should be managed effectively. This can be achieved by:

• Using a PSA (see Chapter 7) to measure and record utilisation trends over time.
• Making one partner responsible for the firm hitting utilisation targets.

- Ensuring that pipeline visibility is apparent for one to two months ahead.
- Using employees on the bench before using contractors (although there will be exceptions).

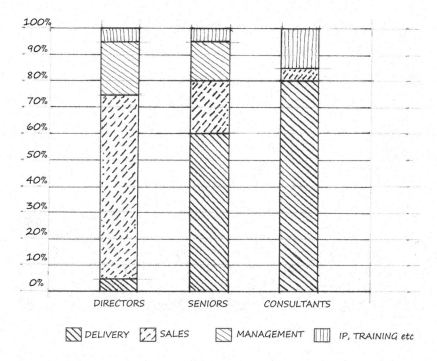

Figure 3.9 Common utilisation targets for different grades.

How?

Business models: move over Maister?

Let us assume 'why' and 'what' are defined, for now. You've got your niche, culture and value proposition sorted, but a fundamental question remains – *how* are you going to win? The answer to this is your business model, which I define as *the way you organise to achieve competitive advantage*.

David Maister, the don of consulting insight in the 1980s and 1990s, defined three business models with different forms of leverage: Brains, Grey Hair and Procedure. Brains and Procedure were, he argued, polar opposites in terms of client risk, fees, leverage, competition with other consultancies and customisation. Grey Hair projects are in the middle (Table 3.4).

Table 3.4 Maister's classifications of consulting companies

	Problem focus	*Solution focus*	*Typical staff*	*Cost*	*Leverage*
Brains	Complex, relatively unique, one-off problems.	Innovative. Diagnosis intensive.	Intelligent, creative, younger.	High	Low
Grey Hair	Uncommon for the firm but common in the industry.	Expert.	Experienced, older experts. Many partners.	Medium	Medium
Procedure	Common.	Standardised. Execution intensive.	Mostly junior.	Low	High

Whilst I use these simplifications occasionally later on, I would argue that these models have been mixed up considerably by digital technology. Consider Exlirr, who amid the COVID-19 pandemic began publishing daily insightful data-driven presentations about the virus and its impact – most definitely fitting in the Brains box. Yet consider that the value provided was driven by their technologies: APIs to external databases, powerful data analysis software and semi-automated presentation software. It seems to me not only that the Brains, Grey Hair and Procedure models are much more converged now than they were 20 years ago, but also that 'Procedure' doesn't really capture the huge transformation offered by digital to the average consultancy. The early versions of technology that Maister may have seen (for example, ERP) might have fitted with commodified work and low-cost pricing, but this is no longer the case.[15]

Moreover, as the 'built to sell' model of consultancy growth has gained in popularity, buyers are less keen on investing in firms where the brains or grey hair can walk out of the door after the earn-out period. They now look for IP, such as digital products, but also internal processes and procedures, that shift the asset base of the firm from people to the firm.

There are also other trends that have disrupted Maister's classifications: the younger age of consulting firm founders, the propensity of buyers to value digital assets and internal processes over key individuals (especially those coming up to retirement), the decline of the 'master-apprentice' form of consultancy, the market shift away from strategy and towards digital and the ubiquity of information that was previously the preserve of top firms. I could go on, but let us now focus on more innovative business models which I've seen work.

Innovative business models

Despite everything I've written above, it should be noted that the traditional cost-plus, leveraged business model for consultancies is alive and well. Many consulting firms (successful and otherwise) have at their heart a team which costs the partners X and is sold out at 3X or thereabouts. The key to the cost-plus business model is providing systems, resources and training which allow juniors to be safely leveraged to do more valuable work. In other words, the value of the people you offer is increased, and thus the price can be increased.

Whilst the cost-plus business model is still dominant, there are an increasing number of complementary and alternative business models that complement existing approaches. Many fast-growing consulting firms combine traditional consulting with recruitment, training or venturing services. The splendidly named Wyndham Plumptre, founder of The Upside, told me: 'we see ourselves as a talent incubator. Everything else just follows from that. If you've got great people and invest in them, you will get great consulting and great new businesses from them'.

Let's say you are a standard time and materials[16], leverage-based consultancy. These are examples of analogue ways in which you might add to or even supplant your existing business model (we deal with digital opportunities shortly):

- Use a network of skilled associates rather than full-time employees.
- Place individuals or small teams with client employees to support them implementing their own projects.
- Offer expert one-to-one advice rather than project implementation.
- Provide a research-only service and provide recommendations for implementation work.
- Provide a membership network with access to peers, bespoke research and talks and networking events.
- Provide a benchmarking/maturity service.
- Provide accredited training to clients and other consultancies.
- Develop products and services which are licenced to other consultancies or to clients themselves.
- Design the entire company and its services as a franchise for other consultancies and consultants.
- Develop a powerful network with innovative suppliers and act as a broker and advisor for client access.
- Create a hybrid recruitment-consulting firm where high potential hires are trained, used as consultants for a period and then placed as client employees.

The choice for any (or none) of these is of course highly dependent on the firm, its lifecycle and context. Some of these choices are more fundamentally strategic and some are more tactical, but tactical decisions that are successful will often have highly strategic implications. In my coaching, I often find that what has started off as an experiment for clients has become dominant and, in turn, fundamentally transforms what the firm is and how it operates. The key, as we will see in Chapter 5, is to experiment often in small ways, test ideas with 'safe' clients and go all in on ideas that appear to be winners.

B2B service vs. software vs. platform business models

The business models detailed above do not need to be enabled by digital technology, but they generally are. Digital offers an opportunity to deliver value and thus revenue without consultants, thus creating potentially infinite levels of leverage. Over 80% of the firms I studied used some form of revenue-earning digital offering. Sometimes these were stand-alone services such as video courses, apps or software-as-a-service (SaaS), but more commonly they were digital assets that were used by teams in conjunction with their standard consulting work. This includes databases, algorithms and software which they used to add value or reduce costs for the client.

SaaS or apps have potential to break the time-revenue link in a variety of ways (see Table 3.5), and provide the ultimate way of capturing, codifying and improving the firm's expertise and experience.

Table 3.5 Software business model options

How is the software distributed?	Who owns the code?	How is revenue generated?
Local/On-site;	Proprietary (firm);	Licence;
Cloud;	Proprietary (client);	Usage-based;
Hybrid	Open source	Advertising;
		Support-based;
		Transaction fee;
		Freemium;
		Subscription;
		In-app purchases;
		Tiered

Digital has also enabled an alternative innovative business model based on 'platforms'. 'Platforms' simply act as mediators, enabling interactions between synergistic groups, for example, buyers and sellers (Table 3.6). Platforms pre-existed the internet (think auctions) but have been accelerated by developments in technology (think eBay, Amazon, Uber, etc.).[17] I remember back in 2001, losing a strategy argument at '3', the mobile operator, as to whether we should build our own products and services or become a platform for others – the firm went with the former. I'm biased of course, but it is rare that a firm which specialises in X can do Y as well as the Darwinism of the market.

Table 3.6 Traditional vs. digital vs. platform business models

Traditional business product	Digital business model	Platform business model
Newspaper (analogue)	HBO	YouTube
Encyclopaedia Britannica (books)	www.britannica.com	Wikipedia
Walmart (shops)	Walmart.com	Amazon.com
Harvard University MBA	Harvard Distance Learning MBA	Udemy

Whilst platforms are most common in the software world, some consultancies have followed the model to enable interactions between experts and buyers (consider Co-match, Newton-X, Transparency Lab, Alphasights or GLG). One consultancy I have advised for some time, Digitopia, began as a digital maturity consultancy offering one-off engagements, but realised that with some investment, they could create a platform where, for a subscription, firms would have access to a plethora of maturity benchmarks and indexes which could also be built by others but hosted on the platform (for a cut). This transformation accelerated not only their growth but also their attractiveness to buyers, as platforms tend to be stickier and offer higher revenue opportunities than mere software packages.

It is worth considering however that platforms traditionally have two common challenges. The first is ensuring that producers that use the platform produce sufficient quality not to damage the platform brand. Amazon has increasingly had this challenge as cheap sellers flood the platform and buy fake reviews. The second is the chicken-and-egg challenge of having enough users (for example, clients) to attract producers (for example, consultancies) and having enough producers to attract clients.

This all said, the multiples that are paid for software and platform businesses (typically 20–30 times EBITDA) are much greater than for standard consultancies (×7–12 EBITDA). For consultancies that have the opportunity, an obvious way to push up the multiple is to incorporate revenue-generating software or platforms.

One innovation exercise I've tried with clients is detailed in Figure 3.10. The choices are detailed by the client and it often provokes a good discussion and some new ideas.

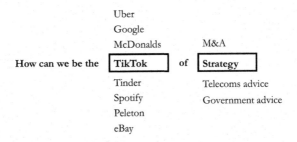

Figure 3.10 Brainstorming innovative business models (example).

Alliances

A few of the firms that I've studied also emphasised how alliances or partnerships with other consultancies helped them grow. These were generally focused on providing a broader or deeper offering to clients where a small solo firm might be insufficient. Alliances or business partnerships often start off as simple mutual introduction arrangements with firms that are working upstream (for example, strategy) or downstream (for example, implementation) from each other or are horizontally aligned (for example, in different markets or functions).

A study in 2021[18] found that alliances and partnerships were likely to fail when there is no clear strategy to the partnership, when insufficient resources are put into the partnership and when there is a lack of cultural fit. Alliances were most successful when there was not only a strong mutual benefit to each consultancy, but also to clients.

To this end, being clear on the purpose and outcomes of, and responsibilities and incentives in, potential partnerships is crucial. A frank conversation with potential partners should be clear on the potential risks and seek to gradually build trust over time though face-to-face time and a willingness to put 'skin in the game'. It is also important to develop the governance mechanisms and agreements suitable for each stage of the relationship. It may be useful to develop metrics by which the success of the partnership can be monitored and review these regularly to assess whether expectations are meeting reality.

Consultancies which might benefit from partnerships or alliances might answer 'yes' to more than three of these questions:

- Do your clients have common needs that fall outside your scope?
- Are there upstream, downstream or horizontal capabilities that would enable you to offer more value to existing clients?
- Are some great potential clients unapproachable because you are too small?
- Do you often find yourselves working for clients before, after or at the same time as other consultancies?
- Do you know of consultancies which operate in the same sector or service that might offer additional depth or breadth to your offering?

Of course, if you are developing a partnership with a larger firm or even a smaller firm with deep pockets, an alliance may offer the chance to test the waters of a potential purchase or investment down the line.

Networks: good and bad

Network business models provide value to clients based less upon what the consultancy produces and more upon the ideas and the experiences with which they are connected. The most basic example is the associate model which, aside from the recent reversal due to legislation in some countries, has been on the increase for 20 years. Although associate models don't generally deliver increased value (to the consultancy) over traditional consulting (see Chapter 8 for a discussion), other models might. Given the rapid pace of technological development, an increasing number of consultancies are focusing on building strong relationships (partnering, investing, affiliating) with innovative new firms rather than trying to develop innovation in-house. As Stephen Newton (Elixirr) told me, 'you can't out innovate the market'.

Another model for network-based consulting are globally distributed groups of similar small firms that join together to offer clients international expertise. They seek to do this without the hassle of a central office and overhead. The challenge comes, however, when these firms seek to sell. Since they are generally made up of separate legal entities, they often try to form a larger company in order to sell: the spokes on the wheel create a central hub, in order to offer an international consulting firm for sale. Such firms often (rightly) see their international presence as a powerful selling point, but risk underestimating the complexities a buyer would face in taking on such a firm. Whilst not impossible to sell, this type of organisation is often trying to put the genie back in the bottle – to effectively 'reverse engineer' the company which can involve several challenges. One is creating a central body that is both funded by the individual firms and has the power to direct them. An associated challenge is presented by the politics of individual firms relinquishing sufficient controls, finances, practices and even incorporation to allow them to act as an individual entity with a new leader. Network-based consultancies also face further challenges, needing sufficient common IP (both internal and external) to guide the practices of the firms and needing to overcome the fact that different partners are likely to have very different requirements for a sale. This can be complicated further by differing cultures and legal requirements. A final common challenge is that the different path dependencies, cultures – and sometimes founder egos – of different firms coming together often creates a hydra that is difficult to manage centrally.

Capabilities

The final answer to the question of 'How?' concerns the capabilities of the firm. By capabilities, I mean *the accumulated knowledge and skills embedded in a consultancy's organisational systems and routines which give it competitive advantage.*[19] In short, these are the things which improve the performance of the firm in the long term.[20]

A consultancy which improves its capability improves its value to employees and clients, and can thus increase its quality of delivery and prices. There are six ways in which capabilities are developed. In Figure 3.11, the big square represents a consulting firm. It has valuable inputs in the forms of recruits, suppliers and partners and market information. Its two outputs are project delivery and client relationships, which, in turn, feed back into the value of the consultancy (say with more experienced consultants, client goodwill, testimonials and referrals). In order to turn these inputs into outputs, the firm implicitly or explicitly relies on six capabilities, all held together by management systems.

If these capabilities are cultivated, systematised and improved, they provide the architecture for increasingly high-quality work, happier employees, better clients and higher profits. Of course, these capabilities can often be strengthened with clear processes or even automation, and their relative importance will shift depending on your business model and the maturity of the firm. It is worth examining the future emphasis on capability during the annual strategy review.

Each of these capabilities is covered in detail at various points in this book, but here I emphasise how they work together:

1. Leadership capabilities **improve the motivation and understanding of employees to achieve the firm's strategy.** Leadership capabilities are

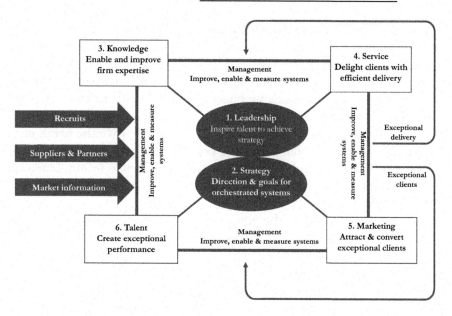

Figure 3.11 The six capabilities of consulting firms.

developed in the senior team through the mindsets and traits (integrity, reassurance, persuasion). The leadership capability is perhaps the least easy to control, change and systematise, which is a pity because it is by far the most important contributor to the success of the firm.

2. Strategy capabilities are not concerned with *what* strategy you pursue but *how* you do strategy. Strategy capabilities help **improve the firm's direction, focus and positioning**. They are the boss of capabilities, in that they drive and co-ordinate all the other capabilities listed here. In the long term, strong strategy capabilities create faster growth, less competition and higher profits. It means developing robust processes around such things as market research, competitor analysis and innovation. It does not mean spending a month or a year creating a huge strategy document that lives and dies in someone's drawer.

3. Knowledge capabilities concern the capturing, storing and sharing of experience, research and knowledge in order to **improve the firm's expertise**. These take experiences from work on a client site, lessons learned, research and innovation, and capture and share them in the in the firm's methods, databases, training or systems. Knowledge is also to be garnered through experimentation, the firm's external network and stakeholders, research and training. You can't deliver up-to-date expertise and increase your prices if you're not investing in your knowledge.

4. Service capabilities are externally focused. Value here is added by translating the talent and knowledge internal to the firm into products and

services through the creation of solutions which attract clients and solve their problems efficiently. These capabilities **improve the firm's delivery** and can be enhanced through external suppliers such as technology providers, associates, software and database licences, knowledge partnerships, training providers, research suppliers and even clients themselves. These all provide additional value for the firm.

5. The marketing capabilities are the assets which **improve the firm's client base**. It is marketing that builds the bridge between the services you offer and the challenges and opportunities that the client is facing. Marketing capabilities include business development more generally and the capacity to price intelligently.

6. Talent capabilities allow the firm to **improve the value of the firm's people**, both in terms of their own motivation and alignment with the firm, but also in terms of the quality of their work. This capability is a key asset of a people-based consultancy and acts as a signal to the market of the firm's pedigree. Whilst strong HR advice is important, the talent capability of the firm should not be outsourced to HR and should instead be led and driven by a partner.

Different firms place different emphases on different parts of this model, yet even in a firm of one, it is worth examining each box and arrow in Figure 3.11. Ask yourself how you can contribute to the value that your firm adds to its inputs in order to create better outputs.[21] Managed well, these capabilities produce a virtuous cycle of value which is reflected in the firm's performance.

Table 3.7 Bodies vs. services

	Selling bodies	*Selling a service*
Invest in......	Employees	Systems
Fees are.....	Finite	Unlimited
Payments are	Time-based	Value-based
Asset is....	Unreliable	Reliable
Recruits are......	Highly skilled, expensive	Lower skilled, cheaper
Leverage is....	Low	High
Quality is.....	Inconsistent	Consistent
Knowledge is.....	Tacit	Codified

As we discuss later, certainly for firms that sell for high multiples, these capabilities should be systematised rather than held in the heads of various partners. This gets to the heart of the difference between a consultancy that sells
bodies compared to the one that has systems that generate leveraged assets
(Table 3.7).

Growth finances: cash flow, investment and borrowing

An interesting divide between leaders who are still growing their firms and
those who have sold their firms is that the former often proudly tell me that
their growth is funded solely through cash flow and the latter often tell me they
wish they'd borrowed or sought investment for faster growth. Of course, the
evidence base is biased, but once you know you have a solid firm with great
growth prospects, there is an opportunity cost to *not* borrowing/seeking investment for growth.

Let's start with cash flow. If you are going to grow solely through cash flow, then
it is important to manage this well because professional services are incredibly
sensitive to cash flow challenges. This is because invoices are often paid much
later than salaries. As the COVID-19 pandemic demonstrated, three months
of losses or one big client refusing to pay can quickly lead to a situation where
staff are not paid and bankruptcy is not far off. Strong cash flow management
for a consultancy prioritises the following:

- Get paid upfront or as soon as possible. As we discuss in Chapter 6, project
  or value pricing is best for this.
- Get invoices paid within 30 days ideally. For anything later than 60 days
  add charges if you can.
- Ensure promptly paid invoices are the responsibility of your project man-
  ager and linked to their bonuses.
- With problem clients, usually a 'letter before action' will do the trick.
- Where possible, develop assets for recurring revenue.

As your consultancy grows, a useful metric is cash flow per partner, which can
also be written as:

$$Cash\ flow/fees \times fees/staff \times staff/partners$$

Cash flow can also be maximised by what David Ogilvy described in his Principles of Management:

> To keep your ship moving through the water at maximum efficiency, you have to keep scraping the barnacles off its bottom. It is rare for a department head to recommend the abolition of a job, or even the elimination of a man; the pressure from below is always adding. If the initiative for barnacle-scraping does not come from management, barnacles will never be scraped.

As a solo consultant, scraping barnacles often involves attention to your salary (did you really need the new Mac Pro?), but later is primarily concerned with the salaries of others. To some extent, salaries can be mitigated through significant performance-related bonuses, a 'high stepped' three-year salary (low in the first year followed by significant increases) or equity in the firm. More strategically, developing a strong recruitment and development programme will allow you to create better talent at a lower cost.

Alternatives to growing from cash flow are growing from debt or taking on an equity partner (which can sometimes be a strategic investor such as another consultancy). Balance sheet debt these days is relatively cheap and there are usually tax benefits. Equity investment can be a benefit if the investor is providing additional expertise, a route to new clients or partnerships or a potential buyer at the end of the journey. Otherwise, equity investment for growth at an early stage is a more expensive option. I detail the use of private equity to support the exit of one or more partners in the final chapter.

The most significant early investment seen by my interviewees was Roger Carlile, who grew Ankura from nothing to a £500 million business in five years. Roger acknowledges his good fortune in raising £100 million in funding after the first year. He didn't particularly want that much money, but the investors, with whom he had an existing relationship, didn't do deals for less than this. It was a nice problem to have. This injection allowed the firm to recruit 150 employees and buy some well-aligned competitors, even if it also raised significant challenges for building and maintaining the firm technology, culture and systems.

What, who and when?

The strategy and plan

I have put a template for a strategy and plan at www.joeomahoney.com. I'm a fan of keeping the strategy short, displaying it publicly and revisiting it frequently. Again, don't try to be vanilla or everything for everyone. Writing the strategy and plan should be iterative, not sequential and both should be 'live' documents that evolve.

We have already covered much of the strategy *process*, but here is a guide for formalising it. It should be tailored to suit your stage and preferences, but a typical structure may go as follows:

- **Why?**
  - o **Values**: the principles and standards that provide the basis for your culture.
  - o **Culture**: the norms and attitudes that will guide your activities.
- **What?**
  - o **Ultimate goal**: what do the major shareholders want this firm to achieve and in what timespan?
  - o **Mission statement**: an inspirational statement of (i) the ideal difference you want your firm to make, (ii) to the stakeholders who you serve and (iii) how you will achieve this.
  - o **Niche positioning**: what clients (business and role) will you serve? What need will you fulfil? What will you do? This should link to your marketing strategy and plan.
  - o **Unique Value Proposition**: why would clients select your firm above others?
  - o **Competitive positioning**: where will you be compared to the competitors?
- **How?**
  - o **Business model**: how does the firm generate value, both for its clients and for itself?
  - o **Capabilities**: what capabilities must the firm develop in order to support and drive growth?
  - o **Competencies**: what key skills and attributes do our people need to have to support growth?
  - o **Services**: what services, platforms, software and products will you have?
- **When and Who?**
  - o **Three-Year Goals**: revenues and margins; projects and clients; people; capabilities; systems; milestones.
  - o **One-Year Goals**: revenues and margins; projects and clients; people; capabilities; systems.
  - o **Plan**: to achieve one-year goals detailing activities, responsibilities and deadlines.
  - o **Success measures**: how will you quantify progress?

- **Finances and risks**
  - o Sales projections
  - o Headcount and salary projections
  - o Projected capital spending
  - o Projected operating costs
  - o Investment/capital requirements
  - o Projected valuation
  - o Risk register

Aside from the strategy and plan itself, the *process* for strategising and planning is probably the most important process in a growing firm. I suggest using the process as a way to engage and motivate employees and key clients. Involve them in the different aspects of the plan and bring the parts together at a one- or two-day off-site event where it can be developed, challenged and brought together. This is more fun and inclusive than a PowerPoint deck and you may get ideas you weren't expecting.

When crisis hits

This book was written during the COVID-19 lockdown. Whilst it has been an awful time, it has afforded me a unique insight into why some of my interviewees and clients did better than others. The lessons here are reminiscent of those following the 2008 recession and the 2000 crash. In these downturns, five things made a difference. In order of importance, these were:

1. **Luck**: some smaller firms just happened to be in a sector (say healthcare during COVID-19) or services (delayering or crisis management) that were in demand. Those lucky 15% actually grew in the recession.
2. **Pivoting fast**: one of the unique benefits of smaller firms is the ability to pivot quickly. A new website and LinkedIn profile can be created in a day and relevant thought leadership written and disseminated within a week. Some firms did exactly this and turned a crisis into an opportunity for growth. Close communication with and research on the changing client market should lead this shift.
3. **Business development**: hunkering down on sales, in some cases, prevented the loss of existing clients. Paying greater attention to the pipeline and marketing intensively paid off for many. One client of mine had great success with shifting their pricing to success fees, whilst another (who had reserves) offered to postpone billing for clients who were struggling. Remember that in recessions, digital advertising costs tend to fall. It is a good idea to try to get an early view of what will happen to the pipeline by

phoning key clients and watching any announcements. If you have non-exec directors, then these should be encouraged to make referrals.

4. **Cost management**: moving quickly to cut associates and cutting all costs that do not impact sales (especially bonuses) put some firms ahead of the curve, so that declining client revenues hit the bottom line less hard. Where (the weakest, junior) employed staff had to go, this was done quickly and fairly. In some firms, salary cuts were made across the board and many placed this burden especially on senior staff. KPIs such as cash in the bank, debtor days and pipeline metrics should be reviewed weekly.

5. **Shifting client relations**: some consultancies not only shifted what they were doing for clients but also how they worked with them. Shorter return on investments made clients feel the work was worthwhile, and greater attention to communicating the benefits of work almost goes without saying. Following up quicker on debtors is also crucial.

6. **Communications:** being honest about the firm's prospects and intentions will stop rumour-mongering. The best firms reassured employees with projected stages of what they expected to happen, and how the firm would react in each of these stages. Communications were used to both clear the air and focus attention on what needed to be done if the firm was to survive.

Some larger firms had also strategically sought to develop counter-cyclical services, which meant they did well in the downturn, but this was relatively rare in firms with fewer than 100 employees.

Takeaways

- Successful consulting is achieved by passionate experts delivering outstanding value to clients. Consistently improve your value by capturing experience, learning and experimenting.
- Your overarching strategy should focus on the 'Why?' of the founder(s). This should be mirrored in the 'Why?' of the firm: its values and culture.
- Move towards a clear, in-demand niche with high fees. Ask yourself how you could treble your fees.
- Defining and pursuing a focused niche based upon market research, buyer research and competitor analysis is a far superior strategy than simply doing what you have done in the past. A niche can be expanded during growth, but this should be done strategically, not (just) in response to chance.
- Your UVP is the foundation of what the firm is. It summarises why clients should buy from you, and forms the foundation for your culture, capabilities, strategy and services.

- Have a vision of the type of firm you will become, but pivot quickly when necessary.
- Develop and update a growth plan detailing dependencies, costs, revenues, clients and hires.

Case study: Solidiance

The power of local knowledge

If anyone has a claim to cosmopolitan man of the year, it is perhaps Damien Duhamel the co-founder of Solidiance. Born in France, Damien grew up in North Africa and in the South Pacific, and studied in Australia, the US, Singapore and Vietnam. I'd list the places he's worked, but there is a word limit on this book.

After finishing his degree in 1995, Damien returned to Vietnam and, realising that the only option local companies had for external advice was to fly in very expensive consultants from large firms, set up a boutique consulting firm that helped foreign companies enter the country. His niche here was to offer himself and an increasing number of local recruits not only as a more cost-effective alternative, but also as an alternative with more significant hands-on knowledge of the region than many competitors. In some ways, it was a trial run of what he was going to create later on a much larger scale.

The Vietnamese firm grew to 18 employees, but after five years Damien decided to make a shift. The limitations of the Vietnamese market and the excitement of the Dotcom boom elsewhere eventually persuaded him to sell the firm in 2000 and join a company (which eventually became Aegis PLC), where he was promoted to lead the Singapore office. Following his success in this role, Damien became Managing Director (Asia Pacific) after two years. Six years later, having deepened his experience, he decided to begin earning profits for himself rather than other people.

Built to sell

As with many successful founders, Damien left with a significant network and with more work than he could handle alone. His first recruit was

Heiko Bugs, who he invited as a partner because their skill sets complimented each other's weaknesses. Damien says jokingly: 'we have this husband and wife relationship...I was looking for someone who was the opposite of me: someone who would say no to me'. From the beginning, the company was grown to be sold:

> from day one we positioned ourselves to be in the best position to sell: multi-national clients, barriers to entry, and a pan-Asian presence. We had very strong auditing and proper accounting to ensure our books were good. There was no monkey business.

They expanded offices aggressively, opening two in the 2009 recession, typically using a senior manager to start the office and employing young local experts who would work hard and be keen to learn. They would typically wait until they had three to four projects in a region before opening an office, but of course the cost-benefit ratio was different, whereby some offices (for example, Malaysia) were much cheaper than others (for example, Japan).

Solidiance planned their niche as one that would both provide barriers to entry and be attractive to buyers. Their first principle was to only work for multinational companies in order to have larger revenues and profit margins. Their second was to be pan-Asian, so they could provide a total solution in that geography. Their final principle was to work in B2B in order to create barriers to entry to other firms without the knowledge. This last point is interesting. As Damien explains:

> if you are consulting for Haagen-Dazs, everyone understands the market. But if I speak about cement, bolts and chemicals, you are dealing with huge spenders, but they are industries that require deep understanding and that everyone else dislikes. We like these 'dirty' industries – I like to be on the site in a hat and boots. We like it rusty, dusty and rusty.

The company grew out of its own cash and at no point did they take on debt or external investment. As they grew, they allowed more partners to buy into the company, but for 15 years they decided to open new offices rather than take dividends. They avoided taking on non-billable people during growth: 'we never had an HR person; we never had an IT person. We delegated a lot of power to local office managers to make decisions'. They even developed their own ERP/customer relationship management (CRM) system internally which Damien argues was 'a critical part of our success'. The system was designed to be intuitive and needed no staff training.

Solidiance focused exclusively on helping clients grow fast in Asia, growing from two staff and one office in Singapore to 120 full-time staff. Whilst they help many companies (50% US; 20% Japanese; 20% European) strategically expand into Asia, they also have sector specialisms in, for example, automotive, healthcare and construction, and service specialisms in innovation, sustainability and healthcare.

The firm grew rapidly because clients liked the fact that the team was experienced in many different cultures, which provided an advantage over other firms that might fly in teams. As they grew, they established expertise in most key Asian markets. Their clients were exclusively multinationals and the firm focused on delivering high-quality services which resulted in 90% repeat business from their clients. Increasingly, they developed methods and processes for their work, but were also aware that these could often 'turn off your creativity and innovation' – using these was a question of balance.

Running and selling a multinational

As the firm expanded, the number of offices increased. However, the firm kept one profit and loss (P&L) account in order to avoid office competition between business units. This was important because clients might approach their local office with a request for a project in a different country. A single P&L helped with sharing knowledge and clients. The centre also took all the 'red tape and admin' away from the local offices allowing them to focus solely on client work. Co-ordination was also helped by the founders having significant visibility to and of the local offices. The CRM/ERP system provided the owners with high levels of visibility, and two-hour weekly calls were had with the office managers. However, the centre sought to avoid stepping on the toes of office managers: 'we gave them freedom to execute, and they came to us if there were problems they could not solve'.

By 2016, Solidiance had grown to 16 international offices, from Abu Dhabi and New Delhi to Yangon and Sydney and increased their size by 25% when they bought China-based consultancy *Technomic Asia*. In 2017, they expanded to offices in the US and EU to better serve their clients in that space, and in late 2018 were bought (though the Japanese prefer the term 'merged') by a Japanese pan-Asian consultancy YCP to strengthen their own regional presence. Their case deserves attention as a study in creating value across a region, not just a country.

Notes

1 Source: Equiteq (2018) *The Knowledge Economy Global Buyers Report*. Equitq.com.
2 Lafley, A.G., & Martin, R. (2013) *Playing to Win: How Strategy Really Works*. Boston, MA: Harvard Business Review Press.
3 If you wish to expand the questions that contribute to your strategy, see Watkins, M. (2007) *Demystifying Strategy: The What, Who, How, and Why*. Boston, MA: Harvard Business Review, September. For consulting firms, this may be overkill. In addition, the why/what/how questions are also used in Sinek, S. (2011) *Start with Why*. London: Penguin.
4 Note that this is a retrospective calculation of the 'successful' firms. For the new founder, if the opportunity cost, the failure rate and the cost of capital are considered, one can see why it is not a universally popular activity!
5 Stephenson, G. R. (1967) Cultural acquisition of a specific learned response among rhesus monkeys. In: J. Kuhn (ed.) *Progress in Primatology*. Stuttgart: Gustav Fischer Verlag, pp. 76–80.
6 Hinge University (2019) *Professional Services Guide to Research*. Virginia: Hinge.
7 Frederiksen, L. Harr, E., Montgomery, S., & Taylor, A. (2013) *Inside the buyer's brain*. USA: Hinge Research Institute.
8 Such an activity could usefully be supported through an MBA project with your local University.
9 Carman, J. M., & Langeard, E. (1980) Growth strategies for service firms. *Strategic Management Journal*, 1(1), 7–22.
10 Hinge Research Institute (2018) *High Growth Study: Consulting Firm Edition*. Virginia: Hinge Research Institute.
11 Scott, M. (1998) *The Professional service firm*. London: John Wiley, p. 23.
12 Whenever you give a discount, please charge the full price on the invoice and then *show* the discount. This avoids the client thinking that you are permanently cheap.
13 Readers of *Private Eye* will note the vast number of consultancies providing 'free' advisory work on power government committees and boards: they do not do so for the love of their countries.
14 See Chapter 1 of Maister, D. (1993) *Managing the Professional Service Firm*. New York: MacMillan.
15 Oddly, Maister also argued that consulting firms grew primarily to keep good people. His argument was that if the firm wants to maintain its leverage ratio AND keep hold of its ambitious people, it will need to promote a certain percentage of those people in order to maintain their loyalty. This creates an 'escalator effect', whereby many of the employees become more senior and eventually want a share in the partnership. In the spirit of having a smaller slice of a bigger (and growing) pie, most founders will accept this but tie the partnership in with sales and margin targets. Whilst this may be true in large firms, I found little evidence of this in smaller firms that were growing. Growth was primarily driven by founder mindset.
16 In service firms, it's more accurate to write 'time and expenses', but hardly anyone does, so I won't either.

17 Zhu, F., & Furr, N. (2016) Products to platforms: Making the leap. *Harvard Business Review*, 94(4), 72–78.

18 Consultancy Growth Network (2021) Alliances Survey.

19 Day, G. S. (1994) The capabilities of market-driven organizations. *Journal of Marketing*, 58(4), 37–52. I've amended George Day's definition here.

20 I ask my MBA students 'what things can a consultancy do to increase profit per partner?'. They generally reply with: put up prices; increase leverage ratios; sack seniors and employ juniors; cut salaries. I then ask, 'what things can a consultancy do to increase profit per partner *without damaging the firm in the long run?*'. This is a harder question to answer, and one I address in Chapter 8.

21 This theory is an extension of the resource-based view of the firm where knowledge is seen as a resource asset, but also a capacity for innovation. Note, theories of PSF strategies tend not to distinguish between client-facing service development or knowledge development, often assuming that the only important knowledge is that which is deployed in client engagements! Moreover, as much of the research on PSF strategy was done pre-2010, the transformational role of digital in every aspect of the supply chain (suppliers, firm, client engagement) is often missed. For example, Hansen's piece in *Harvard Business Review* in 1999 makes a distinction between 'reuse economics' and 'expert economics' (p. 109) that misses two modern developments: first, the extent to which digital allows reuse (databases, rules, codified processes) and expertise (AI and machine learning); second, innovative (expert) service provision is now generally predicated upon the reuse of different internal assets.

4
Marketing for growth

What are investors and acquirers looking for?

The best form of marketing is great value being delivered by passionate people. This will lead to testimonials and referrals (that are not only more effective than any other form of marketing but also cheaper). Unfortunately, as the firm grows, it becomes harder to deliver consistently outstanding work and even when this is achieved, referrals alone rarely generate the high levels of growth that investors prize.

Thus, as firms get larger, investors will look for marketing *systems* that generate and keep high-spend, repeat-business clients. Buyers will *ideally* be at the CXO level of blue chip firms with which the consultancy has established long-term relationships. Consultancies rarely tick all of these boxes, but ones that do generate high multiples of valuation because buyers are more assured that performance will not fail after an acquisition. Even when partners are involved in the marketing and sales process, which they should be, investors and buyers look for marketing systems that efficiently, consistently and systematically attract the right mix of ideal clients to the firm:

- 'Efficiently' here means a *relatively* low-cost per client acquisition.
- 'Consistently' means that buyers will look at the 'fullness' of your pipeline over several years.
- 'Systematically' means that marketing should not *depend* upon the contacts (or even the significant efforts) of the managing partners in the firm, and instead should rely on internal systems and processes that make marketing the responsibility of everyone in the firm.

In addition to strong marketing systems, buyers prize a strong, recognisable brand which communicates the firm's Unique Value Proposition (UVP). This is important in positioning the firm to clients and buyers, but a strong brand

DOI: 10.4324/9781003149217-4

alone is insufficient to fill the pipeline. For this to happen, more targeted, pro-active work must be done to build systems which make marketing work.

Buyers will also be looking for a diversified portfolio of clients. Typically, this means that no more than 25% of your revenue comes from any one client. They will also look for high levels of repeat business, i.e. consistent work from the same client. A firm with 60% repeat business would be seen as strong by buyers and 80% would win a premium. This is partially because repeat business is often a signal of the quality of your firm, but also means the marketing and sales efforts can be focused on expansion rather than the replacement of clients.

The strategy and planning of marketing

Marketing strategy

Seventy-two per cent of Professional Service Firms (PSFs) rank 'attracting and developing new business' as their top challenge,[1] and this is not surprising. Small firms tend to rely on their personal network and burning the midnight oil to generate leads and referrals. However, as the firm grows, personal connections are generally insufficient to fill the pipeline and employees are generally less likely to work as hard as founders. To avoid this trap, marketing to new (and existing) clients becomes crucial. Provided you are in a reasonable niche, the main symptoms of failing to invest sufficient time and money in *good* marketing are a feast-famine cycle and poor-quality clients.

The fundamentals of marketing are relatively simple: first, understand the major challenges/opportunities of your ideal clients; next, describe the consequences and experience of these in the clients' language so that the client knows that you 'get' them; then, describe how your services will address the challenges/opportunities and provide evidence that they work; and finally, measure lead engagement, improve the marketing efforts and repeat. The rest of this chapter aims to help achieve this by detailing what a strong marketing strategy and plan looks like. Your marketing strategy must attract the best clients for your firm and continually improve the process by which this happens. This involves six activities, covered over the course of this chapter:

1. Having the right Unique Value Proposition.
2. Understanding the needs of your (ideal) clients.
3. Creating the right brand.
4. Developing stretch pipeline targets.
5. Creating marketing systems which improve continually.
6. Creating a marketing plan.

Having the right Unique Value Proposition

In the previous chapter, I detailed how to create your firm's UVP, and this is the starting point for your marketing. Your UVP should provide the backdrop to your messaging so that your client is clear not only on your service offering, but also on the principles that drive your culture, values and purpose whether this is innovation, quality, value, speed and so on. This is important because clients do not buy on price alone. Indeed, when examining 30 years of research on client buying, *Harvard Business Review*[2] research found a hierarchy of 'elements of value' which influence client buying. These fall into five categories:

1. Table stakes: meeting the requirements at an acceptable price.
2. Functional: addressing the company's performance needs.
3. Ease-of-doing business: time, effort, cultural fit.
4. Individual: the emotional-, personal- and career-related wants of the buyer.
5. Aspirational: improving the vision for the future, hope or social responsibility.

The research shows that most business-to-business companies focus on providing value at levels 1 and 2, but rarely market or deliver value in the other three levels. It also shows that many companies are missing a trick because, for example, most of what is prized by clients focuses on 'ease-of-doing business', so focusing on this will provide a unique competitive advantage away from cost and functionality. Therefore it is crucial to think widely about what value your firm is generating for clients above and beyond delivery.

Understanding (ideal) client needs

When did you last ask your ideal clients what their major challenges are in your area of expertise? Firms that do frequent client research (i.e. at least every quarter) grow 50% faster than those who do only occasional research.[3] This is primarily because doing more research allows you better insights into client challenges and to adjust your sales and marketing efforts accordingly. It is also because the very process of research can build better relationships with clients, enabling conversations, generating insights and making them reflect upon their own needs.

When undertaking client research, your primary research questions should be something like:

- Which are our target markets? What are the trends here?
- Who are our target clients? Where do they gather (physically and online)?

- What are their major challenges/opportunities? Which of these are not being met sufficiently well?
- What language do target clients use to describe these challenges and their consequences?
- Who are the key decision-makers and influencers in these clients?
- Where do these decision-makers go for information/support/ideas?
- What information, technologies, research, contacts or publications might be useful to these decision-makers that we can help with?

Doing frequent market research should not only provide you with updates about what your clients think of your services; it will also reveal the things they need which you are *not* doing. In order to steer clear of your own confirmation bias,[4] it is also occasionally advisable to get an external firm (or MBA student if you are not flush) to do this review for you.

Branding as strategic positioning

There are two views on branding. On the one hand, branding specialists like to tell us that 80% of the value of a company is in its brand (well, they would, wouldn't they?). These experts often forget that a strong brand is usually built on years of hard work, innovation and strong leadership. This is why companies decline when they rely solely on their brand, failing to invest in innovation and quality.[5] On the other hand, more traditional partners (especially in the UK and oddly ex-Big Four) have raised an eyebrow when I've suggested they invest in their brand. For some, branding is seen as a bit gimmicky – something for the cheap-suited, salesy types that inhabit less professional domains.

Although it is important to be realistic about the limits of branding, it does play an important role in visualising and communicating what you are to employees, clients and buyers. It cannot cover up your weaknesses, hide shoddy work, poor hires or a weak strategy, but it can help amplify your strengths.

As an example of good *visual* branding, look at the website of Exellys. The brand is aimed at their young, tech-savvy audience. Their entire business model relies on attracting and keeping the best talent, and so they position their people right in the centre of everything you see. Having worked with them as well as interviewing them and some of their clients, it is clear to me that their visual branding fits well with their strategy, deliverables and value proposition. As another example, examine the fantastic positioning of Elixirr as 'the challenger consultancy'. They even made their own Amazon Prime series to cement their reputation as innovators. Now, the actual names 'Exlirr' or

'Exellys' aren't outstanding, and nor are their logos. The value of their brands is that they are genuine and consistent: their value proposition, their culture and what they actually do are all aligned and their brand reflects and amplifies this (Figure 4.1).

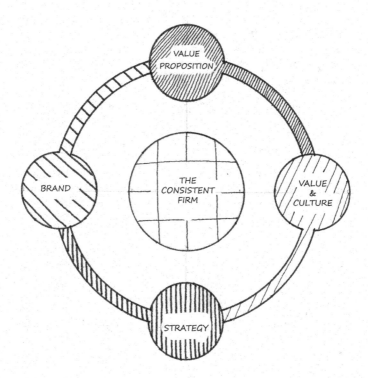

Figure 4.1 The brand in a consistent ecosystem.

Your brand should mirror and help recreate your culture, strategic positioning and UVP. Whenever there is a shift in one, the others should also be reviewed and potentially adapted. If these points are inconsistent, either your employees or your clients are going to be disappointed. If you don't have an innovative culture, you can't deliver innovative services. The same is true of quality, agility, fun, value, cheapness and any other adjective you might aim for. Clients will certainly check out your website, but they might also check out what people are saying about you on social media, what your ex-employees are saying on Glassdoor or even what reviews you have on Facebook or Google. This doesn't mean that everything must be perfect, simply that a firm that promises X and delivers Y to its staff, clients or buyers is likely to diminish trust quickly.

A rebrand can be prompted by a shift in strategy or more commonly, newly available revenue, which means you can afford more than a visit to Fiverr for a logo design. Rebranding can be costly but is often worth it when integrated with a strategic review. Angrez Saran of 8Works told me:

> We bought in a branding person who'd been recommended. It was a very tough experience being told that the way we positioned ourselves and the way we brand ourselves was wrong. We spent all of our time talking about the 'How?' rather than the 'Why?'. She repositioned the language and everything else and rebranded us in a way which had a phenomenal impact on our business and our revenues. And it was very simple, but very, very tough to do.

The results can be surprising. Mark Palmer, CEO of GoBeyond, told me:

> That's why this whole repositioning and rebranding had such a big impact. From the client feedback we were told clients weren't bothered by our method! The method was what got us excited, but clients were telling us 'please just park your methodology - we're not excited by it'. So we fundamentally repositioned ourselves and rethought what we did and how we did it.

I've put some of the slides I use for rebranding exercises at joeomahoney.com for your use. In my experience, the bigger the group involved in this project (over say three), the worse the final result will be, although the ongoing approval of the managing partner will be important.

Rebranding can be expensive (typically 5% of revenues) but this will depend on your size and how much you want from it. At a minimum, you should be looking at doing market research, re-positioning, crafting your messaging and finding a new tagline (if not logo). At the most, you might include a website redesign and rewriting, a new marketing strategy and plan, messaging and brand style guidelines. The balance between DIY and professional third-party support is one each firm needs to work out, but I would suggest the latter is worth the investment.

Developing stretch marketing targets

The stretch targets for your marketing and sales pipeline derive from your business strategy and plan. Your growth targets should translate into metrics for growth in target markets and services which can also be placed alongside investment decisions. In Table 4.1, I've given an example which also shows target return on marketing investment. In reality, this would vary considerably by type of firm and growth stage, and the presentation will depend on the preferences of partners (many prefer traffic light colours!).

Table 4.1 Example marketing targets (revenue target/investment)

	Market 1	Market 2	Market 3	Total (ROI)
Service 1	£250,000/ £15,000	£120,000/ £5,000	£50,000/ £5,000	£370,000/ £25,000 (14.8×)
Service 2	£120,000/ £20,000	£50,000/ £10,000	NA	£170,000/ £30,000 (5.7×)
Service 3	£50,000/ £10,000	NA	NA	£50,000/ £10,000 (5×)
Total	£420,000/ £45,000 (9.3×)	£170,000/ £15,000 (11.3×)	£50,000/ £5,000 (10×)	

The presentation of such a table might be extended to include headcount investments, the maturity of services being offered and the expansion/contraction of the markets and services. This may be overkill for some small firms, but it is important to remember that marketing is one of the easiest ways to burn through money. If return on investment isn't measured, then you may as well be John Wanamaker, who, according to some, wrote 'half the money I spend on advertising is wasted; the trouble is I don't know which half'. There is no excuse for this in the digital age.

We deal with pipeline management in Chapter 6, but the target figures you set need to be translated into the number of clients that are needed and what this translates to at each stage of your pipeline. For example, a typical pipeline might be broken down into the conversion ratios in Table 4.2. If the average client spend on Service 1 in Market 1 is £50,000, then to achieve the target revenue of £250,000, the consultants in that division need to be having an awful lot of conversations. Of course, such figures are always speculative and approximate – many meetings will come from previous clients, referrals or completely out of the blue (although these assumptions can be built in). Yet as we see later, in the internet age, what was once 'out of the blue' is now often quite traceable: LinkedIn Insight, Facebook Pixel, Google Analytics and other software give you the ability to trace interactions with your social media, website, webinars or ads, and the conversations generated.

The key question that should drive your marketing research is *where do our best leads come from*? If the answer is still 'the contacts of the founders', then you're not just selling at a sub-optimal rate you are also probably on your way to a long earn-out. In the next section, we look at how to avoid this.

Table 4.2 Example conversion ratios and targets for Service 1/Market 1[6]

Stage	Conversion Ratio	Target	Numbers Needed
1. Conversations	NA	£22.5 million	450
2. Meetings	10:1	£2.25 million	45
3. Proposals	3:1	£750,000	15
4. Deals	3:1	£250,000	5

Creating marketing systems

Once you have your targets, it is crucial that you build systematic, logical processes to support your marketing efforts. Systems and processes are not everything, as consulting is still very much a relationships business, but it is wrong to think of systems and soft relational forms of marketing as opposites. In reality, the former will support and accelerate the latter.

Your marketing systems should create a continuous improvement cycle (shown in Figure 4.2), by which the effectiveness of your marketing is measured and improved constantly. The key questions to guide this process should include:

- Where are your (quality) leads coming from?
- Which marketing is most effective?
- What is the cost of acquiring a client for different marketing channels?
- What are the conversion rates at different stages of your pipeline?
- What can be improved in the system?

There may also be subsystems within your marketing system. For example, you might have a system for LinkedIn which adds leads to your network, sends a message, reviews engagement with your posts and follows up with more person-alised messages. You might find trending topics in your area, write blog posts about them, measure engagement and improve. Whatever it is, it is worth drawing out the system, understanding what can be automated or outsourced and identifying where you (or the relevant senior) can most add value. Whilst there are many software systems that will help you measure, track and record your sales and marketing activity, the software itself won't make you use it sys-tematically. This is a mindset factor, and something that needs dedicated focus led by a partner.

Marketing systems, as with all systems in a growing consultancy, require the capture and codification of expert knowledge, from the partners and seniors, but also from experience and research. It means that a reliable, predictable and

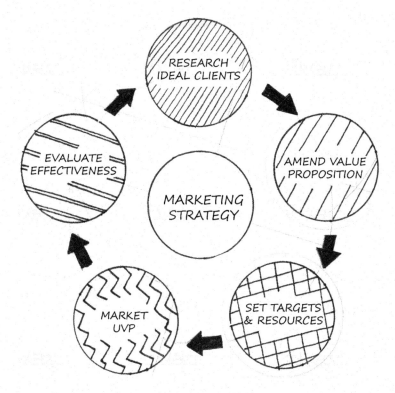

Figure 4.2 Continuous improvement cycle for a marketing system.

consistent process supports and then displaces the reliance upon key individuals in the firm. Remember that systems are scalable, people are not.

Marketing plan

Let us assume that you know your niche, your target client roles and avatars, your UVP, marketing positioning, strategy and messaging. What is left? A well-developed marketing plan that will implement the strategy and achieve the growth goals of the firm. Whether your activities are online or physical, a marketing plan should typically involve the following steps:

1. Define your objectives (for example, new leads, branding, recruitment).
2. Define target audiences (for example, potential clients, influencers, referral sources, specific firms).
3. Identify where these audiences gather (both online and offline).
4. Specify what you want the audiences to 'do' after being engaged and how they will do it.

5. Select the appropriate campaign route.
6. Specify the measures that are important.
7. Plan the campaign (what, when, how, who, when).
8. Create great content.
9. Run the campaign.
10. Review, reflect and improve for next time.

Many marketing plans I have seen are quite general and talk about visitors, likes, shares and so on. This is fine, but it is hard to gauge the quality of traffic. It is important that marketing is driving the *right* type of client to your sales teams, and if they are not, this needs to be addressed quickly. Ideally, these are clients that not only want to buy your niche service, but are also those seniors from blue chip firms who are inclined towards repeat business, who do not require procurement exercises and who understand your value. The wrong clients often hamper growth as much as the right clients boost it. By 'wrong' I mean those that have cost-based procurement processes, change their requirements often, invest nothing in their relationship with you and are not prepared to pay for quality work.

Principles of great marketing

What great marketing looks like

Great marketing attracts your ideal clients by making cold 'prospects' (who are oblivious to you) warm (who are aware of you and what you do) and eventually hot (who are ready to buy or recommend you to others). Unless you are blessed with perfect clients from the start, then your client list, like anything else in your firm, should be improving continuously. You should be confident of dropping weak clients because you have a steady stream of new ones.

Great marketing ensures that your value proposition and brand is well communicated and clear to those who *should* know about you: 44% of clients reject a potential consultancy simply because they can't work out exactly how it can solve their problems.[7] It also ensures your positioning in the market is obvious through the various campaigns that are run. For example, high-end firms will win awards, deliver keynotes at conferences and contribute to think tanks, whereas others might focus on LinkedIn, testimonials or simply build referrals organically. As we see later, doing everything is not the answer, but doing a few select activities will let clients build familiarity with you and your expertise.

Know your clients

Better knowing your clients and their needs is a crucial way of improving your marketing and sales results. A few times a year, I am approached by Partners to help improve the sales of a service which has faced continuous client rejection. This is despite spending a small fortune on marketing. This is one step worse than having done no client research at all, as it involves an almost patholog-ical refusal to listen to or accept client feedback. Often, these Partners spend considerable time telling me about the virtues of their service and arguing that clients 'need to' understand how brilliant it is. My pleas for the consultancy to drop the service and conduct research on what their clients really want sometimes fall on deaf ears, and I often feel they think that I'm as 'dumb' as the clients.

It is common practice to advise consultants and coaches to build an 'avatar' (or persona) of their buyer in terms of key demographics. My own view is that objective descriptors (age, sex, income, etc.) are of no use at all compared to a thorough market analysis and the psychological profile of your buyers. The lat-ter can be approximated using any number of tools (a quick one to learn is the DiSC personality typography). I recommend anyone who sells to put a frame-work of their favoured profiling tool up on the wall by their computer and make an approximation of each lead they speak to. There may be a pattern to the buyers in your niche. If you discover it, this could inform the messaging in all of your marketing. However, even if there are no commonalities, it is still great practice for salespeople to understand the needs of individual buyers and tailor their messages and services to specific needs and personality types. Knowing whether a decision-maker is, for example, facts-driven or relationship-driven, an extrovert or an introvert, a controller or a follower can make a huge differ-ence to how communications are drafted and proposals are written.

The (high) cost of client acquisition

How much did it cost you to acquire client X? When I ask my executive class to calculate this, they typically add up the salaried time of the consultants who did the research, bid writing, presentation(s) and negotiation. Those consult-ants should be charged out rather than writing proposals, so our first step is to cost the charge out time. I then ask, "what about all the other bids that failed?". If one in three bids fail, then the cost of acquisition should treble (in the same way that a successful bet cannot be judged against the stake, but against all the other stakes that did not win). Next, the calculation should consider the costs of a new project which are often not charged, for example, for coming up to speed, building new relationships and negotiating the statement of work. If all these costs are considered, it is common that my students' estimations of an acquisition cost increase six-fold. For this reason, it is not uncommon for new projects with new clients to make a loss.

This is worth bearing in mind because instincts tell us that hunting (proactively seeking out new business) is sexier than farming (nurturing long-term, high-trust relationships with clients). It is rare that champagne is popped for a client renewing the same contract that they have had for the last seven years. This is unfortunate, because it is the opposite to how potential acquirers or investors see sales.

Farming is best

Provided it is with the right clients, farming is the key to unlocking sustainable, predictable revenues. It allows the cost of client acquisition to be amortised over several years, generates the predictable revenue required for more effective planning and allows a better leverage ratio (as the consultancy becomes more expert in the client's operations it can use more junior consultants). For potential investors in your firm, farming is important because a high level of client churn leaves an annual gap in revenues that needs to be filled with new sales, which takes consultants away from fee-earning activity, and is therefore a risk.

When thinking about reward structures, it is therefore important that new client acquisition should not be prioritised over old client maintenance. Rewards should reflect not only the lifetime revenues expected from projects, but also build in the amortisation of the cost of client acquisition.[8] Consultancies that are good at farming ensure that each client has a dedicated account manager who possesses the skills that allow them to foster deep, long-term relationships that bond clients to the practice like family. When talking to buyers of consultancies, they generally say that 60% of revenue should come from existing services, 20% from new services with existing clients and 20% from existing services with new clients. Effort and budgeting should mirror this. Also ensure that your marketing and customer relationship management (CRM) system keeps existing clients as 'warm' and prospects – great thought leadership, company events and hospitality should all be targeted at existing clients as well as potential ones.

Hunting is important

If farming is best, hunting is still important. When old clients are no longer the target, still on the rates that you negotiated when the firm was nascent or not generating sufficient growth, it is time to hunt! Hunting brings the promise of *better* clients. There will always be projects that are better priced, more aligned with the firm's strategy and offer more potential for growth or knowledge development. Hunting also allows the firm to hone its client base. A common sentiment from consultancies I interviewed that were great at sales was that they loved the point when they could drop 'problem clients'.

In addition, hunting provides senior consultants with important 'boundary scanning'[9] knowledge about emerging market trends, competitors and pricing as well as their own firm's competitive weaknesses. It is easy to over- (or under-!) estimate one's own attractiveness when in a stable relationship rather than playing the dating game (or to forget that one still needs to be attractive to one's long-term partner). Approaching new clients will give you frank feedback about your relative attractiveness and competitiveness in the market.

I generally suggest both a 'Sniper' and 'Shotgun' approach to hunting new clients (sorry for the rather violent metaphors).

The Sniper involves making a shortlist of 'perfect' firms (between 3 and 20, depending on your size). 'Perfect' here depends on your needs but might include high-spend, high-profile accounts that would be a great fit with your services and value proposition. Approaching these involves more targeted campaigns personalised to the firm and their key decision-makers, detailed research about the firms' trends, use of competitors, announcements and challenges and slower, more personalised approaches from seniors.

The Shotgun is the opposite: a systematised, part automated campaign to target hundreds, if not thousands, of potential clients with a sequence of standardised, though well-crafted, messages. This typically involves a digital media search of relevant LinkedIn profiles and emails and an automated sequence of messages to provide value and build familiarity over time and encourage a conversation. Under 'Digital Architecture' later in this chapter, I give an example of how this can be achieved for a small firm on a low budget.

As I repeat throughout this book, hunting or business development needs to be ingrained throughout the firm. In Chapter 8, I will discuss the different skills that are needed for business finders compared to relationship developers and that *both* need to be recruited and rewarded.

Fishing can work if the pond is well stocked

Less effort than both farming and hunting is fishing.[10] Once the equipment is set up, the bait (what marketers call a 'lead magnet') does most of the hard work. Providing bait for potential clients is not new. Prior to 2000, consultancies would often advertise in magazines offering a free workshop, talk or strategy session. What has changed with the advent of digital is that the targeting of specific potential clients has *potentially* become laser-focused, cheaper and infinitely more measurable. I have worked through an example of fishing in Table 4.3, but we cover this in more detail later.

Table 4.3 The fishing process with example

Step	Example
You identify a niche audience that has a specific challenge that your consulting services can help solve.	On LinkedIn's ads, you specify an audience of Operational Directors in universities in Germany.
You create a targeted, paid advert on a digital site to provide a free resource (for example, e-book; short course; template) that can help the potential client overcome this challenge.	You create an advert: *five short videos to help improve professional service efficiency in universities.* It contains a click-through to your website where the videos are hosted.
The potential client is presented with your ad, clicks on it (triggering a small cost to you) and is taken to your website.	Your ad is presented to 300 Operational Directors at German universities. Sixty of them click on the link. This costs you £15 per click.
On your website, the potential client is provided with more information, and in exchange for their email, is provided with the free resource. After you provide the resource, you show them your services or suggest a call.	Thirty directors provide you with their email (20 of which watch the video until the end). The email is captured by your MailChimp account. After the video, you suggest a 'strategy call' that can be booked there and then.
A series of automated emails with more high-value relevant resources are then sent to the client, demonstrating your expertise with their specific issue.	You have designed a series of automated emails to be sent at specific times to the HR Directors you have 'captured'. Each offers a different resource (for example, successful case studies; e-book) to help with their challenge. During the process, 15 Directors unsubscribe.
In each email, the client is encouraged to book a call in order to see how you can help them solve their problem in more detail.	At the end of each email, and each resource, you ask the Director if they would like a free 'strategy call' to see if you can help or if your tried and tested training course can help them. This is also automated (via Calendly). Five Directors sign up for a call. Down the line, one of them eventually signs a contract.

Fishing does not need to be a hard sell. There are other variants to support your firm and client base. My own view is that the market is full of over-sold lead magnets offering to SCALE YOUR FIRM TO SIX FIGURES A MONTH!!!, and that potential clients have grown sick and sceptical of bombastic, empty promises and automated LinkedIn bots. Offering something of real value that establishes your expertise is sufficient for the right client to pass you their email, but it may suit your business model to then do some individual research to provide the lead with tailored follow-ups rather than simply passing on generic sales material. The balance between tailored follow-up and more generic marketing will depend on the number and value of the leads.

Marketing practice

Digital media

I understand the common wariness many founders have concerning social media, especially around advertising. It is not only a big psychological step from traditional marketing in consultancies, it is also one of the quickest ways to burn cash if you pay for adverts. Often, this fear is compounded by early experiments by founders in blogging, YouTube videos or LinkedIn advertisements, which took up a lot of time but did not work. However, my view is that social media marketing (not necessarily paid advertisements) is very much worth the effort. Research shows an incredibly strong correlation between firms that use digital marketing and growth success.[11] Findings suggest that high growth PSFs:

- invested 25% more effort in digital and content marketing than their no-growth counterparts;
- spent 15%+ of their budget on marketing;
- were twice as likely as low-growth firms to use paid digital ads, videos and automated marketing; and
- used gated digital content which generated 40% or more leads online that grew at double the speed of firms that didn't.

Whilst it is true that consulting sales still depend upon building rich relationships (through testimonials, referrals and follow-on work), social media offers huge value in both achieving these and shifting potential clients from cold to warm. Social media has two fantastic capabilities for consultancies: its ability to provide a laser-like focus on the specific audience you need – according to age, job, interests, location, employer and so on – and its ability to track which of your campaigns are more successful.

With most clients, I recommend five rules for the effective use of social media.

1. Plan. Identify key themes that will underpin all your content. Plan and time-table your creation and distribution process carefully. Execute and improve.
2. Do one thing (generally LinkedIn) very well before you think of moving on to anything else.
3. Create a content reuse process. This might mean that LinkedIn content is automatically reposted on Twitter (or blog content on LinkedIn), but might also mean that 'evergreen content' (i.e. content that is relatively timeless) is reused on LinkedIn several times[12] or that a video posted on your website is edited down into different segments for reuse elsewhere.
4. Never take a lead to a dead end. Once potential clients have viewed your content, there should always be an option to subscribe, book a call or access another piece of content.
5. Occasionally use 'gated' content. This is content hosted on your website that the lead can access after submitting an email. This not only provides you with the potential lead's contact details, but also lets you build up a picture of who else might be interested based on their profile.

Obviously as the firm grows, it will dedicate more resources to marketing and is likely to take on a marketing agency or contractor. I generally advise growing firms to outsource digital media work other than content creation to the experts and experiment with different suppliers for different campaigns. Close direction of suppliers and performance management will ensure you're not wasting money paying a teenager to create GIFs for Reddit.

It is also important to remember that analogue marketing remains crucial for growth. There is a lot of evidence to show that firms that are great at networking, demonstrating their expertise and emphasising value during the sales process, all grow faster. In the sections below, I have treated analogue and digital approaches to marketing as two parts of the overall package needed for a successful firm.

From oblivious to informed

Should we do more videos? Should they be on LinkedIn or YouTube? Should they be live or pre-recorded? Are they better than blogs? What about Pay-per-click? Should we use blogs or write LinkedIn articles? What the hell is a banner ad? The list of potential methods of developing leads is large and growing. Table 4.4 lists most of these in terms of moving clients from cold (do not know you exist) to warm (know what you do) to hot (ready to buy). The cold → warm phase is done by general marketing, but the warm → hot sales phase usually requires some personalisation and human interaction.

Table 4.4 Digital and analogue ways to develop leads

	Moving clients from cold to warm	*Then from warm to hot*
Marketing activity	Conferences; Cold calling; Direct mail; Website and SEO; Awards; Sponsorship; Exhibitions; Social media posting; Paid ads; Infographics; Lead magnets; Reports; Free benchmarking/maturity study; Podcast; Public speaking; Publishing; Blogs; White papers	Free training; Webinar; Video conference; Testimonials; Dinners; Meetings; Calls; Free training; Referrals

It's all rather overwhelming if you're not a marketing expert, but it needn't be! Fortunately, the clearest and most common sense explanation of marketing practices I've seen is provided by my business partner and friend Martin J. Williams. After following Martin digitally for five years and admiring his insights, I approached him to join one of my firms as a partner. What follows is a simplified excerpt of Martin's contribution to one of our programmes.

Moving a client from cold to hot requires a kind of *education*. The client may need to be taught about your existence and ability to find a solution to their problem. They may even need to be taught why they have a problem in the first place. Figure 4.3 shows how this education can be achieved by building trust through a series of marketing touches, moving leads from the bottom to the top of the pyramid. This is also a nice inversion from the usual 'funnel' that markets use and emphasises the journey a potential client must take from being completely oblivious about a firm through to slowly building trust and familiarity until they are ready to buy.

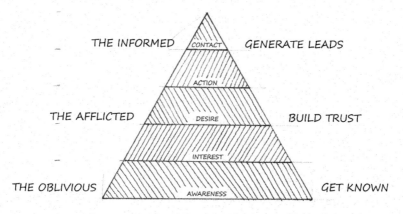

Figure 4.3 Pyramid of Trust: moving leads from oblivious to informed.

Martin's view is that it doesn't matter so much what route you choose up the pyramid, so long as you have a defined and systematic path. To make this easier for us, he has recreated the pyramid with different marketing channels (Figure 4.4). The exact position of each marketing channel, the number of levels to the top and the route to the top will be entirely dependent on the firm itself, but the principles governing your choice of route should remain the same.

Figure 4.4 Climbing the pyramid of trust.

In summary, although there is no 'right' route up the pyramid, the route that is designed should:

- educate a prospect about their challenge/opportunity with insights, cases and thought leadership;
- build trust through a progression of 'touches' with the firm;
- focus on one route up the pyramid (at first) rather than doing everything;
- choose methods which show-off your strong points;
- never have a dead end; there is always an obvious next step[13]; and
- have an option to contact you directly at each step.

Good advice on each individual method is freely available on the internet,[14] but here I want to emphasise four tips which many forget. The first is that, with regard to digital content, doing something is better than doing nothing. It is easy to start burning through time and money planning, executing and editing the perfect video, blog or book. Focus on the 80:20 and get it done! For the small firm, many authentic but rough videos are generally better than one polished video. The second tip is to focus on creating 'evergreen' material that can be reused. People often think that potential clients will get sick of seeing the same material. In my view these people over-estimate how much the client thinks about them. The third tip is to outsource what should be outsourced (don't try to do paid ads yourself, for example) and keep what shouldn't (don't get third parties to write your content). Finally, rely on (and improve) the system. The cycle of setting targets, measuring and improving is the only way you will know if your marketing is getting better. Using LinkedIn Pixel and Google Analytics is a great way to see the impact of your activity.

LinkedIn

Whilst LinkedIn has 'only' a quarter of Facebook's nearly three billion users, it is aimed primarily at business people who wish to connect with others. As such, a LinkedIn user is much more likely to 'stop the scroll' for business content that they find interesting than the very same user on Facebook, who will be likely thinking about friends and family. In my view, LinkedIn is *by far* the most useful social media platform for consultants to find and increase the number of potential clients. LinkedIn Sales Navigator also offers a level of precision in marketing that was previously unimaginable: I recently helped a Scottish strategy firm craft a successful marketing plan which included a LinkedIn campaign which targeted Chief Strategy Officers in the manufacturing industry that had been in their roles for less than 90 days and who had been educated in a Scottish University!

As well as targeted ('Sniper') campaigns you can also easily scale your audience through automation ('Shotgun'). Now, this isn't for everyone, but there are dozens of LinkedIn software automation tools (see, for example, LinkedIn Helper or Meet Alfred). As an example, some simple automated tasks might include:

- Sending a personalised connection request to all of your second connections who are directors in large automotive companies in the US and following up with a thank you when they connect.
- Finding the emails of all CEOs who went to your University and using that database to create a LinkedIn mail sequence.
- Sending a LinkedIn message to 500 senior managers at Ford, followed up by a personalised email a week later to those who do not respond.
- Keeping track of which potential clients visit your profile and then emailing them so that your outreach is not cold.

Automated campaigns be reasonably successful in generating leads for smaller consultancies but it depends on how searchable your buyers are. These campaigns are most powerful if they are combined with your website, a CRM system and good digital content. Below, I detail an example of the digital activities small firms often undertake (this is one variant of many – please tailor it to your own needs):

1. Dig out the avatars/profiles of your idea buyers and the challenges they face that you can solve.
2. Create a landing page on your website that starts with the main challenge your clients face that you solve and explain why and how you can help. Provide testimonials and great content on this page. Use your best IP. Use video as well as using text. Create an easy way to contact you directly to discuss further and a subscription button for regular quality thought leadership on this topic.
3. Integrate your subscription button with a CRM like ActiveCampaign so that lead emails can be captured and organised. Create a subscription button on your landing page so it captures and passes on emails to your CRM system (for example, ActiveCampaign).
4. Create an email sequence in the CRM system with high-quality content that goes out monthly to the captured emails. This will build familiarity and trust in your expertise. Perhaps link to the occasional free webinar.
5. Use a LinkedIn automation tool to connect with as many of your target people as possible with a message that is interesting but not at all salesy. You need to smile at someone before you ask someone out on a date.
6. Use automated LinkedIn messaging to provide this group with valuable content once a month that is not salesy, but shows (i) you understand their pain points and (ii) you are an expert in this area. Have a link to your landing page at the end of every message. If available, use their email for your CRM system (and add in any other email lists you have accumulated over the years).
7. Once you are familiar with the messages which drive ideal clients to your website and to calls, think about the costs and benefits of experimenting with paid advertising on LinkedIn. This should use a very valuable lead magnet (for example, a report; live webinar; or benchmarking tool) to drive people to a (new) landing page and capture their email for your CRM sequence.
8. Monitor the effectiveness of your marketing campaigns with Google Analytics and LinkedIn Insight, and improve.

This is just an example. It may not be suitable for your firm at all. Providing the work on the avatar and the content is done creating this system will take a digital agency as little as five days and will cost you around £3,000. If you know what you are doing, you can get this done well using mTurk or Fiverr for about £1,000.

Together, the logical combination of your website, LinkedIn profile, CRM system, email and so on is called a 'digital architecture'. This is simply a system which ensures your marketing components are logically connected: that good content pulls the right people to your website, that their details are captured, and that these details are used to provide ongoing high-value content. For small consultancies that have little experience in marketing, it can be a bit confusing, so I've created a sample of a simple digital architecture in Figure 4.5.

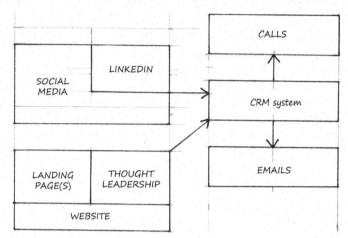

Figure 4.5 Example architecture for digital marketing.

However, you should also note that the Scatter-gun approach to digital marketing, whilst potentially effective, can also be self-defeating, especially for larger firms. If not used intelligently the apps can end up sending irrelevant messages, which are obviously automated, to leads or – even worse – existing clients. Done badly, it is akin to cold calling, getting the targets name wrong and the realising the target was already a client. Additionally, if the LinkedIn algorithm notices that you are spamming thousands of people who you are not connected with, you can expect a warning and then a suspension. As I say, this type of architecture isn't suitable for all firms, but can help some.[15]

Websites

You wouldn't believe the number of my clients who tell me 'our website is in the process of being revamped', only to admit later on that this has been the case for a year or two. There are so many bad websites out there that I felt this really needed a small section. A good website is a hygiene factor: 23% of consulting acquirers rule out firms because of poor-quality digital content and 30% of potential clients rule out firms because of an unimpressive website.[16] I'm sure you think your website is fine (in the same way that your clients think their DIY 'strategy and plan' is fine), but if you directed and led the design and build yourself, it probably isn't. The odds of you having great aesthetic, messaging and design sense are roughly the same as the next person in the street having great accounting skills.[17] The best approach is to trust the good designers over good partners when it comes to the web. Your UVP, strategy, niche and messaging should drive the form, function and aesthetics of your website.[18]

Your website should prioritise content that builds credibility and familiarity. Professional reports or videos should include cases, testimonials, research, thought leadership and team biographies. As a guide, it is advisable to do less, better, than more, worse. Your website is your potential client's window into your firm, and there is no better place to communicate your UVP properly.

It is also important to consider the role of Search Engine Optimisation (SEO).[19] Whilst digital agencies will often tell you that SEO is the number one method to generate leads, the simple truth is that management consultancy clients do not find their consultancies by searching for services on the internet. This method is ranked ninth by buyers after (in order of importance) referrals, previous experience, industry word of mouth, solicitation from a consultancy, viewing that consultancy's materials or speakers and seeing consultants quoted in leading publications.[20] This said, clients *do* search for advice and insights on the internet. If you are in a well-defined niche and have made yourself a category leader, doing basic SEO on your content pages is a relatively cheap way to ensure that you are found, *should* a client ask the relevant questions on Google.

What is more useful than 'onsite' SEO is having trusted websites link to your own (known as 'offsite SEO'). Any thought leadership that you host on your website (including reports, blogs, videos and so on) should be easily shareable by others on social media, their own blog and other websites. Think about other places that your client will be looking: websites, blogs and industry/sector/service experts. It is worth reaching out to these (with a view to adding them to your mailing list) and introducing yourself, preferably with one or two of your best thought pieces or research. It is relatively simple to automate not only the publication of your blog to LinkedIn and Twitter, but also to follow and target suitable accounts in the hope of further interaction.[21]

Awards

The pros and cons of applying for awards is a question that often divides my clients, so it is worth some reflection. Three quarters of the firms I interviewed had won awards of various types and many of them mentioned the benefits. Sarah William's firm, Virgo Health, won a 'Communique Award' for 'New Launch of the Year' in their first month and, she told me, 'we launched in front of 1200 people…. and the phone never stopped ringing'. She went on:

> we won loads of awards. We thought it was really important to enter our work and ourselves. It essentially acts as a benchmarking exercise. So it's

not just the fact that if you if you win, or even n if you get placed, you get some nice publicity out of it, and it's great for a recruitment tool. But it's also a brilliant organisational self-development tool. It was a lot of work to do this every year, but it paid back in dividends. It was really worth doing.

In short, I would argue that awards are great if they fit with your strategy. If it is strategically important to you to be seen as the best place to work and attract great employees, to be the most creative and attract the right type of project or to run the best projects and price yourself at the top of the market, then awards are a great way of both signalling and benchmarking your efforts. However, it is important to keep your overall strategy in mind. Everyone would like to price themselves at the top of the market and attract the best employees, but is it *important* to your strategy? Sometimes the answer will actually be 'no'. There is nothing wrong with that – you just need to ensure that your marketing tactics are driven by your strategy.

Thought leadership

Planning thought leadership

It always amazes me how many otherwise great consultancies actually generate quite weak thought leadership. This is troubling, because the clients I interviewed ranked thought leadership as one of the most effective ways for a consulting firm to market its services. Half of clients read thought leadership pieces and around 25% of these have contacted an author,[22] making the investment in thought leadership a no-brainer for the firm that wants to illustrate its unique value. As we shall see later, thought leadership also provides a significant boost to business development, can be developed into tools or services and is a great support for recruitment. Spencer Land, an experienced non-executive director, told me, 'all senior/key hires I've recruited over the last 10–12 years have mentioned engaging with our thought leadership out in the market as a positive sign about the business'. I recommend all my clients to have a sequence of high-value thought leadership pieces that are sent out to new connections on LinkedIn and on email at least every six weeks. This can be automated of course.

Finally, thought leadership is considered an asset by acquirers if it is relevant, actionable and well-received by clients. In the words of one buyer of consultancies: 'some firms can demonstrate that their thought leadership leads to conversations, and these conversations lead to sales. This is the Holy Grail for thought leadership'.

As with most other activities in a valuable, growing consulting firm, effective thought leadership needs to be systematised. At a minimum, this means developing a plan that answers six key questions. These are outlined in Table 4.5. It is not essential to answer all items with a 'yes', since simply asking yourself the question can be enough to prompt thinking about these issues. Of course, size will guide the investment in and sophistication of your thought leadership.

Table 4.5 A basic structure for a thought leadership plan

	Guidance	Checklist for specific thought leadership pieces
Why?	Great thought leadership is driven by your marketing priorities and consistent with your UVP.	Does it link to our UVP?
		Is it driven by our marketing priorities/ strategy?
		Have you defined the outcomes you want?
		Will you know how successful this piece is?
		Do you have success targets and measures?
		Does it link clearly to the services we offer?
Who?	Being clear about your targeted readership (including gatekeepers) means your work isn't wasted.	Am I clear on who we are targeting?
		Have we asked them their research needs?
		Have we specified how they prefer to consume data?
		Do we know what we want our reader to feel and think?
What?	Excellent content is innovative, based on credible research and has a call to action.	Do we have a clear call to action?
		Is the message innovative (to the client) or provocative?
		Is the research capable of supporting your argument?
		Is the research investment worth the outputs?
		Has this type of research been done better elsewhere?

How?	Quality professional production of visuals is crucial. Think about three types of output for every piece.	Does the messaging suit the audience?
		Is it written (or attributable) to an expert?
		Are the graphics eye-catching and memorable?
		Can the content be used in different formats?
Where?	The distribution should be multichannel and focus on places where your targets gather.	Have we thought widely about distribution channels?
		Do we have the right distribution channels planned?
		Have we considered paid advertising (especially social media)?
		Does the format match the channel?
		Is someone tasked with capturing metrics from the channel?
		Have we listed the key influencers who will be contacted?
When?	Not all thought leadership needs specific timing, but in some cases this may increase your visibility.	Do we have a sensible launch time?
		Are we launching concurrently with relevant events?
		Are we targeting clients at the right point of their life cycle?
		Is the piece 'evergreen' or will it become less relevant over time?

Good thought leadership begins at the top of the table with your marketing priorities – your UVP, the various services you offer and your target clients that year. An annual workshop can build on this and prioritise thought leadership ideas based upon your area of expertise, changes affecting clients and the services you offer. Table 4.6 represents a brainstorming exercise that can help you with this. Detailed 'state of the sector' reviews based upon significant research can also be powerful tools for signalling expertise and driving leads, but not all small firms will have the resources or opportunities to achieve these.

Table 4.6 Generating thought leadership foci

Unique value proposition.....

	Megatrends (global)	Industry trends[23,24]	Current changes	Social media insights	Client changes/ concerns	Depth of our expertise	Client research needs	Thought leadership foci
Service/Market 1								
Service/Market 2								
Service/Market 3								
Service/Market 4								

Prioritising areas of focus is the beginning rather than the end. Sometimes you might start out with an original insight, hypothesis or argument based on your existing knowledge or gut feel (for example, that traditional leadership training rarely works). Other times, you might initiate a round of research to explore something you feel your clients would be interested in (for example, what do innovation award winners do better than other firms?).[25] Regardless of the questions you begin with, you should make sure that each links back to your UVP. For exploratory research, you won't know what you're getting (in Year 1 at least), but you want to feel confident that the results will be of interest.

It is also worth considering that although most good thought leadership is based on evidence, the type and credibility of evidence can vary significantly. I would urge you to think creatively and widely when considering evidence types. For example, if I post a poll on LinkedIn or Reddit, I now typically get the same number of responses (around 300) as I would have from a formal paper-based survey sent to thousands of recipients. Posting a poll a month provides me credible evidence which I can use to write a report or include in a book (ahem!). So, when using evidence, do consider case studies, polls, publicly available data, endorsements, worked examples, your own internal data, freedom of information requests and surveys. I should also stress here the importance of thinking creatively about internal data. Consulting firms with many projects under their belts often underestimate how a simple aggregation of data (such as project success factors; over-run causes; major risks) might be of great interest to their clients.

Surveys can be especially powerful, not only because they generate compelling visuals – which the busy executive prefers – but also because the results can be turned into a benchmarking or maturity tool. When I first joined academia, I led a research project on innovation in the consulting industry. I decided to use the results of a survey I had run to create an app which would benchmark any firm that wished to input their metrics and automatically generate a 'recommendations' report. Within three weeks, I had 58 contacts from firms asking me to help them improve their levels of innovation. Rightly or wrongly (in my view, usually wrongly) the 50% of potential clients that 'underperform' against a benchmark worry about what they are missing. If the benchmark creates a number of measures then most firms will underperform in one or more areas. If your system can automate recommendations (as mine did), then this will provide opportunities to push relevant services.

What good thought leadership looks like

Once you have a set of thought leadership priorities, these can be assigned and executed. Outstanding thought leadership has the following features:

- Says something new, differentiated and interesting (at least from the client's perspective) about something clients care about.
- Has a specific call to clients to consider doing something different.
- Is based on empirical evidence (for example, trend analysis, research, statistics).
- Links the solution to the issue to one of the firm's services.
- Introduces the authors first. Readers want credibility.
- Highlights the research and analysis you have done.
- Uses visuals that get the message across (many users will only look at these).
- Ensures that the title conveys the key message.

There are many potential output formats available (see Table 4.7) and every piece of content should be distributed in more than one way. Ideally, your overall marketing architecture will drive traffic to your website where the main content will be hosted and shared.

Table 4.7 Ideas for thought leadership distribution

	Physical	Both	Virtual
Paid (typically)	Conference Trade event	Book PR campaign	Social media advertising Influencer campaign Apps/interactive tools
Unpaid (typically)	Dinner/ drinks Roundtable Seminar	Report Infographic Industry association Magazine/newspaper Podcast (invitation/own)	Blog Webinar (live) Webinar (recorded) Social media Email

Finally, it is important to remember that, as with all intellectual property, thought leadership needs to be managed, ideally through a strong knowledge management or CRM system. Sending relevant thought material to actual and potential clients at the right time can tip the balance in terms of sales and relationship building. Moreover, related thought leadership pieces can be accumulated in order to create a book or e-book in the future.[26]

Takeaways

- Buyers want a marketing *system* which efficiently, consistently and systematically fills your funnel with the right type of warm clients.
- Great marketing requires that your strategy, marketing, messaging and sales are driven by the problems, language and needs of your ideal clients rather than what you or anyone else in your firm thinks.
- Farming and fishing are superior to hunting due to the high costs of client acquisition of the latter, but hunting is usually necessary for growth.
- Buyers do not (just) buy on price and functionality; your values, vision, culture are important.
- Investing in quality (not necessarily expensive) marketing which includes market research, branding, messaging and UVP development is one of the best investments you will make.
- Managing and measuring your pipeline and linking this with marketing and sales activity will help prevent the feast-and-famine cycle and provide consistent cash flow for growth.
- Invest efficiently in digital marketing: create, disseminate, reuse and measure the success of your thought leadership and lead magnets.

Case study: Quick Release (QR_)

When launching new products, automotive companies and their suppliers face complex challenges. They have to co-ordinate different data, systems and processes, all the while getting quality products to market as fast as possible. Misunderstood or mismatched data on product information, issues and operations can lead to delays and quality issues. QR_ helps automotive companies become more efficient in their development and launch of new products by helping them address these data challenges.

Rob Ferrone first identified these challenges when working at Ford, where he realised the potential of working independently with Ford's suppliers to integrate them more effectively with the motor giant for new product launches. Starting as an independent consultant in 2000, Ferrone eventually brought on the brother of a close friend, Adam Grant, and formed a company in 2003. In late 2004, however, work began to drop off and the pair decided to take some time out to work on the business. In hindsight they had spent 'too much time' locked in a room designing a business and not enough time understanding the market, asking who might need their service and how to get in touch with those people at the right time.

'We wasted a year', Ferrone suggests. 'If we had seen the bigger picture, we'd have accelerated a lot quicker... Building the company administration as you go is the most effective way to do it'.

In 2006, QR_ 'got a big break' when invited to Cologne by a large automotive supplier, Faurecia, which led to orders from other suppliers and prompted the need to grow the company. However, whilst QR_ took on one extra person, their aversion to risk prompted them to work with associates rather than recruit employees. Moreover, their growth was primarily reactive in response to enquiries rather than proactively investing in marketing.

During this period, the flatmate and friend of Adam Grant, Adam Blomerley, began to get more involved in QR_, sitting in on discussions and doing some of the finance work. Eventually, in 2007, Blomerley joined the company as a contractor. A year later, Blomerley approached Ferrone and Grant with a five-year plan (the first of several) to grow the company more proactively and strategically. Ferrone says, 'it needed someone with that vision to grow the business'. Grant and Ferrone accepted Blomerley's offer to buy into the company. In addition to an ambitious growth target of 50% annually and a shortlist of target clients, the plan also helped provide a narrative to both clients and potential employees around the promise of a larger, more professional company in a few years' time.

Frustratingly, Adam Blomerley, the then CEO of QR_, doesn't have the wrinkles and grey hair common among many growers of successful consulting firms. 'I never finished puberty', he says, laughing. Whilst this isn't true biologically, he does undeniably bring a youthful positivity and enthusiasm to our conversations. In terms of leadership roles, it was clear that Blomerley had the 'infectious ambition' for a leader, whilst Ferrone had the trusted network to focus on developing clients. Grant, meanwhile, was 'all about execution and quality'.

For the first ten years, QR_ offered roughly the same service to a growing list of clients in the automotive sector, but as their value proposition and the measurable impact of their work became clearer, they began diversifying. QR_ began offering three levels of service which were: (a) time and materials to work on projects, (b) outsourcing data projects completely to simply work on a deliverables basis and (c) improving the client's capability at managing data. This diversification created new revenue streams, but also created tensions between different internal teams as well as challenges around capturing knowledge and competence for intellectual property.

As QR_ grew, they took several approaches to maintain quality and growth:

- Embedding sales as a behaviour throughout the organisation.
- Capturing project experiences in intellectual property and thought leadership.
- Internally developing software for consultants to improve their performance.
- Evidencing and demonstrating the financial value of QR_ work to clients.
- Professionalising and improving the people management side of things.
- Building a clear project management methodology for client interventions.

Yet growth was not without its challenges. As the company grew and the governance moved from a democratic to a functional model, Ferrone reflects that initially:

> we split things up by what we had the strongest opinion about rather than what we were experienced, or knowledgeable about.... In retrospect perhaps we should have got, say, the [professional] HR manager in sooner rather than it being me, who was not an expert at all.... It was like driving with the handbrake on in many ways because we had less time to be close to customers and projects and were sub-optimally delivering our internal roles.

Blomerley agrees and suggests that as the company experimented with different ways of promoting, recruiting, assessing, rewarding and communicating with employees, many began to experience change fatigue.

A second challenge was getting the right people in the right management roles. As the company grew, good consultants (often graduates) were promoted to team and project leaders, then to sales managers and then to Associate Directors. However, this was neither a recipe for getting the best people in the right place nor for doing well on the sales front.

A third challenge was around values. Early on, as with many IT or data-focused companies, the demographic of the company was primarily male, young and white, and the culture more 'laddish' than anything else. Eventually, an informal workshop to focus on culture was headed by

Blomerley's brother, who had worked for E&Y. It culminated in a new set of values for QR_:

- Producing quality work.
- Cultivating genuine human relationships with clients and within the team.
- Providing excellent, fast client service (initially termed 'the perfect butler').
- Being innovative, creative and curious.

These values helped employees to make decisions that were aligned with the strategy direction of the company. The values were built into performance reviews and appraisals to make them more embedded.

Both Ferrone and Blomerley are very upfront about the mistakes the company has made and often comment that they 'are still learning' and 'continue to mess some things up', but they were clearly doing something right. By 2019, the consultancy had grown to 211 full-time consultants. The founders were at the life stage where they wanted to take cash out of the firm, and in 2018 had set the goal of being the most recognised brand name in their niche. After being approached by several companies for a purchase, they eventually sold to Alten, a French multinational engineering services company. Alten was attractive because its biggest clients were the perfect accounts for QR_ (although Adam notes that this cross-selling is more complex in practice than in theory).

None of the senior team suffers from an ego issue and none had worked in consultancy before. They are strong examples of the humble mindset, accepting their limitations, asking for help when they need it, both externally (using trusted advisors) and internally (by listening to feedback). The fact that they worked with people they liked and that the Directors were linked by friendship helped this effort enormously. The appearance of Blomerley and his ambitious growth mindset was crucial in creating a new trajectory for the company. But so too was the founders' willingness to see how Blomerley's competences would make up for gaps in their own.

Notes

1 Propero (2017) *Marketing Priorities for Professional Services Firms Report*. London. https://www.properopartners.com/2017-report/.
2 Almquist, E., Cleghorn, J., & Sherer, L. (2018) The B2B elements of value. *Harvard Business Review*, 96(3), 18.

3 Frederiksen, L., Harr, E., Montgomery, S., & Taylor, A. (2013) *Inside the Buyer's Brain*. Virginia: Hinge.

4 Klayman, J. (1995) Varieties of confirmation bias. *Psychology of Learning and Motivation, 32*, 385–418.

5 This is often, although not always, marked by the shift from a private firm to a listed firm. Sadly, in most forms of shareholder capitalism, shareholders want short-term returns and high dividends which often results in low investment, training and innovation. Consultancy founders who sell to a listed company should not underestimate the shift that will occur. If you think branding causes profitability rather than vice versa, then what happened to the Enron or Arthur Andersen brands to cause their collapse?

6 It is only in small firms that one would expect to see a table! As soon as possible, firms intent on growing should move to professional services automation software or a sales system (see Chapter 7) that tracks marketing and sales in a more consistent and presentable way than I have illustrated here.

7 Hinge Research Institute (2015) *Referral Marketing for Professional Service Firms Research Report*. Virginia: Hinge.

8 McDougall, D., Wyner, G., & Vazdauskas, D. (1997) Customer valuation as a foundation for growth. *Managing Service Quality: An International Journal, 7*(1), 5–11

9 Schwab, R. C., Ungson, G. R., & Brown, W. B. (1985) Redefining the boundary spanning-environment relationship. *Journal of Management, 11*(1), 75–86.

10 Distinct from 'phishing'!

11 Frederiksen, L., McVey, S., Montgomery, S., & Taylor, A. (2012) *Online Marketing for Professional Services*. Virginia: Hinge.

12 Many clients are worried that the same people will see the same content repeatedly. This is not usually the case. A typical LinkedIn post will be seen by 5% of your contacts, and the algorithm is pretty good at ensuring similar content is viewed by different people. The exception is if one of your posts is massively viral, in which case your network might want to see it again!

13 On this note, I've seen a few business cards with a QR code that takes the person to a video about the problems the firm solves.

14 More reliable advice is available from Martin at martin@consultingmastered.com

15 Personally, I've done a complete U-turn on LinkedIn. When I started out in academia, I saw it as completely over-valued and pointless. However, when I started my own consultancy on the side, I used LinkedIn to simply send an introduction to founders of new consultancies with a short video of a key insight on growth I'd recorded. After this, I never had to do any outreach or marketing. Indeed, after six months, I turned the tool off because I was over-booked and my existing clients did my marketing for me. As I have written before, if you are a small consultancy in a good niche it is hard *not* to get oversubscribed with the systematic use of digital marketing.

16 Hinge Research Institute (2015) *Referral Marketing for Professional Service Firms Research Report*. Virginia: Hinge.

17 It was a sad moment in my life when I realised I had no aesthetic taste. The directors of a charity I founded and chaired had an intervention regarding the website,

logo and branding I had chosen. I now begrudgingly admit they were right, but isn't it odd that we can take more offence when told about our lack of aesthetic judgement as opposed to (nearly) any other skill set? Cerys, if you're reading this, I'm sorry about the dragon.

18 If anyone wishes to delve into great web design, the best book I've read on it is (still) Steve Krug's (2006) *Don't Make Me Think*. New Riders: CA.

19 A useful part of a SEO project is to undertake a key word search: the phrases people are *actually* using when searching for your services online. These words, where appropriate, should be used in the content you write to maximise the chances of their being found in searches. These words can also usefully be used in URLs, page titles and metadata. There are also other services that can be undertaken at the same time as doing an SEO project, including creating an XML sitemap and running error reports, which will make your website a better place for visitors. Using Fiverr or Amazon Turk, you can typically find someone to do all the services above for less than £200. On this note, I would urge you not to buy back-links to your website in an effort to 'trick' search engines – a service that many online contractors offer. It doesn't work and can actually damage your visibility.

20 Consultancy.UK (2017) How do buyers of consultancy services find | research consulting firms? https://www.consultancy.uk/news/14790/how-do-buyers-of-consultancy-services-find-research-consulting-firms

21 Useful software if you are doing this in-house: Storychief, Curata and Open Site Explorer.

22 SGR (2017a) Five quick wins for your next piece of thought leadership. Source Global Research (blog). https://www.sourceglobalresearch.com/five-quick-wins-for-your-next-piece-of-thought-leadership/ 13.12.17.

23 Hinge Research Institute (2018) *High Growth Study: Consulting Firm Edition*. Virginia: Hinge.

24 It might be useful to do a PESTLE analysis for some of these columns (Political, Economic, Social, Technological, Legal, Environmental).

25 Remember, there are thousands of MBAs and MScs looking for summer projects!

26 For a detailed breakdown of how to write quality thought leadership, I recommend: Prizeman, T. (2015) *The Thought Leadership Manual*. London: Panama Press.

5
Building intellectual property, services and products

What are investors and acquirers looking for?

Intellectual property (IP) is one of the most important qualitative measures buyers cite when looking to acquire consultancies. Without IP, the value of the firm is, give or take, the present net value of contracts plus the reputation of the firm. In these cases, buyers are typically purchasing the skills of the individuals and the client connections that would be useful to the aquirer. Either way, this tends to result in cherry-picking by the buyer, a relatively low price multiple for the firm and a very long (up to five years) earn-out period. This is not to say that firms without strong service IP cannot be successful, simply that in the PE and M&A game, strong service and operational IP can have a significant effect on the valuation of the firm.

For buyers, strong IP doesn't just reduce the risk of the purchase, it also provides them with a quick way to offer their own clients your products and services. Imagine you are a strategic buyer with 500 clients. Strongly packaged IP, especially if it is independent of people, provides you with an immediate proposition for 500 additional revenue streams! Thus, when asked what IP should achieve for the buyer, purchasers gave the following preferences in order of importance (highest to lowest): adding to future scalability, differentiating the services of the firm, improving the visibility of the firm, and revenue generation.[1] The position of 'revenue' in last place indicates the power that good IP has to drive scale for firms without directly generating cash.

When it comes to services, strategic buyers are often looking more for specific profitable products that they can cross-sell to their own existing client base or for services which fill a specific gap in their offerings. Private equity (PE) buyers are generally looking for services that have potential to grow sales fast. This is not an either/or choice, but a question of emphasis: often PE will buy a firm that has developed services which are useful for their 'stable' of invested firms,

DOI: 10.4324/9781003149217-5

and strategic buyers will certainly pay a premium for a firm that has services which are highly profitable in their own right.

Both PE and strategic buyers generally prefer commodified products and services based around IP. It minimises costs and protects them from the risk of key people leaving. Both forms of buyers will also do due diligence on your past projects, looking not only for evidence of success, but also seeking to understand the quality management processes that enable them.

It should also be stressed that digital products and services attract a premium, both in terms of the numbers of interested buyers and the price they will pay. This is because digital breaks the link between headcount and revenue. Yet, it is not just the specific products or services that are of interest to the buyer, but also the processes by which services are continuously developed and improved. This pertains to both the systems for assessing which services *should* be developed (i.e. those relating to strategy) and also those which underpin the development process itself.

All this said, when it comes to the sale, it is insufficient to simply *possess* IP. Nearly 50% of buyers report that they find it hard to understand how the consultancy's claims to IP actually link to its bottom line.[2] Typically, only between 20% and 30% of firms are perceived as clearly communicating the value of their IP.

Intellectual property

Types of IP

Intellectual Property not only includes the services and products that are delivered to clients, but also the operations and business development processes, methods and technologies that firms commodify over time. Table 5.1 highlights these different categories and provides examples of each. All these categories help the firm add leverage, value, scalability and efficiency.

When it comes to buyers' and investors' preferences, we know that revenue-generating IP is in first place, but not by as much as many might expect (see Figure 5.1). For obvious reasons, buyers look for recurring revenue IP rather than revenue dependent upon constant sales efforts. Over 60% of buyers say that recurring revenue is 'extremely important' for them, although this is much more important for PE buyers (67%) than strategic buyers (45%), and much more important in the US (75%) than in Europe (42%). In other words, if you do not have any recurring revenue, then perhaps focus your attention on European strategic buyers! The reason for this is that PE tends to be more focused on future financial returns from your services, whereas strategic buyers, whilst not uninterested in this, are more focused on the strategic synergies be-tween the two firms.

Table 5.1 Categories and examples of IP for methods and tools

	What does it enable?	*Examples*
Business Development	Selling more, dearer, faster at lower cost to you.	Bid management process; Marketing analysis processes; Case studies; Thought leadership practices; Pitch methodologies; Proposal templates; Sales training and mentoring systems; Brand
Delivery	Scaling and standardising by enabling high-fee work by cheaper consultants.	Peer group networks; Expert groups; Accreditation; Simulation; Licencing; Database access; Research reports; Benchmarking/maturity indexes; Video courses; Apps/software; Games; Research report/survey; Franchising; Project methodologies; Templates; questionnaires; process maps
Operations	A more effective business infrastructure that continuously improves.	Knowledge management processes (i.e. capture, storage, improvement, sharing); Business plan; People processes; CRM process; Pricing methods; Resource planning; Sales forecasting; Project management methods/tools; Forecasting process; Business model (for example, partnerships); CRM processes and data; Contractor relationships database; Strategy

Your *type* of firm (Brains, Grey Hair or Procedure – see Chapter 3) will influ-ence the focus of your IP. Brains firms will tend towards strong marketing IP, especially in the form of thought leadership (see Chapter 4): IP that *demon-strates* rather than *captures* experience and expertise (for example, thought leadership). Since the problems they solve tend to be relatively unique and the solutions they develop relatively creative, there are often low levels of service IP. This said, there are strong opportunities for these types of firms in operational IP and it is something that many neglect until it is too late. The Special Air Service or Navy Seals frequently solve one-off complex problems, but this doesn't influence the systematic rigour of their training, communica-tions and planning.

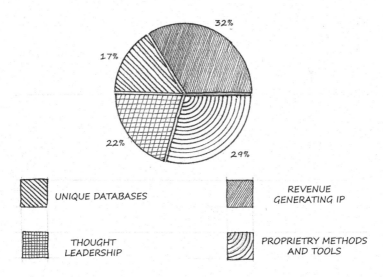

32%

17%

22%

29%

UNIQUE DATABASES

REVENUE
GENERATING IP

THOUGHT
LEADERSHIP

PROPRIETRY METHODS
AND TOOLS

Figure 5.1 Buyer preferences of consulting IP.

At the other end of the spectrum, procedure or IT-led firms will (or should!) often have strong levels of IP throughout the firm: well-defined products, operational processes and sales IP. Space for creativity and innovation is still important and still the basis for long-term competitive advantage, but this tends to be generated at the more senior levels as juniors are often maxed out with utilisation. I would urge this type of firm to think about slightly lowering target utilisation levels in exchange for greater involvement of juniors in IP development. Types of IP should also reflect the firm's Unique Value Proposition (UVP), whether that is making clients quicker, cheaper, higher quality or bigger, it should help define your IP priorities.

Managing IP

Managing IP is almost as important as creating it, because a central focus for IP is to continuously capture improvements. As firms grow in complexity, they will need to create processes for IP storage, sharing, use, improvement and retirement. As someone that has been forced to use terrible IP systems as a junior consultant, I can point to a few important insights in its management:

- Take the system seriously as an asset. It has the potential to significantly improve the value of the work you do, and thus your pricing.
- Make someone senior responsible for ensuring a clean, fast, accurate and useful knowledge/IP system.

- Request and use frequent feedback from people who have to use the system, especially juniors.
- Measure the usage of IP and prune what is not useful.
- Use version control.
- Invest in a great search function and encourage sensible metadata.
- Subject matter experts should be gatekeepers in maintaining quality.
- Protect it: for example, what needs password access? What can be kept on laptops?
- Ownership of IP must be clear in contractor and employee contracts.

The great news for most managers of internal IP is that there is now a variety of inexpensive software solutions that can help. Platforms such as Guru start from $5 a month per user. A good PSA will also help codify and automate processes and communication, and software such as MethodGrid provides sophisticated knowledge management systems to better manage, store and communicate internal IP.

There is, of course, no point having a great IP system if there is no IP created in the firm. The creation of IP should be led by a partner and should be prioritised for practice/business unit leaders. My own recommendation (and something I have done here) is to separate out IP priorities for internal processes and external services, perhaps with different leaders. They should lead to:

- Standardising and codifying common delivery activities, methods or processes.
- Capturing knowledge that is valuable to the client or to the firm.
- Creating, standardising and automating internal business processes.
- Timetabling and standardising important events such as strategy development or market research.

A useful way of improving internal IP is to focus on the business processes of the firm and gather ideas for developing the speed, efficiency and quality of these. Priorities for IP development should be communicated clearly to everyone in the firm. Ensure that there is time made available to work on IP and that the work is incentivised to illustrate its value. This said, it is also important to incentivise the right thing. I have seen a few firms incentivise the creation of IP through appraisals or even bonuses, only to find that a vast amount of time has been spent creating templates, tools and processes which do not align with the firm's strategy or priorities. I have put together a workshop template at joe-omahoney.com which should help you identify and develop your IP priorities.

The final issue you will encounter when developing IP is how to protect it. Generally speaking, getting *legal* protection for management IP is often difficult. In most countries impossible or very difficult to protect management ideas through patents. However, some protection can be given through the use of trade marks (for brands, names and logos), trade secrets (confidential information that provides economic benefits) and copyright (in the consulting context, usually for thought leadership). As a rule of thumb, the more commodified a service or product (i.e. codified, branded and standardised), the easier it is to protect. However, as I know from personal experience, IP lawyers are very expensive, and unless you have a large purse and are confident in your claim, it is generally better to focus on being ahead of the competition rather than suing them.

Many of my own clients worry about sharing their IP in marketing with potential clients, but my experience suggests that the more you share, the more successful you will be. These days, information is not a scarce commodity; it is freely available to anyone with an internet connection. What *is* a commodity, however, is visibility. In the process of democratising knowledge, the internet has become a shouting match for millions of people who want to sell to your leads. The easier you can make it for potential clients to access your ideas, the more visible and trusted you will become. This said, it is still worth making every effort to be clear with your employees, associates and clients concerning the ownership of IP. Being clear about this in contracts can act as a deterrent and also put you on more solid ground should a question of ownership end up in the courts.

Product and services

The benefits and costs of commodified consulting

For most consultancies, the most valuable IP they can develop are their services. The traditional service strategy of professional service firms is based around leveraging juniors. Prescriptive, codified methods, processes and templates allow junior staff to in theory produce the quality work of seniors, but on a lower salary. Despite frequent trumpeting about the death of traditional consulting, this model is still alive and well. Moreover, developing codified services offers a number of additional benefits, in addition to leverage:

- A more predictable, transparent and consistent service.
- A focus to capture and share experience.
- An asset which can be continuously improved and does not disappear when employees leave.
- A reference point for training and development.

- Greater potential to licence and franchise the service or, indeed, the whole firm.
- Greater potential to use junior staff, or automation, and reduce cost of delivery.
- Codified services fit well with fixed pricing which is generally superior to other methods (see Chapter 6).
- Productised, tangible, branded services can build greater client trust and understanding.

However, although codified services create leverage opportunities, these are still generally tied to headcount. Breaking out of the headcount = revenue equation offers consultancies significant opportunities to generate cash without paying people, and thus create very large profit margins. Contrary to prophets of the digital revolution, opportunities to do exactly this have always been there. Retainers, for example, go some way towards this, as does value-based pricing, benchmarking, selling research reports and access to peer networks.

Yet, it is certainly true that digital offers *new* ways to break the link between people and revenue. The collapse in cost in developing and using digital services also means it is no longer the preserve of big firms. Apps, video courses, automated benchmarking and report generation, training simulations and Software as a Service (SaaS) can be created relatively cheaply and quickly through outsourced developers, cloud-based platforms and cheap DIY software ('low code' or 'no code'). Recurring revenue linked to digital assets rather than headcount is also something which buyers particularly look for, especially if they are PE investors. You may be surprised about the potential for this in your own firm, once you start to investigate. Digital can also allow your firm to 'leave behind' something for the client offering additional value or revenue streams.

Once built, there are also old and new ways of 'sweating' these assets: licencing, franchising, co-investing, partnering, selling the service outright and pay per use are all ways I have seen consultancies use digital assets. Some also give access away free of charge, as part of a 'freemium' service, in which users upgrade or are encouraged to buy higher value (often more traditional) services.

It is perfectly possible to grow and sell a firm that has no commodified services. A handful of my interviewees did exactly that. These firms are generally 'brains' firms which focus on creative solutions to one-off problems that are typically highly priced. Their founders are often ex-partners from firms like McKinsey &Co. or BCG and had the credibility and contacts to charge very high rates for their bespoke work (£8,000–10,000/day would not be unusual). This said, these firms *did* possess 'IP' of sorts in the ways in which they created and resourced their bespoke solutions – a 'method for their methods' – so that their model was still efficient. Additionally, much of the presentation of 'bespoke' work is often more rhetoric than reality, as consultants compensate for the loss of pride often associated with delivering standardised solutions.[3] In one case an (anonymised) founder told me that she actually moved away from standardised work because she found it boring: 'It made us a lot of money, but I really wasn't interested in it. I like solving complex problems in a creative way'.

Finally, I would note that some firms I have coached have eventually turned their services and methods into licenced assets. As the risk here is that licensees steal the IP, this usually requires a more intense and enhanced effort of 'productisation' that might involve:

- Building a very strong brand with powerful thought leadership.
- Having as much legally protected IP as possible.
- Creating as much 'hard to imitate' content in the IP as possible (for example, software).
- Acting as a sales channel for licensees.
- Assuring quality by insisting on regular certification and training.
- Having a clear, contractual agreement, whereby licencing is revoked if the brand is threatened by a licensee.

I am currently helping a firm called Chameleon Works turn a service they have been using successfully for some time into a product that is licenced to other consultants. The service is a combination of two passions of the founder: wine tasting and MBTI personality testing. The service is based around using wine tasting to develop insights into leadership, sales and communication for executive teams, and as such has huge potential as a fun, unique and insightful way for other consultancies to develop business with new and existing clients. Whilst the founder, Deborah, has done all the relevant copyrighting and trade marking, it is really the quality, branding and maturity of the service that allows her to be confident that her product will dominate any potential competitors.

Service strategy

The aim of your service strategy is to ensure your services are getting you to where you need to be in terms of sales, markets and your UVP. But there are common pitfalls that have solutions in service development. One of the most common is outlined by Angrez of 8Works:

> How do you stop this whole hamster wheel of running project every six to eight weeks and then finding another project? You deliver work, find work, deliver

work, find work....We changed our offering not to just do the six to eight week sprints but to also actually design clients a new vision, purpose, or operating model. We created a 'transformation hub' that would run for three to six months to build capability in the client, to design change but then also execute on it.

The 'hamster wheel' is no one's friend, and if you can find a way to move upstream or downstream for longer projects or even create recurring business models (discussed later), you will make your life much easier.

With my own clients, I often run an annual workshop to explore (i) which services are most and least successful? (ii) what new services/markets should be prioritised? (iii) whether the services are achieving synergies? (iv) which existing services can be improved? I have put a slide deck that you can use for running this workshop at joeomahoney.com. Below, I give an example of the service/market matrix I use with some of my consultancy clients (Figure 5.2). It depicts three existing services at various stages of development in two existing markets and two services under development (indicated by the incomplete circles). The traffic light system (here it is shaded instead) represents the profit brought in by the service (high, medium, low) and the letter represents whether sales are increasing at 20%+, 0%+ or decreasing. The incomplete circles show the 'completeness' of new services in existing markets or existing services in new markets.

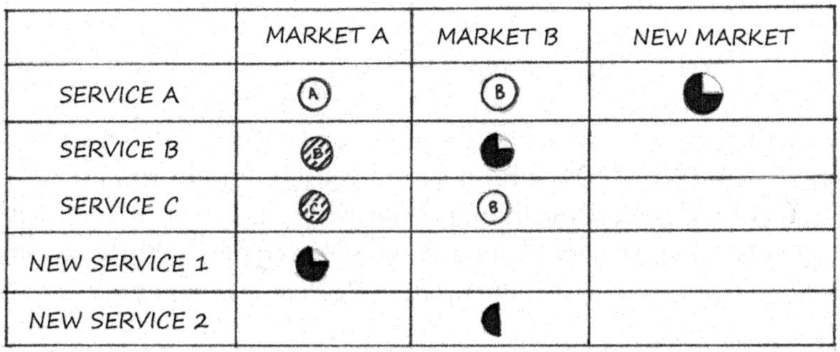

	MARKET A	MARKET B	NEW MARKET
SERVICE A	(A)	(B)	◖
SERVICE B	◉	◖	
SERVICE C	◉	(B)	
NEW SERVICE 1	◖		
NEW SERVICE 2		◗	

Figure 5.2 An example of a service/market matrix.

Beyond a simple visual of the success and progress of current activities, the matrix is also useful for identifying future activities: in this case, moving services B and C into the new market and New Services 1 and 2 into all markets. It can also be used as a basis for assigning budgets, targets (margins and revenues), headcount and recruitment. As a note here, I would stress that this is only an example. You should have a process that suits your stage of development. In addition to aiming to turn the matrix green, you should also consider retiring products that fail to grow for two years or more (excluding recessions!), especially if the margins are not great.

When assessing the potential of new markets, it is worth creating a structured scoring process with weighted items such as market size, competition, market growth and existing client presence as well as contacts and experience in the market. This will allow you to have a rational discussion about which markets have the most potential. For new services, as there are costs involved (including research, development, testing, branding and associated thought leadership), you are really building a business case for an investment, and so some market research will be needed involving actual and potential clients.

Concerning whether to initially diversify services or markets, the former is more common than the latter, but it depends on the firm's context. Some services are suited to only one market, which means it is often easier for the firm to grow by diversifying services, whilst some services are fairly generic, and thus adjacent markets are easier to target. No matter, if you decide to move into new markets, it is worth thinking about potential partners who might give you easier access to markets – firms that are already present and are aligned to you but that might initially pass work your way in exchange for a commission or a reciprocal relationship. It will also be worth considering bringing on associates or staff with existing experience and contacts in these markets.

A final note on strategy concerns recessions. You should be aware of the extent to which your services depend on economic good times. If the answer is 'a lot', then seek to develop counter-cyclical services or markets which might keep you afloat during another recession. The consulting market in general is not heavily affected by recessions, but this average picture disguises a split between 50% who do badly and 30% who do very well. To ensure you are not in the former category, it is worth thinking about what might sustain you when the worst happens. Greg Alexander, founder of SBI, told me that his firm's strength in recessions was crucial in driving up the price paid for the firm.

Service development

I've created a full template for a service development workshop at joeomahoney.com, but we can note here that service development should have three features. The first is a strategic review of the market needs. This should result in a formal workshop to shortlist ideas for new service development. As developing new services is a fast way to burn through resource (especially if software-based), a business case should be built and low-hanging fruit prioritised. Start with the market, look at your capabilities and existing offerings and score ideas and solutions by cost, benefit, cross-selling potential and strategic fit.

The second is articulating and codifying what you already do. My own clients are occasionally sitting on a wealth of data about previous projects or clients, or market research that they have done, without realising its value to clients. I have already pointed to the value of internal data for thought leadership, but it can also be useful for service development.

Finally, continuous improvement. Staff, especially new hires, should be encouraged and rewarded for improving services each time they are implemented. Small changes should be captured automatically; larger shifts – for example to software – should be built around a business case.

Typically, consultancies start off doing 'customised services' (a different service for each client) and then, with at least some of their services, move to 'productised services' (typically a fixed price service with a 'standard' methodology or process). Most small consultancies stop here, but both customised services and productised services are 1:1 offerings which require effort for every extra client. The next stage is 'products' – off-the-shelf purchases which requires minimal effort and cost for every additional client. These might include purchasing an online course, a research report or a webinar place. This is great because finally the link between time and revenue is broken. However, there is one final step which we can call 'Product as a Service' (PaaS) which is a product that has recurring revenue typically in exchange for ongoing access: an annual subscription fee for research reports, a monthly membership fee for database access, annual user fees for benchmarking access. Of course, not all customised services can be transformed into PaaS but it is worth thinking about the ones that, with some work, can. The reason most software companies attract a sale multiple three times higher than those of consultancies is because they tend to only operate PaaS.

Many consultancies find developing new products difficult, so I've included a basic method below. It should of course be edited depending on the consultancy and service:

1. Use your market research to identify client needs, competitor offerings or relevant trends.
2. Capture tacit knowledge that is commonly used and create more if needed.
3. Conduct a research exercise (for example, similar products) to boost the efficacy of this knowledge.
4. Abstract and categorise what you have captured into simple types.
5. Break down further until you have a detailed method. Support this with templates, checklists, databases and so on as needed.
6. Create the client journey/experience emphasising points of personalisation and attention.
7. Share the minimum viable product with client(s) to gain feedback and improve.

8. Create the process/instructions on delivering services to clients.
9. Outsource, automate or delegate simple parts of the process where possible.
10. Package and brand consistently with the firm's brand and UVP.
11. Supplement with added value products (for example, video/software).
12. Undertake thought leadership on the value of your service/product.
13. Improve, reduce delivery costs, increase value and innovate in pricing.

Point number (2), capturing tacit knowledge, is an art that many firms would benefit from learning. Some very bright seniors often start with a view that what is in their heads can't be codified, and to some extent this is true. However, this kind of stubbornness can lead consultants to overlook the possibility of at least codifying *aspects* of what they do. If say 60% of knowledge *can* be captured and codified, seniors will be free to focus their time on the 40% where they can really add value. This is the basis of effective leverage. One of the training courses I created for a larger firm involved an interview process, designed to show firm experts how to effectively capture their tacit knowledge. The interview focused on the questions they ask (subconsciously or consciously), the differences they note between good and bad practice and the implicit process they follow when approaching common issues. Consultants often found that aspects of their work were more procedural than they initially thought. The ultimate aim is to develop a service or approach that is repeatable by juniors and thus scalable.

When converting tacit to codified knowledge, it is useful to consider all the options available for developing the IP. Below (Table 5.2), I've created a short list of tools, methods and approaches that can be used. It is important to stress that it is a big risk to jump straight into the expensive software development of stage three or four. Start with your clients' problems. Develop a minimum viable proposition, test it and continue this so that your development is iterative rather than linear. During the development, you might also consider innovative forms of pricing. I discuss these more in Chapter 6, but giving serious

Table 5.2 Components for service development

Templates and tools	Train the trainer	Video Course
Processes	Simulation	Apps/software
Peer group network	Database access	Gamification
Expert group	Research reports	Research/surveys
Accreditation	Benchmarking/maturity	Crowdsourcing
Network introductions	Capacity development	Methods and methodologies

consideration to whether a service should be free, licenced, pay per use or even franchised can make a huge difference to profitability.

Buyers emphasise proprietary methods and tools almost as much as they do products and services. This is especially so if the services have been licenced outside the firm (think Six Sigma or Prince 2). The difficulty with many of these is that they are often part of trends or fashions that go out of date (think Total Quality Management or Business Process Re-Engineering). These can certainly be updated to reflect the new fashions (think Agile or Scrum). Of course, it is a rare firm that can develop a Six Sigma service that is licenced globally; however, if you have chosen your niche well, it may well be possible to develop a proprietary method for your area. This may start off as something relatively simple but can be reviewed each year to see if there is potential for further development. Once you have made a start, it may be worth partnering with academics, trade bodies or institutes to help develop and even accredit the IP.

Improving services

Your service strategy should be reviewed every year and additionally during any significant market or firm change. Service strategy reviews are crucial to the growth of the business because they identify when it is time to create, retire, improve or expand your service offering. The thoroughness and complexity of service reviews will depend on the firm's own maturity, but should include something like the items listed in Table 5.3. You could evaluate these items using a score or traffic light system. The benefit of the former is that you can scale and weight different criteria, but I personally prefer the latter as it shows me immediately what I need to work on.

The outcome of the service review will be a set of actions that aims to turn all the colours to green. If the service is not yet completed, integrated or profitable, then what actions need to be taken to improve this? These actions should feed into a service plan, the progress of which can be reviewed. It may be the case that not all lights *can* actually be green: some services can't or shouldn't be completely commodified and some may never be well integrated or aligned. It is important to go about your service review with a sense of realism!

Innovation

I wanted to add a brief note here on innovation. Genuine innovation is a key source of competitive advantage for consultancies. Indeed, in their detailed analysis of consulting metrics SPI found that being innovation focused was the number one predictor of high performance – above leadership, communication or strategy.[4]

Table 5.3 Example Service Review Scorecard

Criteria	Things to consider
How aligned is the service with our value proposition and strategy?	Does the service fit with our 'why' as a company and our culture? Does it help us get to where we want? Will it drive new business?
Is the service commodified?	Does it lend itself to leverage? Can any of it be automated/digitised? How dependent is the service on person-hours?
Is the service well managed internally?	How well do we manage the leverage and utilisation of the service? Is it smoothly implemented? Do we capture learnings to improve the service?
How well does the brand and language of the service fit with the current zeitgeist?	Are you talking about BPR when you should be talking about Lean? Is the service packaged, described and branded effectively? Does the service link clearly with current thought leadership?
How is the service selling?	Churn? Market penetration? Client feedback? Success rates (perceived and actual)?
How profitable is the service?	What share of revenues and profits? Is it growing or declining?
How complete is the service?	Is the service new, developing or mature? What priority is it for us?
How aligned are the staff?	How much knowledge do they have of the service? How many times have they implemented/delivered it? Are they behind it? Apprentice/master/expert?
How competitive is the service?	Competitors? Competing on price? Are we market leaders on this service?
All services: Are the service well integrated?	Do they have horizontal or vertical cross-sell opportunities? Can they be offered to all sectors that you serve? Are there overlaps or gaps? Does one service logically lead to another?

A few years back, I led a two-year study of innovation in the consulting industry, funded by the UK government.[5] The study focused on very large consultancies and found that levels of innovation were generally quite low, because a period of declining profit margins (driven by procurement and more savvy clients) meant there was less investment in innovation and more focus on standardisation. This obviously causes a challenge for large firms because innovation is the number one requirement of clients who have themselves delayered and automated to the point where internal innovation is often limited.[6]

Following the research, I was contacted by many large firms who wanted help with their innovation. However, few were prepared to change their culture, take the pressure off utilisation rates or recruit a different type of person. When I suggested to a leading strategy firm that perhaps the best vehicle for my recommendations on creativity was not a PowerPoint deck, I was met with blank faces. The consequence is that many large firms seek to enhance their innovation by buying exactly the sort of firm you are probably leading now. Their success at this is often limited as the smaller firm is often (though not always) absorbed by the larger, losing its distinctiveness and sometimes many of its key people.

The lesson for most smaller firms is to maintain the space for innovation that is often missing at the large firms. This means keeping abreast of new ideas, investing in service research and development, experimenting with joint partnerships and co-innovation projects, taking on people outside the standard MBA route and nurturing innovation as a core competence through culture, reward and training. This, ironically, is rarely in spite of codified processes, but *because* of them. Systems not only help free up the time and space for innovation, but also provide methods for systematising, capturing and exploiting it.

Takeaways

- IP builds assets for delivery, operations and business development in the firm instead of its people and is crucial for buyer interest. It is also crucial for scaling the firm and enabling leverage. It should be led by a partner. Maximise margins through leveraged, unique IP.
- Standardise internal process and activities by strategically and systematically capturing useful knowledge, storing and sharing it effectively and improving it frequently. Automate and outsource work where quality will not be diminished.
- Products and Product as a Service are cheaper to deliver, easier to scale and can lead to recurring revenue that breaks the link between income and headcount. This drives high multiples of EBITDA.
- Consider the extent to which your services are recession-proof. If you have a weakness here, consider developing counter-cyclical services.
- Services should be developed and expanded into new markets strategically. New services should be developed through a methodology which starts with client needs and ends with continuous improvement.

- Putting innovation at the heart of your firm's strategy and capabilities prevents *clients* commodifying your work, ensures you stay ahead of the competition and justifies higher prices.
- Prioritise sharing your client-facing IP over keeping it secret. In the digital age, information is not scarce, but client attention is, and sharing more often helps gain the latter.

Case study: Water Street Partners

In strategy consulting, where salaries are sky-high, it is rare to come across a firm that matches the margins achieved by Water Street Partners (WSP), a boutique joint venture specialist. Equally surprising is their annual revenue per consultant which was around £1 million, putting them on the same rung as McKinsey, Bain and BCG. This was achieved at utilisation rates that hovered around the 60% mark.

So how does a firm, started only in 2008, grow to hit these figures and then sell only 12 years after inception? The pedigrees of the founders David Ernst and James Bamford do not hurt. They founded and led McKinsey & Co.'s joint venture practice and by the time they left, had established their reputations through over 150 articles in publications ranging from the *Harvard Business Review* to the *Financial Times*. Their careers also provided them with enough capital to have a running start with five employees, one of whom, David tells me, 'was one of the best researchers in the world'.

Yet this is not a story of an easy ride. Soon after WSP was founded, the longest recession in living memory disrupted their core business. Initially, WSP focused on a subscription service where they provided data, best practice and benchmarking information on joint ventures for leaders in this field. Given the huge sums and risks involved with joint ventures, a few firms were happy to pay around £100,000 a year for this expertise. When the recession bit and client discretionary spend was cut back, however, the founders looked to increasing their management consulting work, advising on the strategy, governance and structuring of joint ventures. The subscription business continued until 2009, when it was reinvented at a lower price point and then, in 2016, halted completely.

Even so, the databases, best practice repositories and market reports developed for the subscription business still provided the staff at the firm with a powerful arsenal to attract and delight clients. When they founded, there were very few specialist consultancies in the joint venture space and none with the reputation of the founders. Business grew rapidly and the generous non-compete contracts the founders had signed with McKinsey & Co. allowed the firm almost free rein in the market.

As with many successful firms, WSP focused entirely on quality client delivery. This, both David and Jim tell me, was their 'primary metric'. Incredibly, given their sizeable margins, David tells me, 'we never really focused on financial metrics. Initially, given the recession, we wanted to make sure the pipeline was full, and we were working with the right clients doing the best work we could'. The strategy paid off: the firm was rated #1 in the industry rankings for joint venture consulting and over 50% of their clients were from repeat business.

Yet, premium delivery and fees require quality talent, and attracting people from top strategy firms was always going to be challenging. James tells me, 'if you're at McKinsey, and you're a strong performer, why you would ever leave is beyond me.... so we struggled to pull people from there'. Their target became two groups: people who McKinsey should have recruited but didn't, and good transaction attorneys in big law firms. James tells me the latter that they 'had great transferable skills, but often weren't happy in their jobs'.

This case has many features of best practice start-up. It shows the success that can happen when growing consultancies focus on a profitable, low competition niche, invest strongly in growth, focus on high-quality delivery and pivot quickly in response to market changes. However, no case is without its challenges, and when asked about these, James mentioned two things. The first was governance. Whilst he and David held the only voting rights in the company, they took a participative approach to decision-making. As with other successful founders, such as Stephen Newton at Elixir, James felt this could sometimes slow things down and lead to sub-optimal decisions. The second challenge was establishing a strong culture in a small firm when people were on the road so often: 'We have a great space on the river...but on any given day we have say 5 people in an office...So we'd have discussions about culture and stuff, but travel and physical size of the office made it difficult'.

Despite these challenges, the firm eventually chose Ankora from their potential suitors, a relatively new consulting firm with big growth ambitions. The deal was completed in 2000. One reason for their choice was that Ankora gave them the space to keep their brand and identity as opposed to much larger firms who would have simply absorbed the people.

Notes

1 Equiteq (2019) *The Knowledge Economy Global Buyers Report*.
2 Equiteq (2017) What buyers of consulting firms look for and how they will determine value in 2018. YouTube. https://youtu.be/GTc9fURaUxI
3 This tendency is explored in: Visscher, K., Heusinkveld, S., & O'Mahoney, J. (2018) Bricolage and identity work. *British Journal of Management*, 29(2), 356–372.
4 Service Performance Insight (2020) Professional services maturity benchmark. Deltek. www.SPIresearch.com
5 If you are interested, see these two references: O'Mahoney, J. (2013) *Management Innovation in the UK Consulting Industry*. In Haynes, K., & Grugulis, I. eds. *Managing Services: Challenges and Innovation*. Oxford: Oxford University Press, pp. 83–104. O'Mahoney, J. (2011) *Management Innovation in the UK Consulting Industry*. Report for the Chartered Management Institute.
6 SGR (2020c) *A Theory of Everything: Rebuilding the Consulting Model, Capability by Capability*. Source Global Consulting. April.

6
Business development

What are investors and acquirers looking for?

When I asked one PE investor what they looked for in sales, she replied, 'it's not complicated Joe: good clients who spend more money each year'. However, it actually *is* complicated, because the systems and people to effectively find and keep those clients are fairly rare in consultancies.

Buyers want your sales team to be hitting the figures I have emphasised throughout this book, a minimum of 20% annual growth on 20% EBITDA. To minimise risk, they would rather that no single client contributed more than 25% of the firm's revenue and would prefer blue chip and board-level clients as these are more valuable contacts for the buyer interested in cross-selling.

To make this happen, much has to happen behind the scenes, and buyers would like to see systems that are measured and continually improved. This doesn't simply concern IT systems such as CRM, but also systems of training, recruitment and rewards which place sales at the centre of the organisation. This effort should also shift the responsibility for sales away from the founder and to the wider team, de-risking the business and removing a major limit on sales potential.

Sales strategy

Mindset (again)

Whilst there are many exceptions, most founders who start their first small consultancy come either from a large consulting firm or a senior management position in a large company. In most cases, unless they were a partner, they will not have done much business development and often feel resistant to it. This is a tragedy because without sales the firm will fail. In my advisory sessions, which

DOI: 10.4324/9781003149217-6

here generally turn into coaching sessions, several things have commonly happened to this person.

- They have spent too much time and money on marketing in the (often subconscious) hope that this will supplant the need for sales.
- They have wasted days locked in a room doing sales planning, strategising and research, getting their fonts just so and spending as little time as possible talking to potential clients.
- They are sometimes actually great at the relationship side of business development but falter when it comes to negotiating and closing the deal, often giving discounts before they are even requested.

What to do? Here is what works for my clients that are shy of sales:

- Believe in your expertise and your services. Read previous testimonials and remind yourself of your successes. Remind yourself that even without any expertise, an objective, independent view is valuable in its own right. You are an expert who can help people. Your sales job isn't to persuade everyone to hire you but find out if they are in that group you *can* help and tell them how.
- Let your marketing, branding and thought leadership do most of the work. Clients want to know (i) can you do the work well?; (ii) will you make their lives easier?; and (iii) can they respect you? By the time you speak to clients, you should have answered those questions for them with testimonials, thought leadership, videos and case studies. If the answer to these questions is no, you shouldn't be working with them anyway.
- Stop selling and start consulting immediately. In my own work, I love problem-solving and I'm good at it, so I just start doing it as soon as I speak to someone. It is less like selling and more like giving the client a live preview of your capabilities.
- Do not wait until clients are looking for people to fix their problems. By then, it is too late, and you may end up in procurement hell. Instead, target your thought leadership, marketing and messaging to when clients are setting their priorities and prioritising issues (rather than solutions). Seventy-one per cent of clients say they want to be contacted earlier by consultancies,[1] and the earlier you engage, the more time you have to build a relationship and show clients that you understand their challenge.
- When it comes to a sales event, some shy consultants 'act out' a specific personality that helps them say things they wouldn't normally be comfortable with. One of my clients channels Ruby Wax and another, Alan Sugar. I've no idea if this works as a sales tool, but apparently it can make the process feel more comfortable.

- Others reframe the sales meeting. Some focus on simply getting to a 'no', arguing that they are not trying to sell, but just need a decision. Others frame sales as a skills development exercise, often doing ten calls in the morning to get the day started.
- Clients primarily buy on trust. This is trust in skills (your people can do the job), trust in your values (your people won't let the client down outside of the job) and trust in your firm (the brand, not just the people). The best way to build trust is frequent touches and honesty. Building trust is better for sales than any trick or technique you will learn in a business development seminar.

From you to them

Early on, the responsibility for sales lies with the founder(s), and clients are usually simply buying the time of that person. Logan Naidu of Dartmouth Partners told me:

> How do you make sure that one or two individuals don't own all the relationships? We were like that for the first three or four years. Despite my best intentions, the client know they're buying you, they're not buying Dartmouth. My regular routine was Tuesday, Wednesday and Thursday nights out with clients selling daytime meetings, constantly. But the growth of the business has been focused around creating an organic sales engine outside of your two or three main people.

When the sales engine is not expanded beyond the founders, things go wrong later in the growth cycle. As Greg Francis of the Access Partnership told me:

> For years I gathered all of the business development to myself, which is of course a single point of failure and absolutely stupid in business terms. But I thought it was enabling capabilities of a different sort in the people we were hiring. While that might have been true for a while, it certainly wasn't a roadmap for growth. So we had to reinvent our company to have more commercial awareness across staff which had never been a requirement, which was very difficult.

Whilst it is difficult early on, a CEO or founder needs to transition from marketing and selling services to marketing and selling the firm. Shifting the focus from you to other seniors takes time, but typically involves the following movements:

1. A system of recruitment, development and incentivisation of capable and connected seniors mentored *and delegated to* by the partner(s) to support

delivery and sales. These should be introduced to existing clients with reassurances about the quality of work, but should also begin to sell more commodified services to new clients (I cover this more in Chapter 8, on talent).
2. Purchase of an integrated CRM system that is used strategically and systematically to build intelligence on and relationships with client stakeholders.
3. Placing (the right) sales at the core of the business. As the business grows this must be reflected in recruitment, development, promotion, rewards, performance management, communications and culture.
4. Continuing development and improvement of strong sales IP to guide and feed the business development process.
5. Recruitment of experienced juniors to work on more commodified work. For existing clients, this might initially be 'back-office' work. Juniors can be increasingly exposed to sales training, mentoring and experience.
6. A cascade of sales meetings focused on measurement and improvement integrated with developments in propositions and marketing.

Even after sales have become integral to everyone in the organisation, partners should still spend the majority of their time on business development. David Maister's recommendation of between 70% and 80% of partner time on business development is still the target I would suggest for firms with more than 20 employees. The exception is the *managing* partner (or CEO), who should spend an increasing amount of their time running the firm as it grows.

Success in sales for a consultancy requires technical competences that we discuss shortly, but most important of all is a deep cultural awareness throughout the firm that, for the company to thrive, the pipeline must constantly be full and that this is everyone's responsibility. Furthermore, if juniors are to become seniors, they must already be adept at business development and know that this is a large part of their own success in the firm. In larger firms, I generally suggest including business development time as part of the utilisation target for all grades. It is harder to measure, but psychologically it will reinforce the importance of sales to the firm.

Your consultants must develop an instinct for sales. For example, they should have at least (say) four proposals in front of clients and (say) 20 presentations, seminars, meetings, conferences or referrals on the go. Equally, maintaining close relationships and providing value outside of projects to existing clients is important. The key competencies for sales will depend on the firm, but research shows that the following are important for successful sales in professional services:

- A strong personal network.
- A 'visible' brand as an expert in the relevant industry/service.
- Confidence in one's expertise and a willingness to challenge the client.
- Strong interpersonal skills which build trust.

Generally, the maturity of your sales functions will match the size of the firm (see Figure 6.1). This is not to say that later stages are 'better' than earlier ones, as each stage should match the capabilities of the firm. There are economies of scope and scale to establishing mature systems in a large firm that simply don't exist for a small firm.

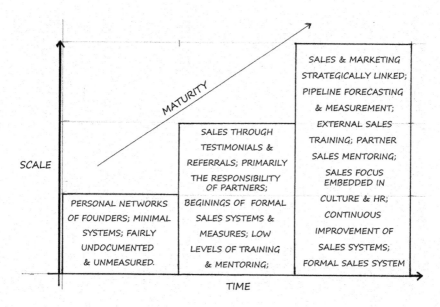

Figure 6.1 Example maturity levels for a consultancy's sales function.

Strategy and plan

Your sales plan should extend and implement your marketing strategy (Figure 6.2). Whilst your marketing strategy moves potential clients from being oblivious to informed, your sales plan enters in to move them from a state of engagement to signing a contract and ideally becoming an advocate for your services.

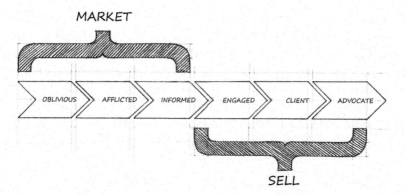

Figure 6.2 The new client journey.

An interesting comment from one of my interviewees was that marketing should be prioritised over sales. The reason, they argued, was two-fold. First, by prioritising marketing, you are investing in the asset of the firm rather than events. Second, by prioritising marketing over sales, you are less likely to be held hostage by dominant rain-makers who can threaten to take 'their' clients elsewhere. I am not convinced that the two need to compete however. The former, for growing firms, is more embedded in systems and content whereas the latter is embedded in the skills and culture of the firm.

It is also worth emphasising that not all sales are equal. Your sales plan should focus on investing in your core high-margin, high-revenue services (Figure 6.3). This also means either improving or dropping those areas which do not deliver on this.

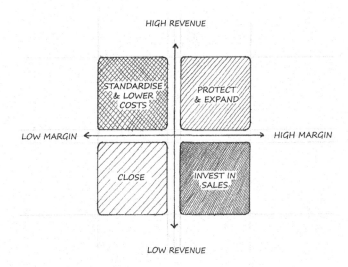

Figure 6.3 Sales priorities for growth by client type.

Even a solo consulting firm needs sales targets if it is to have any direction and ambition. As firms grow, these headline figures must be broken down into business units (usually service or industry lines) and to individual clients or partners, depending on your preference (see Figure 6.4). These should be tied into individual targets for seniors. This should be a two-way relationship where feedback from individual clients and seniors feeds into subsequent target setting on the basis of client/industry opportunities and new service development.

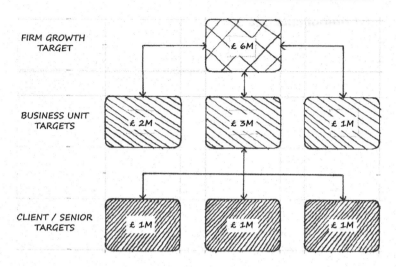

FIRM GROWTH TARGET

£ 6M

BUSINESS UNIT TARGETS

£ 2M £ 3M £ 1M

CLIENT / SENIOR TARGETS

£ 1M £ 1M £ 1M

Figure 6.4 Cascading sales targets.

The targets should feed into individual plans for each client. The focus, once again, needs to be on the *right* sales – the ones which fit the core proposition of the firm.

The sales plan should begin with high-level sales targets (targets for qualified leads, proposals/presentations, contracts, conversion ratios), which are then broken down for priority sectors and services and target clients (organisations and roles). If the firm is big enough, targets should be assigned against specific leaders who may break these down into targets for individuals in their teams. Once the 'what' is set, then the 'who' and 'when' and 'how' can be detailed (see Table 6.1). I've put a template for a sales plan at joeomahoney.com, but a good PSA/CRM system will have this integrated.

As I discuss below, the implementation of your sales plan is contingent on your pipeline. If the pipeline is looking weak, planned activities should be accelerated or bought forward. If the pipeline is too full and additional resource is not available, activities should be postponed. Additional sales activity should also be linked to specific marketing campaigns, such as new thought leadership or services.

Finally, I would stress that in larger firms, a crucial link for sales is with the teams doing the implementation. In pursuit of growing sales, some consultancies bring in specialist sales resource, but the danger here is that this resource sells anything they can to hit their targets. The results can be poor project quality and dissatisfied clients or projects which distract the firm from more useful activity.

Table 6.1 Components of a consulting sales plan

	Components	Examples
What?	Target revenues, firms, roles for sectors and services. Target pipeline measures and conversion ratios.	Twenty per cent revenue growth overall. Twenty-five per cent growth in telco and 15% growth in media. First contract with TelcoUSA (minimum £55,000), 15% growth in all clients; increase qualification by 15% and target pipeline ratios of 12: 3:1.
Who?	Who is responsible for each target? Targets for business units, leaders and teams.	John responsible for TelcoUSA; Claire responsible for media; Ahmed responsible for telco. Ahmed's team targets to follow.
How?	Ongoing tactics linked to specific marketing campaigns (for example, referrals, renewals, upsells, cross-sells, new prospects, new segments). Specific activities for specific roles. Investments.	Sales effort to follow marketing campaign for TelCom Conference this year; 25% increase spend on LinkedIn ads = target of 15% more qualified calls. Sales campaign to 'capture' Telco USA. Claire to increase farming revenue from media by 30% and new business by 10%. Launch of new report to be supported all through emails to contacts.
When?	Monitoring points; dates to link with marketing campaigns; key client events calendar (for example, trigger events, conferences, release of results).	5th June, outreach to TelcoUSA Director at TelCom conference to coincide with marketing campaign. 2nd February, Ahmed to discuss expansion of project in ClientX to non-core services.

Formalising sales

The sales process

My interviewees' firms went about sales in a variety of ways. For some, reputation for quality drove potential clients to their door and sales was simply a matter of correctly qualifying clients for the right projects. However, in most other firms, strong sales were generated through establishing strong relationship with clients, but also developing strong systems for sales. As argued above, developing IP for sales, improving sales, diminishing costs and reassuring buyers are crucial.

Better understanding the perspective and milestones of your clients' decision-making will allow your people a better engagement with the process and how deals should be managed. Ensure you formalise from the client point of view, not your own. At one level, this is about understanding your major clients buying processes and how you can help them efficiently at different stages. But this might also involve changing only the language you use to your clients' perspectives. For example, 'initial meeting' might shift to 'understanding pain points' or 'presenting solution' might become 'compare solutions'. However, more generally, there is often a mindset shift needed by consultants (including partners) to understand that the best way to know what and how to sell is to ask the clients themselves. This shift also requires an understanding of what information and insights will best incline the client to buy from your firm. Sellers who provide unique insights *and* follow a formal process are 30% more likely to be high performers than those who do not.[2]

With these things established, what does the sales process itself look like? Sales tend to be initiated by three triggers. The first is when marketing hands leads over to sales for a more personalised and human interaction. The second is when clients approach the consultancy, often in response to a recommendation or thought leadership. The third is when seniors strategically target clients in one firm in a bid to win specific work. From these starting points, three further things must usually happen in order to maximise the chances of a good sale:

1. The client must be convinced of your expertise and ability to solve their problem or help with their opportunity. If your marketing has done its job, and passed on thought leadership, case studies and testimonials, much of this will have already been achieved. But in the first interaction with the prospect, it remains crucial for whoever is leading the sale to truly wow the prospect with their understanding of the client challenge/opportunity, how it is affecting their firm and the potential solutions. This is crucial in framing your firm as the most likely to help the client but will also help you in negotiations.
2. The problem and challenge must be clearly agreed and understood by both parties. The consultant and the client should help each other understand the potential benefits of getting the solution right and the consequences of doing nothing. This will help considerably when discussing pricing.
3. The client and project must be qualified. This means asking: Whether there is budget for the project. If the client has the authority to authorise spend. If not, what needs to be done to influence the right person? What priority the project is for the client? When is the project likely to start?

Finally, what are the key dependencies of the project and the expected milestones? This information will help you weigh the opportunity in the pipeline calculation (discussed below) and better help the client get the project rolling.

These things are not necessarily done in a specific order (Figure 6.5) and may be spread over several meetings. The next step, if possible, is to having a discussion around the value of the project if it is done well. For value-based pricing, this is crucial; but even with other forms of pricing, it is useful to understand and emphasise the true value of the project to the client (financially, psychologically, personally, reputationally) before moving on to the pricing discussion. For value-based pricing (discussed shortly), this conversation might end with a price range for the project, for example, 'given the value of the benefits we've discussed, how about I develop some options for you priced between £70,000 and £250,000?'.

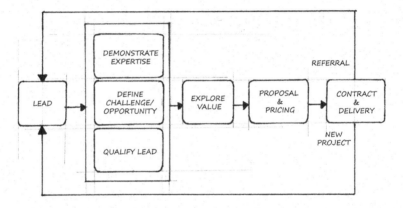

Figure 6.5 A high-level sales process for consulting firms.

A price range is useful because it allows you to give the client options. If you only give the client one price, they only have two options: to go ahead or not. If you give the client several options, this increases the chance of a 'yes' but also allows you to remove options during negotiations instead of cutting your price for doing the same thing.

Your own sales process will of course be more detailed and tailored to the different types of clients you serve and the services you sell. It might include:

- Processes for engaging different clients.
- Guidance on client conversations and relationships.
- The sequence and timing of passing on thought leadership and testimonials.

- Key events in the sales process.
- Creating innovation during the sales process.
- Weekly firm sales meetings.
- Scripts or structures for sales calls.
- Templates for proposal writing.
- Using and managing the pipeline.
- Training and mentoring on all of the above.

For some firms, sales also include other activities. A few years ago, I wrote a paper on how McKinsey & Co. sell without selling.[3] This was very often by exercising 'soft power': alumni relationships, free resource on steering committees, sponsoring conferences, working with top universities, secondments with key clients and working on think tanks. Whilst no small firms have the resources of McKinsey & Co. it is worth thinking about how 'soft power' might work in getting your name in front of key clients[4].

In addition, to the processes *of* sales, there are also the processes of monitoring, supporting, incentivising and goal-setting, which should be given more attention as the organisation grows. One of my interviewees opened up the weekly sales meetings held by seniors so that juniors could dial in and listen. This helped juniors realise how important sales was in moving up the organisation and encouraged them to pursue leads of their own.

Pipeline management

A Harvard study found that firms which managed their pipeline had 15% higher revenue growth than those that did not.[5] Moreover, they discovered that firms which clearly defined the sales process, spent at least three hours a month on pipeline management, and trained their seniors on pipeline management, had 28% higher growth. Pipeline effort is clearly worth the work, and a partner should be made responsible for managing this.

Buyers of consulting firms see a healthy pipeline as one with more than 75% of business booked for the next three months and 50% booked for the next six months. This is the ideal of course, and will depend on the type of projects you deliver, but managing your pipeline effectively is crucial to ensuring that your staff are not over-stretched or underemployed. Most professional services automation software has some form of pipeline metrics which combines the 'heat' of each lead (cold, warm, hot) with the likely staffing requirement. This allows you visibility of resourcing problems on the horizon, which, in turn, should allow you to concentrate your sales efforts, stretch or compress existing work and flexibly use your associates.

A forecast of monthly income can be achieved by discounting the predicted deal size by the chances of that deal happening. This is your Discounted Sales Pipeline (DSP). I've put a simple spreadsheet tool for tracking your pipeline at joeomahoney.com, but here (in Table 6.2) I have detailed a simplified DSP calculation. It multiplies the chances of success of each pipeline stage with the average value of the service being sold and the number of leads at that stage (the bold number in brackets). This provides you with an approximate sales figure for future months and allows you to plan resources accordingly. More importantly, it allows you to increase your focus and effort at different stages of the pipeline to ensure that you are hitting the revenue targets you've set.

As your practice grows and you gather more data on the likelihood of success of different services, your model can be tweaked to be more precise and capture more subtle metrics. One useful metric for growing firms, illustrated in Figure 6.6, is what Equiteq calls the 'pipeline index' which is created by the following ratio:

$$Pipeline\ Index = \frac{Discounted\ sales\ pipeline}{Delivery\ capacity\ at\ full\ sales}$$

If the index is at 1, the two are perfectly matched. If the index is more than one, your resources will be stretched, unless you:

- Use associates.
- Hire quickly (though this should only be done if stretching is a common problem).
- Take people over utilisation targets (not a good idea in the medium to long term).
- Postpone or turn down work.

If the index is less than one, this means you will have consultants on the bench, unless you:

- Increase your sales efforts.
- Bring forward work further down the pipeline.
- Replace associates with employees (though check you are replacing like with like).
- Manage your employees' presence (for example, bring forward holidays, postpone start dates, make redundancies).

It is also crucial to remember that managing the pipeline is not simply about forecasting – in fact, I would recommend separating pipeline management from forecasting. If your discussions focus on close dates, probabilities and deal

Table 6.2 Calculating discounted sales pipeline by client

	No. Monthly Leads and Probability of Success					
	Leads (5%)	Meetings (10%)	Proposal (20%)	Presentation (25%)	Contract (100%)	DSP
Service 1 £10,000	(16) £8,000	(8) £8,000	(4) £8,000	(2) £5,000	(1) £10,000	39,000
Service 2 £20,000	(32) £32,000	(16) £32,000	(8) £32,000	(4) £20,000	(3) £60,000	176,000
Service 3 £50,000	(33) £82,500	(14) £70,000	(7) £70,000	(5) £62,500	(2) £100,000	385,000
Service 4 £100,000	(20) £100,000	(8) £80,000	(4) £80,000	(2) £50,000	(2) £200,000	510,000
					Total	1,110,000

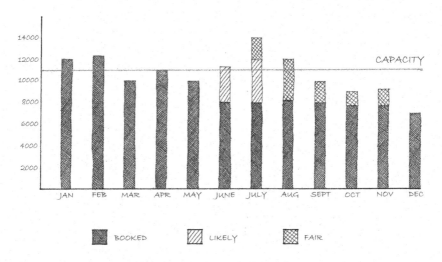

Figure 6.6 A visualisation of a Pipeline Index (Discounted vs. Capacity).

sizes, then you are forecasting. Management means ensuring that the pipeline process is working productively and that all opportunities are being met by a strongly motivated workforce. It is also ensuring that staff understand sales priorities (see below) and that the right discussions and proposals are happening (for example project utilisation and leverage is creating sufficient margins). Weekly sales meetings are crucial to prioritising pipeline work. At strategic reviews, the sales meetings should offer insights as to whether different people need to be recruited at different grades and whether the incentivisation scheme is working.

Finally, I also advise thinking carefully about the client *journey* through the pipeline. It's important that the experience as leads progress from prospect to client is as good, if not better, than their experience working with you. It would be a useful exercise to map out typical pipeline routes and touch points to see how your firm can add value to each client as they progress and follow up with those who fall out.

Incentivising the right sales

'Feeding the machine is our biggest challenge', says Chris Gibson of Pen, which reflects how stressful finding the right amount and right type of sales can be. However, 'right' is key here: the wrong type of sales will pull your firm out of shape, ensure poor quality delivery, over-stretch your people and damage your reputation. You should therefore be clear to all partners and senior managers what the right type of sales are and how many each should be expected to bring in. Ideal sales:

- Fit with your value proposition
- Maximise margins
- Minimise partner time
- Have the right leverage ratio
- Repeat or develop existing offerings
- Are in your target sectors and markets

The prioritisation of the right types of sales can be achieved by:

- Measuring them by market, service, sector, team and consultant
- Frequently and publicly reporting on targets
- Tying targets in with appraisals and bonuses

Generally speaking, larger projects tend to be more profitable because of economies of scale: their set up and partner sales time is usually proportionally lower. Several of the interviewees for this book emphasised that part of their niche was multinational firms, simply because projects were larger and the prospects of repeating successful contracts in other parts of the client were greater.

Advice on selling

Challenge and insight selling

When you buy a widget (can of beans, computer, car), what you get does not depend on you, and if you don't get what you ordered, you can usually send it back for a refund. Selling most consulting work is very different not just because the outcome is generally an unknown and partially dependent upon the buyer, but also because a bad consulting project can actually do damage to the client more widely (imagine if buying a faulty can of beans could destroy the value of your house!).

All these features of consulting work mean that trust is absolutely crucial to business development. The importance of trust is why referrals from trusted sources and previous experience with a consulting firm are the top routes by which clients find their consultants. However, trust can also be built through familiarity, and as we saw during COVID-19, this is eminently possible in the digital age: case studies, webinars, video testimonials and quality thought leadership, all provide potential clients with ways of familiarising themselves with you or your firm. In larger firms, the brand is a symbol of trust, but as Steve Newton, founder of Elixirr, told me, smaller firms cannot rely on this: 'one of the steepest learning curves to overcome coming from a large firm is that you're suddenly without the power of a calling card'.

Whilst traditional approaches to sales emphasise the benefits of the service, the problem is that buyers simply don't trust messages from people they have no experience with. Some time ago, a study by Bain & Co. found that 80% of consultancies believed they sold a 'superior value proposition' to clients, but only 8% of clients agreed.[6]

This is not to say that telling the clients about the benefits and value of your offerings is unimportant, but this has to build on the clients' existing understanding of why they need your solution. This involves what has come to be known as 'insight selling'. In their book of that title, Schultz and Doerr studied 700 business-to-business (B2B) purchases.[7] When they compared those who won a sale with those who came in second, they found a pattern among the winners. Clients reported that the sales people:

- educated me with new ideas and perspectives.
- collaborated with me.
- persuaded me we would achieve results.
- understood my needs.

Indeed, selected consultancies were three times more likely to have educated buyers with new ideas and perspectives than the runner-up choice. Note that the benefits or values of any services are not mentioned here. Instead, an insightful expert educates the buyer about new ways of doing things. Successful consultants make clients more aware of their need for the service and build trust and confidence in the seller's expertise.

Harvard Business Review made comparable observations when they reported on a research study of B2B sales. Some of the results were surprising.[8] In their study they classified five types of sales people:

- Relationship builders create friends and advocates in the client firm.
- Hard workers work longer hours and make the most calls.
- Lone wolves are confident rule-breakers.
- Problem-solvers are reliable and detail orientated.
- Challengers use deep understanding of client business to generate challenging insights.

Challengers outperformed all others. Those insightful and often provocative sellers accounted for nearly 40% of high performing salespeople, which increased to 54% in more complex B2B sales, such as those in management consulting.

This insight is supported and developed by another study of B2B sales,[9] which found that in sales meetings, sellers of B2B services expect to talk about creating value for clients through the products they sell, whereas buyers expect sellers to show a deep understanding to their specific firm, which results in insights about doing things differently.

Challengers go against conventional wisdom. Instead of leading with the benefits of what they are selling, they seek to educate clients about why their firm needs to do things differently. This leads the client to seeing the value of the services on offer. The emphasis here is much more on educating by revealing useful insights rather than simply telling the client about the benefits of service X. One of the key insights from behavioural ('nudge') theories is that when people are more likely to accept change, then they come to their own realisation about its benefits. I believe the success of challengers is based on similar psychology.[10]

In order to achieve the two crucial steps of educating clients and building trust in your expertise, the following are common examples of good practice:

- Research in detail the specific client and firm as well as the industry.
- Understand their drivers, needs and opportunities with which your services will help.
- Provide tailored and insightful content marketing through a sophisticated CRM system.
- Use account management to build strong relationships between individuals.
- In early meetings ensure you listen and learn as well as providing insights.
- Collaborate with clients to explore new angles and innovative ideas.
- Be confident in your expertise and do not be afraid to challenge clients or ask 'stupid' questions.

What clients want

The top three reasons that clients buy consultants are, in order of importance: a good reputation, competitive pricing (though please note, not necessarily the cheapest!) and a good fit with the buyer's values.[11] To a great extent, then, your ability to win at a sale will be determined long before you attempt to contact a lead. Developing this finding is research[12] showing that B2B clients buy value on five different levels:

1. Inspirational value (the ethics, values and vision of the firm).
2. Individual client value (what are you bringing to the person, for example, network, growth, CV material).
3. Ease of doing business with the client (access to seniors, building strong relationships).
4. Function (revenue, costs, quality, innovation).
5. Basics (price, regulatory, specifications, ethics).

The research shows that the more levels that the seller pays attention to, the more likely they are to be successful in their sales. Unfortunately, most consultancies only pay attention to levels 4 and 5 – focusing on delivering good services for a reasonable price. Levels 1–3 are generally ignored, but play a crucial part in moving a sale from 'probable' to 'likely'.

The other important research insight shows us that clients want to be contacted much earlier in the problem journey.[13] A typical problem journey for a client involves five steps:

1. Noticing something is not working well.
2. Identifying the cause.
3. Identifying the solution.
4. Scoping, planning and prioritising the implementation of the solution.
5. Implementing the solution.

If left to their own devices, many clients will arrive at (4) and then send out tenders for solution implementers via procurement. The consultants duly arrive and often find that the problem the client thinks they have and the solution they think they want will not actually help a huge amount. This isn't surprising, as the client manager is rarely an expert in that specific issue or in the research needed to identify the cause and solution. Many clients realise this and 71% of them wish that consultancies had contacted them earlier.

Earlier contact works for both the client and the consultancy, as the former doesn't waste time and money chasing the wrong issue and consultants avoid procurement hell. The lesson here for sales (and marketing) is the value of conducting more informal speculative and open conversations with clients as well as using thought leadership to help clients understand their 'unknown unknowns' (the things they don't know they don't know but are important) and 'known unknowns' (the things they know they don't know but are also important).

Ideally, this will also be done when you are working in an existing client. 'Land and expand' has a bad reputation, but if you are genuinely helping a client identify, understand and solve issues or opportunities, then you are adding value to their firm. Angrez Saran, founder and CEO of 8Works, told me:

> We have a 6–8 week engagement which is our bread and butter, but from there we embed ourselves with our clients helping them build this capacity to deliver change more widely. This gave us recurring annual revenue which allowed us to rapidly grow our business by focusing on new clients.

The importance of working on sales with existing clients brings us nicely to our next topic: account management.

Account management

When I asked Edward Beals, founder of the process change consultancy Loft9, how he managed to grow in such a competitive area, he replied, 'every time we won an account, we had to take it from someone else. It was really competitive'. Their ability to do this, he argued, was down to competitor consultancies taking their eye off the ball once they'd landed a client. This is ill-advised in today's competitive market which will punish a firm's inattention to clients. Two figures from recent research highlight the failure well:

- Sixty-five per cent of clients are ignorant of their current consultancies' offerings.
- Eighty-five per cent of clients' service 'wish list' included services already available from their current provider

This underscores the importance of developing strong communications with the client. This does not happen by accident or as a natural result of the sales process. Instead, it requires a defined process or method that trained account managers can use to shift how your services are seen. Good account management makes the difference between a transaction and a genuine partnership. In the early days, this will typically be done by partners, but as firms expand, engagement managers or dedicated account managers will take on the role.

There are many account management methods to choose from, but at their heart, they all involve:

- Improving communication with the client about your achievements and your potential.
- Developing and deepening relationships with key client stakeholders, especially at board level.
- Identifying new challenges and leads within existing clients.
- Capturing feedback and market intelligence from the client.

- Building projects in the firm for long-term revenue (for example, licencing, annual or cascading projects, joint investment or innovation projects).

Account managers should be trained, incentivised and supported in building client relationships. They should also seek to develop their stakeholder relationships upwards, towards the board, so that there is less chance of a competitor usurping your firm. In addition, a partner should be touching base with the most senior business owners not only to develop new business, but also to understand future plans and check on client satisfaction. Changing trends in the client market should be anticipated by the consultancy through research-driven solid thought leadership and key clients should be invited to be on the firm's advisory board or participate in strategy reviews.

The amount and type of extra effort involved in delighting the client will differ between the start-up and the more established firm. A start-up is likely to sacrifice time to ensure the highest quality delivery in pursuit of repeat business and testimonials. An established firm is likely to have less of an issue with their pipeline and more of an eye on margins and finding more systematic ways of delivering value. This said, firms large and small should think about the items in Table 6.3 as ways of building stronger relationships with clients. Some take more effort than others, but it is wise to systematise many of these activities by making them regular diary entries.

Table 6.3 Strengthening client relationships

Low investment	Regular calls and visits. Forwarding/mailing relevant thought leadership to client contacts. Provision of personal mobile number. Social activities and entertainment. Introductions to firm partners and useful outsiders.
Medium Investment	Free training. Invite to firm offices (for example, for reverse seminars). Research involvement (for example, survey input and output). Off-project advice. Cases written up of successful projects.
High investment	Joint applications for prizes/awards. Co-authored publications. Intra-firm mentoring/work placement opportunities. Joint investment or partnerships, for example, innovation projects.

Strong account management should be supported with a well-managed CRM system. A strong system doesn't simply support the account manager, it also captures and manages their knowledge and reduces the risk of the firm developing a strong dependency on individuals. In addition to the digital capture and processing of client information and communications, CRM can be used to capture much of the client knowledge that normally resides in the heads of account managers.

CRM helps increase profits by improving the value of your interactions with potential and existing clients and spans marketing (designing campaigns and measuring impact), sales (capturing information, supporting and measuring the pipeline) and delivery (upselling in existing projects). Effective CRM results in lower cost of sales, higher rates, longer and more projects, lower client churn and greater loyalty. A well-used CRM system will tell the account manager:

- The history of the client (projects, etc.).
- Who the key contacts are and who knows them in the firm.
- The level of readiness or maturity of the firm.
- Any research on the firm.
- The thought leadership and cases that contacts have been sent.
- Useful details (for example, needs and personalities) of key individuals.

This should be used systematically to build stronger relationships and demonstrate your potential value to each client stakeholder. A great CRM system is also something buyers look very favourably upon.

Referrals

Referrals are the most common route for clients finding out about consultancies. They come with a huge benefit, because the consultancy's value is already framed by a trusted contact of the client. This makes it unlikely that there will be much competition. As you grow, therefore, it is worth establishing a consistent, systematic approach to getting the best referrals possible. This process should also tie in post-project feedback, testimonial gathering and case-writing, but should be primed by mentioning it early on.

Ideally, referral requests will be timed to catch the client in the best mood possible, which means asking at the right time (perhaps over a post-project celebration) and also steering the referral to target the right roles in the right companies. This conversation might also include getting a video-based testimonial which praises your value. First and foremost, you need to ask. Hinge University found that 80% of professional services buyers would provide a referral if asked[14]. If a key client or great case is reluctant, then it is often worth offering a swap for a quality referral (or testimonial) of your own.

However, it is important to bear in mind that 95% of non-client referrals are made by people who have not met you.[15] They are made by people who know that you have a good reputation for working in a specific space. Therefore the best things you can do in order to maximise your referrals are to improve the visibility of what you do and how well you do it, which we covered in the marketing chapter.

Pricing

Ten principles of pricing

Pricing is a craft and mastering it will allow you to generate higher profits. Before getting onto the best pricing models to maximise profits, several principles should be emphasised:

1. Your first focus should always be delivery of great client service. Whilst you must develop your own strategies to maximise profitability, your direction should be informed by conversations with your client about the best way to incentivise their and your teams to create the best outcomes. Does it suit them best to buy time, to have pricing certainty, to buy from a menu of deliverables or to have a true business partner?
2. The only sustainable pricing strategy is based on a *continual increase* in the value of your work and the client's perception of that. A knowledge system which improves your firm's expertise, impact and value as well as a marketing strategy that is entirely focused on your value will allow you to drive higher prices regardless of how they are calculated and avoid conversations about day rates. This will allow you to create higher margins, to hire and train better staff and create a virtuous cycle of value. You want to be forever better, not forever cheaper.
3. A great pricing strategy cannot make up for a poorly selected niche. Your niche provides the ceiling on your fees. A well-selected niche together with a powerful UVP and marketing message will do better for your profits than any pricing model. However, if we assume that you are reasonably happy with your niche, then a focus on intelligent pricing will not only improve your profits but also keep your clients and staff happier due to higher levels of predictability, fairness and performance.
4. Don't compete on price unless your overheads are cheaper because of your business model. This won't apply to most readers of this book for whom the price target should be towards the top of your competitors. We will examine discounting shortly.

5. Generally, consultancies overestimate the importance of cost to their buyers. Frederiksen et al. (2013: 60) found that more than 50% of sellers say price is among the key drivers in a buyer's decision, but only 28% of buyers actually rate price that highly. In another survey of over 3,000 client executives, only 6% ranked price the most important factor when buying consulting services – on average, it was the ninth most important attribute.[16] You may say, 'well I'm sure buyers say that, but....'; however, in my experience and certainly with those firms who grew successfully, value, innovation and impact were all rated as more important than price.[17]

6. Whilst different types of consultancies get their competitive advantages from different types of pricing, generally speaking the *time and materials* (T&M) approach to pricing is wrong for most consultancies. It fails to link revenue to what the client *will* pay or the quality of the work, most clients dislike it and it encourages consultancies and clients to participate in a race to the bottom on price.

7. Even in a well-chosen niche, there are likely to be consultancies offering similar services to yours, including some that you don't know, but more than likely that your client does not know. A client only has so much time to scan the market, and a strong consultancy will ensure that *in their area of expertise* clients should not need to look far. If you have been doing your job in creating and distributing thought leadership, useful connections, research and general educational meetings, it is likely that you will be one of the first ports of call for your client. Even if the client has found similar services elsewhere, your marketing, pricing and framing should differentiate your quality and add value.

8. It is often argued that *value-based pricing* is the ideal solution for the average consultancy or sole trader. However, what many authors fail to note is that value-based pricing is not always suitable, either because it is too hard to measure and the preferences of the client are for something else or because you simply can't generate the value that justifies this type of pricing. Value-based pricing *can* be useful, as we shall see, and the value conversation is definitely worth having. I've put a list of questions you can use to frame value in the client's mind at joeomahoney.com.

9. For most consultancies, mastering *project-based pricing* (a variant of fixed pricing) will be the best approach. It is a skill that is developed with practice, and will allow you to negotiate more effectively, attract more clients and achieve higher margins. Here, it is a good idea to offer different options for the project: gold, silver, bronze levels or specific options which can be removed in order to meet the client's budget.

10. Strong prices are pointless without skills to achieve margins from them. Three things are crucial here: training in pricing and negotiation (too many

partners discount excessively in order to win); a detailed understanding of what the project is *actually* costing the firm (so that pricing and negotiation does not hit the big margin contributors); and strong project management skills especially around utilisation and leverage (so costs on the project are minimised).

What should pricing be based upon?

What drives your pricing (i.e. how price points are arrived at) has nothing to do with how pricing is presented to clients. There are three bases for pricing your services: your costs, the client and the competition. Let's first take your costs. At its simplest, T&M pricing (sometimes called 'cost plus' or 'time and expenses' pricing) calculates the overhead cost of the firm and adds a percentage for target margins to create the target revenue for the firm. This is then divided by the target delivery days for each role so that 'roles × days × price' is equal to the target revenues. In any project, it is important to know the actual cost of overheads by consultant hour (or consultant day) so that your internal pricing can influence your price setting, take account of project costs and easily calculate project margins (predicted and actual). You should know your break-even on every project you bid for, whether it meets your margin targets, and the costs which might be minimised or eliminated should the client object.

Next, let's look at client-based pricing. I don't know a single consultancy that sells into the finance and public sector markets and does not charge them different rates for the same service. Whilst this might flag an ethical issue, in most cases it is because the finance client signals that cost is less of an issue for them and that the value of the output will be worth more. This was most obviously demonstrated in my first consulting gig in banking when the client took the *consulting* team out for a Michelin-starred meal (existing clients please take note!). For client-based pricing, the key is strong negotiation. In the absence of fixed formulae for determining prices, the partner must be able to back up their negotiations with strong supporting evidence, an emphasis on value and a line-by-line justification for deliverables or services.

Finally, competition-based pricing. Michael Porter shows us that there are three competitive strategies: cost, quality and niche. [18] The vast majority of small consultancies should not compete against each other[19] on cost, but on quality or niche which means that cost should be less important to your client. If you have done your annual competitor analysis, you should know their price points and should be pricing yourself towards the top of the pack, as first, this level of pricing is generally not a disqualifier, and second, it can be a signal of quality.

For the vast majority of founders reading this book, it is the client and the competition that should *drive* their pricing, as pricing on your internal costs leaves money on the table in most situations.

Moving away from time and materials

Now we better understand what drives price points: how should the client be charged? There are several pricing models, and below I have listed the four most common with their pros, cons and some advice in using them.

Time and materials pricing (Table 6.4) is, by a hair, the most popular form of pricing by consultancies, used by 48% of management consultancies, 60% of IT consultancies and 35% of advertising consultancies[20]. It is relatively straightforward, but does not maximise profits because fees are generally priced on internal metrics (usually costs + X%) rather than external ones such as the value of the delivery to the client. Strategically, such pricing also does incentivise consultancy efficiency (for example by automating processes), meaning that

Table 6.4 A summary of time and materials pricing

Description
Fee is based upon an agreed day or hourly rate for different 'grades'.
Bill for the time worked plus any material expenses.

Pros	Cons
Useful for unclear scoped projects	Doesn't maximise profit
	Clients don't like the open-ended risk
Useful to utilise unused billable capacity	Encourages consultants to take longer than needed
The consultant's favourite	Can't bill in advance
The simplest structure	More likely to lead to payment disputes
Provides clear understanding of costs	Often used with cap leading to poor quality
	Doesn't lead to more efficient operations for you!

Advice
If using T&M, ensure constant communication with client about current total: no surprises!
Experiment with other fee models to seek advantage vs. competition.
Reward lead partner on project margins, not revenue, to encourage efficiency.

there is a risk the firm may not keep up with competitors in their ability to price low or generate margins. This form of pricing is relatively common in new firms but, in my sample, became less common as firms grew.

Although time and materials is the most common way of pricing consulting projects, generally it produces sub-optimal revenue because:

1. Clients don't like it. They don't like the uncertainty of not knowing what the final cost will be. Indeed, research shows that clients would actually much prefer a higher fixed price than a variable lower price. There is even a psychological term for this called the 'Taxi Meter Effect'[21]: the anxiety associated with ever-increasing costs over which the client has little control.
2. T&M doesn't maximise your potential revenue as it does not consider the amount the client would pay based upon the value of solving the problem, the presence of competition and the relationship you have with the client.
3. T&M doesn't encourage you to be efficient or to innovate. If you are being paid a fixed cost or on the value delivered, there is a huge incentive for you to innovate to improve the value to the client or to do things quicker. Without this incentive you are likely to stay doing what you have been doing.
4. T&M means you can be easily compared with the competition and commodified. Procurement or the client director can easily say 'competitor X charges 80% of your day rate, can you match it?'

In terms of moving away from T&M pricing, if a client insists, a good tactic is to offer it but to make it so expensive so as to discourage the client; but if they insist, then you do very well out of it anyway (Table 6.5).

Table 6.5 A summary of value-based pricing

Description
Sets the price based upon the worth of the service to the client.
Fees are based on specific perceptions and demands of one client segment.

Pros	**Cons**
Potentially higher fees if you can convince the client of value	Competition means it is difficult to convince client (unless you are doing 'rocket science' work)
	Value to the client and budget are usually two separate entities, making it hard to sell the idea

Advice
When setting fees, think about the 'next best alternative' (after you) for your client and the value of your differentiation.

Everyone and their dog urges consultants and coaches to charge by the value they deliver, and there are a plethora of books and webinars on to how frame conversations to achieve this (charges are typically between 10% and 40% of measured value, depending on the project and client). However, the huge hairy horsefly in the ointment is that you can only do this if (i) the client will let you, (ii) it is relatively easy to create unambiguous and fair measures of value, (iii) the competition isn't perceived as better quality than you and (iv) the project lends itself to a value conversation. For this reason, value pricing only accounts for around 15% of all consulting contracts.

Table 6.6 A summary of risk-reward pricing

Description
Base fee + a risk/reward fee based on the outcomes achieved.

The risk/reward element can be fixed or variable.

Risk/reward is based on outcomes (for example, time/cost/scope/quality/ outcomes).

The risk element eats into your profit on the project.

Pros	Cons
Hi-profit potential for great firms	Risk of zero profit
	Can be long hours and stressful
Consultancy focused on	Requires strong monitoring and
Demonstrates 'skin in the game'	measurement
	Risks conflict with the client over disagreements
	Are you only giving your best work if you get a bonus?

Advice
Undertake only with previous clients where trust is a premium (no gaming!).

Agree and test meaningful metrics.

Easier for more commodified work.

Continuous close communication with client on progress towards goals is required.

Risk/reward pricing (Table 6.6) has similar success dependencies to value-based pricing, with a similar upside if all goes well. As with value-based pricing, it is important to define how results will be measured and how disagreements will be mediated, and is best conducted with clients with whom there is an existing trusting relationship.

For most consultancies, mastering *project-based* or *fixed pricing* will be superior to any other approach (Table 6.7). Project pricing, done properly, has several advantages:

- It is attractive to clients because it is easier to budget for and associated with less anxiety.
- It encourages the consultancy to increase their margins through innovation and greater efficiency.
- It encourages the consultancy to think of services as products which are comparable.
- It enables deliverables to be reduced to fit budgets during negotiations.
- It is easier to charge a larger proportion upfront than alternatives.

Table 6.7 A summary of project-based or fixed-fee pricing

Description

Fee is based on total days estimated effort and addition of markup or a fixed sum.

Client pays the same fee regardless of how much effort you expend.

Pros	Cons
Gives client certainty	Quality of work can diminish as hours run out
Easier to charge upfront fees	
Easier planning for client and consultant	High risk on client co-operation
Your efficiencies create greater profit	

Advice

Anticipate and manage change requests clearly and explicitly.

Requires strong time management, gateways and resource management.

Experience and training needed to price effectively.

As you become more efficient, keep the fee the same.

Yet, project (and value-based) pricing is a craft which improves with practice. It requires you to go back through previous projects to see what reasonable prices are and then be quite precise about the various deliverables and stages involved with the project. It also means that you need to have a clear understanding of how different workstreams or deliverables are costed so that when a client asks you to reduce prices, you can shift the value of the deliverables rather than simply discounting. This doesn't mean that the deliverable isn't done, but, for example, a more junior response is used, training is done at the client's site instead of off-site or delivery is virtual instead of face-to-face. Developing a clear view of these options is crucial to well-managed project pricing.

Finally, a note on retainers. A retainer is typically a regular payment by a client to a service provider or an individual to be on 'stand-by' or which includes a basic package of work with an opportunity to pay for more. That payment then enables the client to access the skills and experience of that worker or service provider on demand or for a set period of time. Ideally, if the client does not use the time, they pay the retainer nonetheless and 'lose' the time. Retainers are usually great for two reasons. First, they provide ongoing predictable revenue (which buyers love) but also because it is a chance for ongoing access to the client which is ideal for follow-on work. However, retainers also come with risks. Clients can ask for work at short notice when your pipeline is full or ask for work beyond the specifications of the contract. These can both be managed quite simply through a retainer agreement, which specifies details on notice, adjustments and reviews.

Matching what you do to pricing model

Returning to the different business models outlined at the start of this book (with the caveat that they are rarely 'pure'), the general approaches to pricing are summarised in Table 6.8. I would estimate that 80% of people reading this book will be in the Experience/Relationship model.

'Rocket science' work (typically one-off creative and high value projects) is highly priced not simply because it requires a great amount of (rare) skill, but also because the benefits to the client of getting it done right massively exceed the potential savings of shaving 10% off the price. Indeed, a high price here is, as the Stella advert used to say, 'Reassuringly Expensive'.

Another way of matching your price to what you are doing is to match the stage of the project (see Table 6.9). Here, high potential pricing options are aligned with the project stage. You obviously wouldn't be on retainer for typically one-off work, such as strategy creation or design work. Nor would you charge T&M for ongoing maintenance work (which would quickly become a zero-hours contract!). The question marks around 'design and procure' below really depend on the type of project. As we have seen, value- and risk-based pricing are well suited to projects where agreed, specific and transparent measurements of outcomes are available. These may or may not be available with design and procure work.

Table 6.8 Pricing strategy by business model

Business model	Ideal pricing	Justification	Advice
Rocket science/ Brains	High price	High level of niche expertise mitigates risk. Strong cost: outcomes ratio. Price relatively unimportant to client.	Emphasise risk of sub-optimal delivery. Emphasise your expertise. Ensure client knows it is rocket science.
Experience/ Relationship	Fixed cost/ value pricing	Value pricing can give higher margins if project is suitable. If not, client preference is fixed cost. Cost is important, but not the priority. Price towards top of 'class'.	Emphasise your experience and 'fit' with the team/firm. Negotiate cost on what the client gets, not absolute rates.
Procedure	Low cost	More is more commodified and open to competition. Yet, more standardisation creates opportunities to automate processes.	Emphasise low cost, but also seek testimonials and data which emphasises quality in key areas. Seek to raise switching costs for the client.

Table 6.9 Pricing alignment with project stage[22]

		Time and materials	Fixed fee	Value/risk	Retainer
Project type	Strategy creation	✓	✓	✗	✗
	Design and Procure	✓	✓	??	✗
	Implement and Transition	✓	✓	✓	✗
	Maintain and Improve	✗	✗	✗	✓

Discounting

Despite many 'gurus' telling consultancies never to negotiate, on average actual rates are only 85% of headline rates – especially for juniors, who have the biggest impact on margin[23], and 65% of consultancies admit they discount[24] (I'm assuming others do, but don't admit it). It is simply unrealistic to tell consultancies not to discount. Even if you're avoiding procurement, most clients will ask automatically. This still means that you should try your hardest not to discount. Low-balling usually backfires due to the 'Winner's Curse' (the winner has had to discount so much that a profit is unlikely) and it becomes all but impossible to later raise prices. Discounting is especially common in the US and UK but less so in the rest of the world. Whilst not being naïve enough to think that discounting should never happen, it is worth reminding ourselves of the negative implications of discounting:

- Considerable research shows that clients who receive discounted goods or services perceive them less favourably. For example, Suri et al. found that 'consumers' perceptions of quality and value for the product were higher when price information was presented in a fixed format versus a discount'.[25]
- Once discounting has been done, it is incredibly difficult to raise it to a higher level. Many years ago, I sold an annualised service to a client at a 40% discount (they were my first client for this service), and it took seven years to get it back to the usual price. Lesson learned.
- Price cuts have a disproportionate effect on your profits. A consultancy with a 25% profit margin that continuously discounts at 10% requires a 67% increase in sales to maintain the firm's profits. This can create a vicious circle of low profits → low investment → low quality delivery → price cuts → low profits.

If you are going to cut prices, it is crucial to do so in a way that retains the quality of your brand or earns you concessions that you value. I would advise that any discounts should always be temporary and are marked as such in the invoice.

Negotiation

Negotiation is one of the weakest skill set in many founders' arsenals, especially when compared to procurers, who have often undertaken years of training and whose existence often depends on their ability to trim costs. This is in addition to the tendency of (some) partners to discount in order not to lose a deal. Before long, such weaknesses can seriously eat into margins.

The extent to which you should negotiate should depend on two things. First, your context – are there competitors? Is this a brains or a procedure project? Are you the best in your field? Have you been referred to the client or is this a competitive tender? Second, whether you have been shortlisted. If you get the email telling you that you are in the top three, you are in a strong position and should push back on all but the most minimal discounting. A good tip is to ask what prompted them to select/shortlist you, so as to remind them of how good you really are.[26] Foremost in your mind should be that you are better than the competition (or thereabouts) and so you *should* be more expensive. There is no service in the world where the best is the cheapest. If you experience one of those awful negotiation intermediaries that large clients use to shave another few percentage points from a price at the end of a negotiation, push back strongly. It appears that these increasingly common firms have enough success to justify their existence, but I have never had any client lose a deal following my advice to ignore these entreaties.

Most often, negotiation takes place when there is a shortlist of consultancies. Even at this stage, however, it is highly unlikely that price will be a deciding factor, so do not feel the need to undercut others. You should have a clear idea of the value of the client to you and the minimum margins you can accept for the project. Remember that the price you agree on now could also inform any future negotiations on projects with the same client.

As detailed above, discounting in the first instance should take the form of reducing value – or more specifically, your costs. On a fixed price project, this will be line items, and from a value-based project, it will be the value delivered. If your proposal has included options or a tiered pricing structure, this should be much easier. If this is insufficient then you should have pre-prepared a set of 'swaps' – things that the client can give you in exchange for a small discount, such as:

- A minimum spend over a specific period.
- A position on the firm's advisory board.
- A video testimonial and a joint case-study.
- Introductions to three other CXOs in similar firms.
- Payment in advance or expedited payment.

Whatever tactics you use, it is imperative that your seniors have good external training in sales and negotiation. There are plenty of books out there[27] on

negotiation, but there is nothing like practicing with experts. From my own experience, two pieces of advice stand out. The first is to master the art of silence.
My early preference was always to fill awkward silences with offers: 'if that's too
much, we can always discuss' or 'I know that sounds expensive, but the impact
will be massive' – almost discounting before the client even asked. Not any
more! The second is to invoke policies: 'I'm afraid our policy is not to kick-off
until the initial payment is received' or 'we can't do that as it's our policy not
to discount on senior rates'.[28] For some reason, clients respect 'policies' more
than 'what I say'.

Procurement

When my Dad, who was a senior at what is now Deloitte, suggested pushing
back on prices paid for their lawyers, he was told that 'it really wouldn't do
to question the fees of another professional'. Things have changed somewhat
in the last 50 years! There will be few readers of this book that have not become frustrated with the inefficiencies and stipulations of many procurement
departments. Over the last ten years, I have been involved in two large-scale
projects to help public sector organisations buy professional services through
a consideration of value rather than price. Sadly, the practice is rare, although
there has been some progress. The one benefit of going through procurement is
that once you are on the preferred supplier list or framework agreement, then
you are ahead of most of the competition. Sometimes, for example, in defence
contracts, this can be a barrier to entry to others. However, achieving this
often means signing up to terms and conditions that are not in your favour.

If you have to go through procurement, then most of the advice in the pricing
section still holds. The difference is that you will often be unable to have the
conversation on pricing with someone who is clear about the value of the project. My advice with procurement is as follows:

- Meet the client (buyer) whenever you can and build that relationship.
  Where this is not allowed, talk to procurement where possible. Research
  the firm and get as much inside information about what procurement is
  looking for.
- Work with the client to get around procurement by breaking a project up
  so that it is underneath the radar (usually below the minimum spend for
  procurement visibility). I have known powerful directors simply ignore procurement until the work was completed. Where you already have ongoing
  work in the company, seek to frame the additional project as an extension.

- Whether you are successful or not, seek a debrief from procurement and record this so that you can do better next time.
- In all your communications, signal your value and quality.

Takeaways

- Most of your sales effort is done before you sell. Targeted thought leadership and strong marketing will boost your sales by establishing your position as a quality provider of client value.
- Sales is a skill, probably the most important one in a growing firm. It can and should be learned from experts.
- As an overarching strategy, business development needs to shift from the connections of the founders to a centrally managed capability of the whole firm, especially the senior team.
- Each step of the sales process should eventually become systematised and partially automated, from assessing and approaching leads through to gathering testimonials and referrals.
- A solid sales plan will have a logical progression from the marketing strategy through to identifying key metrics for success, detailing who is responsible and the associated budgets and the tactics by which the targets will be achieved.
- Snipers and shotguns are needed: snipers target a handful of firms with personalised outreach whilst shotguns use a generic message about a common challenge which can be automated.
- Sales skills and competencies should be built and incentivised throughout the organisation and staff trained using external experts. You should explore insight, value and challenger selling to maximise your success.
- A discounted sales pipeline should be used early, maintained and improved to give you more accurate forecasts of revenue.
- You should aim to price towards the top of your (realistic) competition.
- Pricing is best improved through continuous improvement of your delivered value.
- Pricing is a skill which is not developed through T&M approaches. Value and project-based pricing will improve your pricing skill most. They are also better suited for negotiations.
- If you must negotiate, use swaps.

Case study: Elixirr, the challenger consultancy

"I'm a fairly unsophisticated kind of guy"

It is difficult to say what type of consultancy Elixirr is, not only because it doesn't fit neatly into a box but because every time I engage with them, their business model has evolved. In many ways, Elixirr is run very successfully along the lines that McKinsey & Co. adhered to maybe 50 years ago, before it became more commodified and process heavy.[29] Elixirr focuses primarily on strategy work, does virtually no training and instead relies on close mentoring by partners (helped by the 1:9 leverage ratio). It never responds to Requests For Proposals (RFPs) and focuses solely on bespoke, innovative solutions.

Elixirr also explicitly avoids the forms of commodification and process which its founder-experienced in previous consultancies. When I asked Steve Newton, Elixirr's punchy, no-nonsense, South African founder, about the products he offers, he almost winces:

> this business is not complicated. You don't need commodities…We don't go and turn up with a cookie-cutter solution. As [consulting] firms scale, they increasingly become cookie cutters. We are bespoke. I try not to cookie cut anything.

Yet Elixirr is not simply another McKinsey & Co. and Steve is certainly not the coiffured, cultural aesthete one might expect at the top of 'The Firm': 'For a strategy consultant I'm a fairly unsophisticated kind of guy', he says. Indeed, despite what I presume are long hours at the desk, Steve has the outdoor ruggedness that would not have looked out of place in the Karoo a century ago. It is perhaps this untraditional pedigree where Steve's greatest strength lies. He has the ability to think differently and the guts to put those thoughts into action.

Let's take, for example, Steve's argument that innovation from within firms is vastly inferior to a detailed understanding of what is available outside the firm: 'the free market will always out-innovate you. The trick is not to innovate but to dovetail the innovation that is happening with an understanding the clients' needs and then embed that innovation'. This belief drives the company to spend a lot of time exploring Silicon Valley (where they now have an office) scanning for new solutions and businesses that will benefit their clients.

More recently the firm's strategy has been developed into what Steve calls a 'House of Brands'. Determined to avoid the commodification, bureaucracy and standardisation that he experienced when Accenture floated, Steve is keen to acquire innovative, ambitious consultancies, but to keep their brands and structures in place. This, he hopes, will maintain the energy and innovation of smaller companies, whilst providing them with the infrastructure, reward patterns and business development opportunities associated with larger ones. 'This means', he says, 'the founder doesn't see their company torn apart by a corporate buyer and gets to accelerate their client reach in a much bigger set of firms'. All this positions Elixirr as the smaller, nimbler alternative to McKinsey, Bain and Boston Consulting Group, well placed to make the most of the increasingly common frustration of clients with the lack of innovation from large consultancies.

Growth

Founded in 2009, Elixirr depended entirely on work from the personal network of Steve and his four co-founders until 2011. At this point, with revenues of around £3 million a year, the five took the decision to grow the business internationally with the explicit aim of Steve removing himself from revenue earning activity to focus entirely on growing the firm. In 2012, the firm doubled its revenue, and in 2013 increased it by 150%. Year 2017 saw the partners realise their equity through a debt deal, but remain in control of the firm. The same year, they won the 'Best New Consultancy' award from the MCA. In 2017, they were the fastest growing consultancy in the UK and have not slowed down. By the time of my first interview in May 2020 (three months into the COVID-19 outbreak), the firm was predicted to bring in £28 million at around 25% margin and had a full order book for their 100 or so full-time employees. These numbers have improved since then, as Elixirr's clients have increasingly relied on the consultancy for help responding to the post-COVID world.

Elixirr's strategic positioning at the very top of the consulting game means its branding must be spot on. Something is clearly working in this respect, as the firm attracts over 1,000 applications from Oxford and Cambridge every year. Steve doesn't hold much with formal training, but this does not appear to hamper delivery. One client reported: 'Elixirr's people care more about my firm than my own people'. The firm's brand extends to an Amazon Prime series where Steve interviews highly successful innovators whilst flying them in his plane. You can see why some graduates will take the risk to choose Elixirr over the more traditional firms.

Mindset and culture

Elixirr fits squarely into what David Maister called a 'Brains' type firm. Steve's focus on entrepreneurship and innovation is the key differentiator for Elixirr:

> I hire entrepreneurs. I encourage my people to start their own businesses and will support them to do so. This drives an ownership mentality. When I was at Accenture, I didn't feel like an owner, but that mindset is crucial… the great thing about these people is that they have this entrepreneurial edge when they go into our clients.

This sense of ownership has been central to the growth of the company as Steve continuously seeks to align the reward structures of the firm with its market objectives. Prior to floating, principals and outstanding performers in the firm were given the option to put up to 20% of their salary to invest on the performance of the firm. In 2018, this returned 2.2× on their investment. This encourages people in the firm 'to make an active difference in creating value'. Having the downside is important because Steve says, 'you are risking your own money'. The same is true with Elixirr investments in the spin-outs by their employees.

Another feature of the culture is the mentoring programme. Unlike many firms where mentoring is cascaded down the ranks, the partners in Elixirr mentor everyone. This, Steve argues, is important in attracting top talent:

> that's culturally important because our recruits from Oxford or Cambridge will meet the CEO in week one and be mentored by a partner, whereas their classmates who went to McKinsey won't even have met a senior manager yet.

The culture is, however, not without its critics. Reviews of the firm by some junior staff on GlassDoor.com bemoan the lack of a significant HR presence in the firm, and link this to favouritism, low levels of training, high turnover and poor people management. If true, this is perhaps unsurprising as Elixirr is not tailored for graduates who need hand-holding. Steve is very much of the view that 'work-life balance is a first world problem'. His advice for young consultants is: 'instead of walking into your boss's office and asking for a 10% raise, bring in another £100k of value and ask for 20% of it'. Steve's robustness also applies to his leadership style, where Steve is most definitely in charge: 'Consensus is no way to run a business. As the captain, you need to make the calls. Democratic decision-making leads to the lowest common denominator not the best decision'.

Business Development

Steve feels the primary reason for Elixirr's success is 'an unwavering focus on clients and revenue. It's not proposition. It's not skill. It's client relationships and making a difference in every engagement'. He gets frustrated with people who want to talk internally instead of to their clients. He says, 'I've hired a lot of senior people who want to sit in a room creating a proposition. I tell them to get out and talk to the client. Everyone sells'. Steve says:

> Stop seeing sales as a negative thing. Business in about connections, and the real success in business comes from connecting with people…. You can't just create stuff and think it's going to work for you. Delivery is sales and sales is delivery.

In terms of positioning and pricing, Elixirr is very much positioned at the top of the market. Steve explicitly sells on value rather than day rates because:

> As a client, I will pay premium service if I know I'm getting value. Clients don't quibble on price unless they don't believe it's bespoke or if they're dissatisfied. Most sophisticated buyers aren't transactional. If I can't sell on value they go buy from someone else and that's fine.

At the other end of the scale, Steve has no time for the RFP process:

> We do not do RFPs. We have never done RFPs. All procurement care about is unit price. The procurement profession is intellectually bankrupt. They assume everything is cookie-cutter, but the real strategic stuff is never cookie-cutter.

Flotation, not sale

Towards the end of our interview, when discussing funding for further growth, I was told by Steve that that there would be a 'very interesting announcement' in the next few weeks. I presumed it would be a sale, but fast-forward a few months and Elixirr was floated on the Alternative

Investment Market (AIM) – a subset of the FTSE. This is only 11 years after Elixirr was founded. On the question of why AIM rather than selling, he gave me four reasons:

First, Steve didn't want to exit:

> I didn't really start Elixirr with a view to selling. I love business ... I like competitive sports. It's my day to day sport. I enjoy trying to see how well I can do. I don't play basketball, but if I did, I would always count the number of hoops I scored right because why else would you play? So business is the same for me.

Second, it kept him in control of the company:

> Minority private equity looked, and I spent 18 months getting five offers but we fell out of bed each time their desire to control what partners got paid in both cash and equity. They weren't prepared to allow me as the CEO, set the pay for partners so I walked away.

Third, the AIM option provided Steve with the financial resources to exceed partner pay at McKinsey and other top strategy firms. Showing me his salary spreadsheet, he shows how he has aligned the partner pay and reward with the firm's performance, illustrating how on the basis of current growth existing partners can expect to receive packages in excess of competitor firms.

Fourth, the AIM option avoided the long-term value problem of debt. 'You can borrow, buy equity off the partners, and then distribute to others, but you are building perpetual debt. It doesn't monetise the firm at scale in the long term'.

By floating on AIM instead of a larger stock exchange, Steve sought to avoid the shift to bureaucracy and standardisation that many consultancies, including his old employer Accenture, appeared to experience when floating. But this is just the beginning as far as Steve is concerned:

> We're still early, but I can tell you the way my partners have reacted, the way that investors have reacted, the way the business is performing as a result, it's looking promising. I'm not interested in cashing out. I want to be a billion market cap firm. I want McKinsey to turn round in five years' time and go, where the fuck did they come from?

For people who have been waiting for the much-promised disruption of the consulting industry, such an outcome would be no bad thing.

Notes

1 Hinge (2018) *Marketing Planning for Professional Service Firms*. Virginia: Hinge.
2 Challenge (2020) *Prioritising High Performance*. Challenger Insight. Accessed here: https://s.tiled.co/05vpam5/prioritizing-high-performance-new.
3 O'Mahoney, J., & Sturdy, A. (2016) Power and the diffusion of management ideas: The case of McKinsey & Co. *Management Learning, 47*(3), 247–265.
4 Of course, contrary to popular belief, McKinsey partners still need to sell. The firm has a '2:4:8 system': every Director in the firm is required to be working on two assignments, be it in the process of proposing for four more and in communication with eight more prospective clients.
5 Jordan, J., & Kelly, R. (2015) *Companies with a Formal Sales Process Generate More Revenue*. Harvard Business Review, Jan 21.
6 Allen, J., Reichheld, F., Hamilton, B., & Markey, R. (2005) *Closing the Delivery Gap*. Bain & Company, Inc.
7 Schultz, M., & Doerr, J. E. (2014) *Insight Selling: Surprising Research on What Sales Winners Do Differently*. London: John Wiley.
8 Frederiksen, L. Harr, E., Montgomery, S., & Taylor, A. (2013) *Inside the Buyer's Brain*. Virginia: Hinge.
9 Kaski, T. A., Hautamaki, P., Pullins, E. B., & Kock, H. (2017) *Buyer Versus Salesperson Expectations for an Initial B2B Sales Meeting. Journal of Business & Industrial Marketing, 32*(1), 46–56.
10 Thaler, R., & Sunstein, C. (2009) *Nudge: Improving Decisions about Health, Wealth and Happiness*. London: Penguin.
11 Frederiksen, L., Harr, E., Montgomery, S., & Taylor, A. (2013) *Inside the Buyer's Brain*. Virginia: Hinge.
12 Almquist, E., Cleghorn, J., & Sherer, L. (2018) *The B2B Elements of Value: How to Measure—and Deliver—What Business Customers Want*. Harvard Business Review (March–April).
13 Frederiksen, L. Harr, E., Montgomery, S., & Taylor, A. (2013) *Inside the Buyer's Brain*. Virginia: Hinge .
14 Hinge Research Institute (2018) *High Growth Study: Consulting Firm Edition*. Virginia: Hinge.
15 Frederiksen, L. Harr, E., Montgomery, S., & Taylor, A. (2013) *Inside the Buyer's Brain*. Virginia: Hinge.
16 SGR (2018) Source Global Research. *The Global Consulting Market in 2018*. Source Global Research.
17 Concerning the last point, I have found that partners who are unsuccessful in bids often assume (in my view, incorrectly) that the reason was the price rather than the quality of their proposal – who wouldn't!? Indeed, where partners are rewarded by revenue deals rather than margins, they will often pre-emptively bid low or discount too readily when asked.
18 Porter, M. E. (1989) How competitive forces shape strategy. In Bowman, C., & Asch, D. C. eds. *Readings in Strategic Management. Macmillan International Higher Education*, pp. 133–143. London: Palgrave Macmillan.

19 Note that I say 'each other', not other consultancies. As Doolan (2015: 47) points out, 'clients group firms into bands and their expectations in terms of [their] services are conditioned by the group you are in'. He likens this to the star-rating of hotels. Hotels who provide customers with a luxury experience do not see 2* hotels as competition.

20 SPI (2015) *Professional Services Global Pricing Report*. Service Performance Insight: October.

21 Lambrecht, A., & Skiera, B. (2006) Paying too much and being happy about it: Existence, causes, and consequences of tariff-choice biases. *Journal of Marketing Research*, 43(2), 212–223.

22 This table is an amended version of one from my friend and colleague, Martin Williams.

23 SPI (2015) *Professional Services Global Pricing Report*. Service Performance Insight: October.

24 Maister, D. H. (2012) *Managing the Professional Service Firm*. Simon and Schuster.

25 Suri, R., Manchanda, R. V., & Kohli, C. S. (2000) Brand Evaluations: A Comparison of Fixed Price and Discounted Price Offers. *Journal of Product & Brand Management*, 9(3), 193–120.

26 Doolan, K. (2015) *Mastering Services Pricing*. London: Pearson.

27 My favourite is Malhotra, D., & Bazerman, M. (2007) *Negotiation Genius: How to Overcome Obstacles and Achieve Brilliant Results at the Bargaining Table and Beyond*. Bantam.

28 This is actually a trick I use with my two- and four-year-old boys. I have a list of rules (policies) on the wall which seems to have much more authority than simply saying, 'we can't put Felix in the oven because....'.

29 McKinsey & Co. and many of the other large strategy firms have shifted considerably in the last ten years from a 'strategy only', highly bespoke personalised service based around low leverage mentoring of their staff, to doing more implementation, offering standardised services and pursuing higher leverage ratios. The reasons for this are complex but are primarily driven by their increased scale and their diminished profit margins following the decline of strategy consulting, the 2008 recession and COVID-19.

7
Firm design for growth

What are investors and acquirers looking for?

"Simplicity" is what one serial-acquirer told me when I asked him what he looked for in terms of firm design and structure: "complex governance arrangements or inconsistent, or confused, decision-making roles can slow a company down, but also slow the actual sales process down. We haven't got all the time in the world to untangle and understand some of the messes companies get themselves into". Clear, consistent, logical and transparent governance, decision-making and reporting should be the major principles of firm design. Yet, most firms that have grown often do so without these benefits because they are so focused on sales and delivery that they pay insufficient attention to the structures and systems which evolve over time. As new partners join and new practices develop, business reporting and governance can get warped. In the same way that one thins out seedlings to accelerate growth and avoid disease, so to must the growing firm make explicit and strategic interventions to ensure the firm's growth is enabled rather than hindered by its design.

Yet whilst buyers like a simple, clear and logical governance framework that aligns with the maturity of the firm in question, there is no one 'best practice' for firm design. Different types of firms and those at different stages will require different strategies and therefore designs. However, there are still good practices that are common among specific types of firms and at various stages of development.

Governance

Changing governance for growth

Governance concerns the systems of decision-making, control and accountability by which the firm is directed and controlled. At its heart, it is generating

DOI: 10.4324/9781003149217-7

trust for partners, investors, employees, clients and society at large in the stew-ardship of their asset. At their most basic, the rules of governance will be doc-umented in the specifications for the legal entity (for example, a certificate of association, certificate of incorporation and associated national and legal laws), but these are often supplemented by governance documents created by the firm, such as Partnership Charters (discussed below). These will outline the rules for control and decision-making in the firm such as those for voting, quo-rum meetings, the frequency of board meetings and roles and responsibilities. I have put a checklist for good governance at joeomahoney.com.

However, much of what good governance is less formal and ingrained in the cul-ture and ethos of the firm. Some principles for good practice I've seen include[1]:

- Have the difficult conversations early: what if the partners fall out? What if one of us dies? What IP do we own individually? What happens when we sell? What if we disagree?
- Get authorisation for sensitive or risky decisions.
- Be clear on roles, responsibilities and authority.
- Be clear on what triggers salaries, dividends and bonuses (include share options).
- Have a clear, transparent risk management process which includes awk-ward issues!
- Consider how shares would be valued in the event of a forced exit of one shareholder.
- Build a 'share repurchase' agreement into key share agreements so that in the event of death or severe disability the firm can regain control.
- Hold frequent board meetings where risks, finances, progress on the plans, reports and sub-committees are discussed.
- Anticipate disputes in advance and create policies on how to deal with the questions above.

Good governance needs to anticipate and scale ahead of the growth of the firm as it reduces the risk potential of major changes, but the balance needs to be struck between the size of the firm and the levels of bureaucracy and speed in the firm.

As a firm grows, its governance becomes more complicated (Figure 7.1). Laura Empson rightly points out that new governance models solve problems at dif-ferent stages of growth, but also create problems when that firm grows too big for the existing model.[2] A start-up may mirror its governance on its legal own-ership with decisions made through discussion between owners. Ideally, con-trol is moderated through some form of partnership charter, but kept informal.

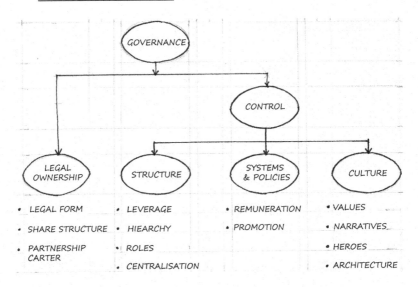

Figure 7.1 Determinants of governance forms.[3]

As the firm grows, this often gives way to some more formal, and some separation of, controls. These are established in role definitions and, as more people are taken on, some form of leveraged hierarchy. Later still, policies around remuneration and promotion have a significant impact on power relations in the firm, and we would also be foolish to disregard the role of culture in having an indirect impact on control, not least through the informal norms and values that influence decision-making.

Decision-making and roles

It is understandable perhaps that everyone who has a stake in the firm may want a say in how it is run, but some partners are clearly either not cut out to be a director or even a manager (some of the best salespeople I know in consulting make awful managers). The answer, once the firm grows, is to distinguish the ownership of the firm (partners) from the people who run the firm (directors). Typically, once the firm gets to about 30 people, the need for processes (and people to own those processes) becomes such that a formal board and specialist senior responsibilities need to be defined. I have personally evidenced this when facilitating board rooms where there were simply too many cooks and too few clearly defined roles. Several times, I have asked 'who is responsible for X?' and either several or no hands have been raised.

As the firm continues to grow to 20 people and beyond, an important form of governance is to have clear, logical and well-communicated roles and responsibilities. This prevents the CEO or Managing Partner being asked every 30 seconds about everything from cleaning the microwave to tax reporting. The progression in firms tends to be from one or two founders to a collegial committee, to a management board of directors. The key here is to distinguish the ownership of the firm (which could be everyone in the firm!) from the directing of the firm, which will be a few key individuals.

Typically, in a firm with three levels of leadership (managers, directors, partners, for example), each tier will have different decision-making authority. For example, higher levels will have more power to authorise projects with lower margins or to authorise spend on say training at different amounts. As the organisation grows and more decisions need to be made, it is important to have clear rules concerning how decision-making is pushed down the organisation to second- and then third-line management. The better more you can clarify responsibilities and guidance to push decision-making down to the lowest possible level, the more time seniors will have for business development and leadership activities.

Depending on the maturity of the firm, roles will have associated responsibilities, authority, budgets and reporting requirements. As the firm develops its second and even third layers of management, the risks of miscommunication or misbehaviour increase and so balancing the delegation of authority with the risk of the decision is an important one to get right. A good example of this is the type of client project that is authorised. If a project is too low margin, too high resource or simply not in the firm's value proposition, the reputational and financial risks are large and the authority for decision-making must be higher up in the organisation.

Partnership charters

It is generally easier to grow a business with one or more business partners, but the risks are much higher should things go wrong. To this end, it is useful to sketch out a charter or agreement which might help in the case of disagreements. The first port of call here is the company constitution – a legally binding document which will usually detail how decisions are made. This needs reviewing when a firm changes or a new partner comes on board.

Beyond the constitution, a charter is (usually) a voluntary agreement aimed at clarifying expectations and anticipating responses to different scenarios. Things that are often in the charter include answers to important questions such as what if…..:

- ….one of us dies?
- ….one of us stops contributing to the firm?

- ....we want to remove a partner who doesn't want to go?
- .... a partner wants to exit before the firm is making strong profits?
- ....we discover a conflict of interest or illegal activity?
- ....the firm trebles in size?
- ....we are declared bankrupt?
- ....we need arbitration due to conflict or deadlock?
- ....there is conflict or disagreement between partners?
- ....the current CEO leaves?

The last of these points is more common than many think, especially approaching sale. A partner who wants to (or is being forced to) exit can hold up the process if they feel they are not being paid sufficiently for their shares. This can be a disaster for the sale. When cash is being used for growth and invoicing takes place at the end of projects, consultancies can be particularly prone to cash flow tightness and reserves to buy a significant shareholder out might be hard to come by. Other questions might be more operational and set expectations for growth and exit:

- How much cash should be kept 'in the bank' for a buffer?
- What metrics should be used to trigger an expansion?
- What will the triggers for exit be?
- What will happen to the firm on exit?
- What guidance should be in place concerning debt?

There will likely always be conflicts as a firm grows, but a clear charter and well-communicated expectations will minimise the opportunities for such disagreements to undo all the great work that has occurred.

Laura Empson's research suggests that governance also changes as a firm grows in response to crises.[4] The first crisis usually occurs for founders who have recruited seniors who expect an increasing involvement in the firm's decision-making processes and share of the profits. The resolution to this crisis is often a 'collegial' form of governance, whereby founders surrender both control and equity to satisfy the demands of senior managers. The next common crisis is prompted by the growing complexity in the firm that strains the efficiency of collegial decision-making which results in disorganisation. The solution is found in governance through committees until the next phase of growth, which leads to a crisis of frustration and so on. In my own data, I found that successful founders generally avoided these crises because they had anticipated the changes that would happen. This knowledge sometimes came from previous experience but also from having a good mentor or having completed an MBA module which warned them about the risks of growth.

Outgrowing the informal organisation

Inflection points

It is growth in employees rather than revenue that shifts firm design. Small firms possess a great advantage in their ability to pivot quickly and rely on the energy and proximity of the founder to drive growth. A new contract or two can quite easily lead to the firm doubling in size for a few years and founders can be relied upon to burn the midnight oil to deliver outstanding work. Buyers rarely invest in teams of this size, but when they do, they are generally buying the team rather than the firm's assets or clients, and therefore arrange long earn-outs. One (anonymised) strategic buyer reflected on their acquisition of a technology consultancy with nine people:

> We had a gap in our tech and needed to scale quickly, and [the purchase] was a great way to get good talent for at least five years. The services they deliver are good, and we might be able to use them, but this was secondary to getting in a great team that will attract others.

Between 10 and 30 employees, things get a little trickier for firm design. At the smaller end of this scale, founders (or increasingly 'directors' now) can still deliver projects, energise the team and manage the firm. But every new employee adds to an exponential growth in complexity, and directors will find themselves increasingly pulled between delivery and leadership tasks. Towards the 30 mark, founders often experience a number of common challenges:

- Clients that push back against founders for not being involved in project delivery.
- An increasing number of errors due to poorly managed information.
- A reluctance or inability to delegate due to the inexperience of juniors or founder psychology.
- Too much founder time wasted dealing with queries from employees and clients.
- Things getting missed because roles are unclear and reporting have not been defined.
- A difficulty for seniors in getting visibility of what is happening in the firm.
- Overlaps or gaps in senior responsibilities.
- An increasing need for professional back-office functions, especially in finance and HR

From a buyer's perspective, purchases of firms with between 10 and 30 employees value a mix of people and tentative assets with more of a proven business model, but perhaps one that is still experimenting with services rather than scaling a core value proposition. When buyers or investors are attracted to these firms, it is often because the services fill a specific gap in the buyer's capabilities. Yet such firms are often a halfway house – lacking the mature systems to reassure buyers and having too few directors to spread the risk of one or more leaving. Buyers also report that sellers in this position are often surprised at the differences in valuations between their own expectations and those of the advisor and the buyer. A long earn-out linked to targets is often used to settle the differences.

Without developing the trappings of a mature organisation (roles, responsibilities, processes, measuring, automation), firms that go beyond 30 will usually collapse back in on themselves when they find out too late that the pipeline has not been kept full or when clients defect because delivery is not up to scratch. Indeed, some firms purposefully reduce headcount at this point, finding that they are comfortable at a specific size (say 20 employees), but that any more causes them to lose what one founder called the 'sweet spot'.

In many ways, the earlier you can plan for this inflection point, the better. In the words of Sarah, the co-founder of Virgo health:

> We didn't ever attempt to run the business on Excel. ...We've been on a time-sheet system and time-management system from the beginning....I have, in my previous life, got involved in some depth with all of the different systems that were then available on the market and so we made a decision fairly early on about which one we were going to go with, and, and we also made an investment fairly soon. I think the benefit of going into a business that you've done before, is that you know what you're going to need, and we didn't even try to do it without it.

There are other inflection points, such as when where the firm starts to move into divisions, multiple offices or even geographies, or where governance or ownership change significantly, but these are outside the scope of this book as they tend to concern very large firms or are relevant post-sale. From my experience and research, it appears that the inflection point of around 30 employees is the one that causes some founders most trouble.

To some extent, this challenge here is one of psychology as much as firm design (see Chapter 2 on mindset). Going above 30–40 people means that the founder(s) can no longer be intricately involved with each delivery (although many try!), and decisions need to be devolved to seniors without the founder looking over their shoulder. If this is a persistent problem, I suggest the founder takes a long look at themselves and asks if they are the right person to take the firm to the next stage. I once coached a CEO who couldn't let go – even after he had left the role. He eventually recruited someone else to lead the firm whilst he became Chairman.

Below, I detail three aspects of design that will help a founder anticipate and grow past the 30 mark: process and hierarchies, PSA and internal platforms. I then show how keeping innovation alive is possible during this phase of codification and formalisation. Finally, I explore how to open international offices – a challenge with which many founders struggle.

Processes and hierarchies

In Chapter 3, we saw that buyers of consulting firms don't simply place a value on revenue-generating assets, but also class *internal* systems and processes as valuable intellectual property. The reason for this is that systems create consistent and predictable results. They shift the focus of attention away from people (assets that can walk out the door) and towards the company processes (which are fixed in place). Internal processes, whether digital or physical, provide a number of benefits. They:

- extract and capture knowledge from unreliable assets (people!);
- enable a single point of improvement so iterative development can occur;
- support low-cost training and role design by showing people what should be done;
- provide documented operations against which culture and values can be checked;
- highlight important decision points which need executive agreement;
- allow easier automation and cost reduction of processes;
- enable lower-skilled/cheaper resources to do the work of seniors; and
- allow the founder(s) to remove themselves from the company with minimal impact.

Before getting onto these details of systems and processes, I should stress here that you should slowly start increasing the work on this area once you grow beyond ten people. Many ex-seniors from large companies who start up by themselves often lose valuable time trying to create systems similar to those they had in their previous firms. It is not only unnecessary for a very small firm, but also a major distraction. You will usually know when it is time to standardise a process because you will notice inconsistencies, variable quality and confusion in the work process. Ideally, things should be tackled before this stage! Additionally, processes should develop and become more detailed as you grow which means they must be attended to constantly – ideally making one partner responsible.

Good processes are codified steps which create valuable, relatively standardised outputs. These might include templates, methods, routines, checklists, scripts, policies or processes, which, in turn, may be written down or captured in software. They should, in the phrasing of Gerber, generate a 'franchise prototype: a business which is process dependent, not people dependent'.[5] Of course, the purpose is usually not franchising, but having systems which allow scaling with minimal deterioration in quality and significant increases in consistency.

Process design simply ensures that the important processes in the firm are captured, efficient, continually improved and deliver high quality outcomes. Typical processes for a growing Professional Service Firm (PSF) include:

- Marketing (for example, from marketing strategy to marketing effectiveness feedback).
- Sales (for example, from lead to post-sales support).
- Delivery.
- Recruiting and onboarding (for example, from role need to onboard).
- Training and development.
- Identifying training needs and training (for example, from appraisal to improvement).
- Thought leadership.
- Task and project management.
- Intellectual property (IP) (for example, from knowledge capture to storage and improvement).
- Back-office processes (for example, invoicing).
- Leadership (for example, how do we develop and exercise leadership effectively?).

There are different routes to designing and codifying a process, which include video/audio instructions, images, checklists, process diagrams and simple templates. The crucial driver of all system design must focus on generating the high-quality output that you wish to achieve, with a focus on the user, who will be learning and following the guidelines. Concerning the first point, you should take time to be clear about what high quality means to the *end user*. In most cases this will be your client, but it may well be an employee, contractor or external stakeholder. One of the most important lessons from many of the Business Processes Re-Engineering failures in the 1990s and 2000s is that users should be involved in the creation and improvement of all processes.

Of course, processes need to be improved and this means having someone senior responsible for managing them. In a previous life, I headed the department of process design consultants in a fast-growing firm that ran very effectively on a process/matrix structure. This combines two forms of reporting and control: the process and the business unit. Table 7.1 provides a simple process template, but there are now many software packages which provide more attractive visual and automated solutions (such as Professional Services Automation [PSA] software, discussed below).

Table 7.1 A process template

Process name:

Improvement responsibility:

Result:

Quality measurements:

Client:

Resources/information:

Step	Description	Accountable	Timing
1			
2			
3			
4			
5			
6			

Once a process has been codified, it needs constant attention to improve it. This should be the job of everyone that is involved with the process and should be the focus of regular reviews. These reviews should also consider the potential for new apps or software to transform or even eliminate the process.

In addition to processes, most firms above fifteen people will need to consider some form of hierarchy. Typically, this starts with the CEO (or Managing Partner) and directors. Directors should not necessarily be the partners – some partners will be great at delivery or sales, but useless at managing and directing. I am currently advising a firm where the founder and CEO recognises that he is not the best person to grow the firm and is demoting himself and promoting someone he believes is more capable. This is the Humble Mindset in action!

I recommend keeping the number of levels in the firm at a minimum until absolutely necessary. I've seen firms of nearly 1,000 employees run successfully with only four levels.

Professional Services Automation

If, like me a few years ago, you have not heard of PSA, you may find the data and processes of your firm are a combination of spreadsheets, apps, Office documents and a few storage platforms like Drive or Dropbox. If you're technologically minded, you may even have connected some of these with software such as Zapier or IFTTT to ensure that at least some of these processes are connected. Yet, you may also have noticed that some integrations are unreliable or impossible; that manual interventions take up an increasing amount of time as you grow; and that the cost of all these disparate apps seems to grow ever skywards.

A growing consultancy has an increasingly large and increasingly complex ecosystem of data, which must be managed effectively if it is going to be efficient, timely and maintain minimal operational costs. Importantly, most, if not all, of these data are interdependent: an upcoming project needs resourcing, planning, reporting and managing, and each of these might trigger other processes such as recruitment, investment or sales.

In the early stages of growth (say 1–5 employees), the major questions around profitability, pipeline, forecasts and project progress can often be answered from the heads of the founders. But soon after, an increasing number of disparate, stand-alone apps can create data silos which are neither connected with each other nor easily analysed and presented to the right people. A number of problems often arise:

- Partners do not have quick and accurate answers to major strategic questions.
- Directors spend too much time answering questions which should be answered automatically.
- Data is inconsistent and updated in different ways at different times.
- Data security is a threat as access by different people in different places is not controlled.
- The dependencies between pipeline, people and profit are not always clear and quantified.
- Clients have limited visibility of the project data that is important to them.

If this sounds familiar, you may be surprised to know that you can buy an integrated system, specifically designed for PSFs, to manage the processes and data for everything from tasks and communication through to resourcing and billing. Many consultants, who have left large companies, may be thinking 'yes, we had one of those, it was called ERP, and it cost us £60m to roll-out'. Fortunately, Software as a System (SaaS) means that the pricing of PSAs is cheap. Avaza, for example, offers a free PSA service for an individual, followed by adding on additional users for around £15 a month.

PSA software aims to provide better visibility, interconnectedness and efficiency of data and processes across organisations and their clients. In both my sample and in other research, PSA has been correlated with better outcomes. Those consultancies I interviewed who used PSA achieved lower operating costs and faster growth. Other research[6] found that the use of PSA was correlated with:

- Seventeen per cent higher revenue growth due to better staffing.
- Fifty per cent higher revenue per project.
- Thirty-one per cent increase in revenue from new clients

When interviewing owners of PSA firms, the mechanisms for achieving these became clear. Behram Khan, co-founder of Avaza, told me:

> an improvement of 5–10% in utilisation is not unusual due to better resource planning: there are fewer status meetings because the data is there for everyone to see, there is less use of email because all collaboration happens on the tasks in the system, and there is less time taken up trying to work out project finance.

The obvious advantage with PSAs, especially for the ex-consultant founder who may not be an expert in forecasting, data management or financial planning, is that it helps these administrative and management tasks to be more integrated, efficient and accurate. There are other advantages as well. One is that you know what data and processes you *should* be defining: PSA companies have developed and refined their systems on the basis of their experiences at thousands of PSFs. Their processes and KPIs therefore have a good claim to be 'best practice'. Whilst every PSF is different, the basic requirements of finding, resourcing, completing and billing for projects are pretty much the same, and a good PSA provider will provide advice on the best metrics to capture for a growing firm. Another benefit is that a PSA also provides advantages to stakeholders outside the firm. For example, clients can be given access to your PSA to see the progress of projects, the management of risks and even sign-off time sheets. Moreover, for buyers or private equity, PSA data provides clear, unambiguous and detailed metrics on the company, which firms without PSAs would spend months collecting.

I offer four final pieces of advice when it comes to the sourcing and use of PSAs. First, it is definitely worth speaking to PSA providers early on, so that you have an idea of the type and format of data that would be useful to capture. This is important because you may develop systems that are not best practice or begin to build 'electronic concrete' that makes it difficult for you to transition. Second, and relatedly, now that many PSAs are so cheap, there is little to be lost by using them early on before you migrate from one spreadsheet and your head to 30 incompatible apps. Third, all the PSA CEOs that I interviewed warned against the dangers of amending their systems too much:

> we often bump up against firms who want us to build around the data that they already capture. The problem with this is that what they capture is often inadequate to the task. Although every PSF is unique in terms of content, the process should be very similar. It's worth bearing in mind that we've developed our processes with hundreds of companies and what we have now is best practice.

Finally, PSAs are much more powerful when integrated with any other systems your company runs such as finance or customer relationship management (CRM) systems. The survey mentioned above found an uplift in all performance metrics if a PSA is integrated rather than stand-alone. Most PSAs will integrate with other software packages (generally SaaS) that are recommended for firms as they grow (see Table 7.2). These days, even solo consultants have financial software that automates invoicing, reconciliation and tax returns. An extension of this is Corporate Financial Management (CFM) or Enterprise Resource Planning (ERP) software. Depending on the capability of their PSA, a growing firm might also consider integrated software for CRM (see Chapter 6), Human Capital Management (for recruiting, hiring, development and performance management) and Business Intelligence (BI) software which helps firms collect and analyse data to support decision-making.

Table 7.2 Use of software by firms of different size (% of firms of that size)

	1–10	11–30	30+
Professional Service Automation	34%	69%	94%
Financial Management	78%	100%	100%
CRM	60%	85%	95%
Human Capital Management	15%	50%	70%
Business Intelligence	25%	35%	55%

Internal platforms

In the chapter on strategy, we looked at the potential of platforms as a service to put together third parties. There is however another way platforms are increasingly used, and that is to structure internal knowledge to help teams deliver to clients. Several high-growth, high-success firms (for example, PostShift) run their company structure on the basis of platforms which offer users a variety of related services to help teams. Here, I use 'platforms' quite generically to be an accessible cloud-based repository of different IP to support consulting work. They might include anything from business analytics software to proprietary benchmarking data to templates for reports.

In this sense, a platform might offer the firm an ability to mix teams and assets to create tailored services for clients whilst retaining some economies of scale through commodification. In other words, a partner or client engagement manager can create a proposition for a client based upon a mix of intellectual property and talent. This might also include third party platforms (for example, software for benchmarking, project management or coding) that offer additional value for the client (see Figure 7.2). The key here is that the value is in the mix that the engagement manager puts together, and it is the knowledge of these internal and third party assets and the skill to blend them into a costed proposition which sets this type of firm apart from the competition.

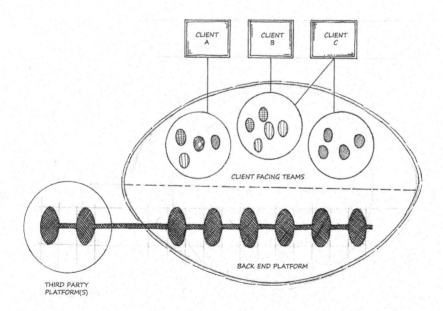

Figure 7.2 IP platforms for proposition development.

Innovation

Whilst process design will cover most of what firms need to do in terms of architecture, one challenge for a growing firm is to maintain innovation when processes systematise and direct the work of people within the firm. In a previous study I conducted on innovation in consulting firms, I found that small firms could generally out-innovate larger firms because their decision-making and implementation of change was so much faster. Of course, at an early stage this may be less relevant to you, but as your firm grows it is important to think about the congruence of your processes and strategy. Conway's Law states that an organisation's outputs mirror its communications systems. It is named after computer programmer Melvin Conway, who introduced the idea in 1967 before it was later proved by MIT.[7] The lesson they emphasised was that if you simply leave your processes and structure up to chance and evolution, you are likely to end up with services which are not optimised for your strategy.

In other chapters we look at how bureaucracy can be avoided through culture, reward and competence management, but here we can consider an interesting alternative for firms pushing beyond the 40-person point. There is an excellent book (sadly, only available in Dutch) by Eckart Wintzen,[8] who details how he turned BSO/Origin from one-man company to a multinational. Eckart hated traditional management structures and felt they inhibited efficiency, innovation and communication. Instead, he used 'cells' to maintain manageable, motivated and innovative teams. Eckart proposed that:

- A company is made of relatively autonomous 'cells' of a maximum 50 people.
- As soon as a cell hits 51, it is split into two independent cells.
- Each cell is led by one leader who is part of the senior management team.
- The leader is responsible for coaching, communicating company goals and culture maintenance.
- The centre of the company is responsible for the 'ground rules', branding and strategic direction.

Having spoken to consultants who have experienced this form of design, it seems to be a successful way of maintaining an 'entrepreneurial culture', even when a firm gets to a large size. Some firms decide to limit a cell to a certain size and have different levels of centralised power. Some, for example, *Nelen-Schuurmans*, have no staff divisions within the company, no IT department and no HR department – each cell is responsible for its own organisation. Others, such as *Corporate Integrity* combine the cell design with cross-company systems for HR, IT, finance and reporting, which provide cells with systems that allow them to manage themselves and report relevant management information. Elixirr's 'house of brands' strategy is not dissimilar.

Opening international offices

As firms grow, they are more likely to open new offices, and the trickiest of these will be those abroad. Around 28% of the firms in my sample opened additional offices in their home country, though this was very much dependent on the size of the country. Another 15% opened offices internationally. Here, I focus on the latter as it is more complicated than, and incorporates the lessons from, the former.

Opening international offices is relatively rare with smaller firms. It is generally more difficult to sell a firm that has a presence in a handful of countries, because a potential buyer will need to also be present in (or have a strategic need to expand into) those countries. Often, as with an over-diversified firm, a buyer will only be interested in one geography and will exclude whatever does not fit their needs. Another problem is that 'expansion to out-of-country markets represents a risk discontinuity'.[9] By this, it is meant that the risk to the firm is increased significantly as opening an overseas office is often akin to starting a new firm. Financial outlays, new staff, new relationships and new laws and rules for operating mean that you have a huge outlay of time, money and management effort. Finally, when the partners and the firm are unknown in a new country, they may struggle to attract quality clients and staff.

Despite these drawbacks, there are situations where some form of office expansion makes sense. This is generally when international presence is fundamental to the business model. One firm, for example, was working for a UK subsidiary of a large pharmaceutical company and was asked to do a presentation on their work at the Paris headquarters, which led to a much bigger and ongoing French project. While working in France, the consultancy realised that the market was less competitive than that in the UK and that they could capture more work with a French office and a partially French workforce.

Another reason to expand is when clients require specific local expertise in overseas territories. For example, one firm initially focused on clients who wanted to move operations from the US to Southeast Asia, then, once established, offered services for moving the other way. A final reason is to make use of relatively cheap but skilled 'back-office' staff. One of the firms I coached through a period of growth were based in Eastern Europe and doing very well, but realised the highest prices were to be gained in the UK. They opened a small office in the UK, whilst the bulk of the work was still done in their home country, the centre of profits slowly shifted. It was important to them to appear British, so the firm headquarters eventually shifted to London and their business development was done by a UK national.

A common sequence for firms that internationalise is:

1. Selling in the home market but delivering abroad.
2. Selling abroad and delivering abroad.
3. Opening an office abroad.

Put like this, it seems simple, but there are complex considerations that partners should consider. There are no definitive answers to these because each will depend on the type of firm and the partners' preferences. In loose order of importance:

National culture: The role of local culture and customs for consultants could fill another book. One of my corporate roles involved taking the business and digital architecture of a successful UK company and rolling it out internationally in Sweden, Hong Kong, Australia, Italy and Austria. This was a baptism by fire. I quickly learned how seemingly innocuous business processes can create significant and often embarrassing cultural misunderstandings. One of my favourite exercises with my MBAs is to ask them what they would do in different international consulting scenarios, and it is usually the cultural nuances that they get wrong, often with the risk of serious offence to clients.

Firm culture: A consistent culture is important, not only for client experience, but also to ensure the overseas office does not feel like a poor partner of the headquarters. It is important that whoever opens and initially runs the new office has been immersed in the culture of the firm and understands its values and priorities. It will also be useful to have frequent rotations and mixed teams, great reinforcing communications and whole company events (from virtual meetings and conferences to awards and celebrations). It is also important that communications are not just one way – that the voices of international offices are taken seriously. One of my old MBA students was part of an overseas office where almost the entire office ended up leaving together and starting up their own firm. The original gripe, which festered, was apparently about the timing of emails!

How to open: Typically, a partner or senior is sent over to manage the office search, recruitment and business development. Subsequently (though not always), the office will be staffed by and transitioned over to local nationals. However, this may not always be the best option. Sometimes a takeover of a small firm, whilst more complex, may allow the larger company a running start.

A senior foreign national may be employed to spend a year at the headquarters to understand the firm's culture before returning to start the new office (the danger here is that they don't want to return!).

Control: Whilst above I emphasised the importance of a consistent culture, there needs to be some flexibility in the process and procedures and rules to fit with local client expectations, and this flexibility needs to be communicated through the hierarchy. Whilst reporting on Key Performance Indicators (KPIs) generally go up the hierarchy, international offices are often given their own profit and loss accounts, which encourages national employees to feel more in control of their firm and their bonuses but can also encourage 'client hoarding'.

Performance reporting

Reporting cascades

A successful firm has a steady rhythm of reporting by which data, ideas, instructions and risks are passed up and down the hierarchy. Initially, this won't be needed, but once the firm grows, it is crucial that key metrics are gathered, discussed and acted upon quickly. The extent to which this is done will vary on the size and culture of the firm, but a typical cascade in a 30-person firm might include some of Table 7.3.

Key performance indicators

Forms of reporting in consultancies are varied and get more complex the larger the firm gets. It appears to me that 'grey hair' experience-based firms tend to measure least and process and implementation firms measure most, with 'brains' firms being somewhere in the middle. Table 7.4 provides a generalisation of the types of KPIs that growing firms use, with the later KPIs being used less commonly and generally only in larger firms.

Certainly, in the start-up period, many of these metrics are pointless, but it is good practice to be clear what metrics are important to *your* firm. I am not a fan of the statement that 'it doesn't exist unless you measure it', but what is measured definitely has a strong impact on the direction of the firm, and poor measures can drive dysfunctional behaviours. Metrics get complicated the more you have as different ways to combine them increase exponentially. As complexity increases, so too do the risks that you are measuring the wrong stuff (or more commonly missing things that should be measured) and that you create incentives to 'game' the metrics.

Table 7.3 An example of reporting and activities by time cycle

Weekly	Sales reporting Pipeline forecasts Work planning (including a utilisation review)
Monthly	Financial performance and forecasting (including cash flow) Budget forecasts vs. actual
Quarterly	P&L revisions and re-forecasting Plan review: revenue, clients, recruitment Investment review Marketing reports
Annual	Strategy review Market analysis and value proposition Business targets review and plan Marketing strategy and plan Competitor analysis IP review Service and pricing review Governance review (including roles and responsibilities)

Two fundamental metrics are worth highlighting. First, profit per partner is generally used once firms are past the 30-employee stage but is important to understand because of the way it is made up. As David Maister pointed out long ago, profit per partner is a key metric for PSFs. I have great fun (well, relatively) with my MBAs asking them to work out how margin, leverage and productivity are calculated, and then why this can be combined to create the profit per partner figure. The three ratios are:

$$\text{Margin} = \frac{\text{Profits}}{\text{Fees}} \quad \text{Productivity} = \frac{\text{Fees}}{\text{No. staff}} \quad \text{Leverage} = \frac{\text{No. Staff}}{\text{No. Partners}}$$

The mathematically minded will know that if fractions are multiplied, we can cancel out the bottom of one fraction with the identical top of another fraction. If you do this with the ratios above, you can cancel out 'No. Staff' and 'Fees', leaving 'Profits' divided by 'No. partners'. This leaves us with the following equation:

$$\text{Profit Per Partner} = \text{Margin} \times \text{Productivity} \times \text{Leverge}$$

Unsurprisingly, this leaves us with the statement that a firm with high margins, productivity and leverage ratios will generate lots of profit for partners. However, we should not leap to the assumption that all these measures should simply be increased. Low leverage firms tend to have higher margins and more productive staff, but also higher leverage ratios. The key is to increase margin, productivity and leverage without damaging the long-term positioning of the firm.

Table 7.4 Frequency of KPIs in different sized consultancies

	KPI used (in order of frequency and firm size)
Finance	Revenue and revenue growth; Margins (total and per client); Profit per partner; Cash flow; Average day rate; Average revenue per consultant; Project contribution margin (remember to include bid costs!); Revenue per project; Margin growth; Revenue and margin by business unit (service/market); SGA/revenue.
Marketing and sales	Pipeline forecasts; Pipeline ratios (for example, bids:wins); Leads per consultant; Sales per consultant; Days sales outstanding; Sales cycle (days from lead to contract); Deal pipeline relative to bookings forecast; Average discount; Sales effectiveness; Marketing effectiveness.
Clients/Projects	Client satisfaction; Client lifetime value; Projects delivered on time; Margin exception reporting; Average project size; Client contribution margin; Client referrals.
People	Employee happiness; Utilisation; Project cost over-run; Employee turnover; Leverage ratio; Billed (fee-earning) vs. non-billed time (back office); Cultural alignment; Diversity measures; Onboarding speed.

The second useful metric is Project Profit Margin (PPM). This can help incentivise partners to sell *profitable* projects rather than *large* projects, and also help avoid them discounting. PPM is:

$$\left(\frac{\text{Actual Profit Margin } (£)}{\text{Actual Sales}} \right) \times 100 = \text{Actual PPM as a \%}$$

The best way to maximise project margins is to make the lead partner responsible for achieving the targets and link this to their compensation.

Fortunately, most PSAs now capture much of this information and present it well, but perhaps capture too many metrics for a growing firm. I believe it is much better to have a handful of crucial measures which are the barometer of a firm. Too many metrics can just have consultants spending too much time capturing and worrying about things that don't matter. If EBITDA is solid and growing and the pipeline is full of good clients, you're not going far wrong.

Takeaways

- Systems and structures of governance should change as the firm matures. Keeping a keen eye on whether your ownership, decision-making, structure and controls are best suited to your stage will help the firm perform better.
- Have a partnership agreement and attend to the role of minority shareholders in potentially holding up a sale.
- Anticipate the firm hitting the 30-employee mark where founders cannot be involved in every decision and all information cannot be tracked on a few spreadsheets. Use PSA early and attend to defining roles and responsibilities before it is necessary. I use a PSA in my solo consulting practice!
- A growing firm will (probably) eventually lose some of its entrepreneurial, family feel. This is necessary for scaling and should be prepared for both psychologically and operationally.
- Give significant thought to how you create, measure and reward your teams. Experiment to see what works best in terms of results and motivation.
- Create, capture, analyse and regularly use clean, accurate data to aid your decision-making.
- Systematise your operations, organization and roles and improve them constantly.

Case study: 1904labs & Avaza

A US-based consultancy, 1904labs, is typical of many fast-growth, entrepreneurial consultancies that help bridge the gap between digital solutions and the humans that use them. The consultancy helps firms build and implement software that has a laser-like focus on the user experience. Their 'Human Centred Designers' (HCDs) take a creative approach to software and data solutions. Whilst their outcomes vary considerably, they have developed an underpinning proprietary method for creating innovative, user-focused solutions called 'HCDAgile'.

Founded in 2016, 1904Labs grew to over 80 employees in just five years. Despite their growth, they pride themselves on a start-up culture which purposefully recruits and encourages entrepreneurial mindsets – something which accounts for their great reviews on recruitment sites such as GlassDoor.

Sarina Handa, the Director of Client Delivery at 1904labs, joined in 2017 when the company had around 37 employees. This is a common point for many firms where they find that disparate apps, spreadsheets and data-bases begin to creak as operational demands test the interaction between different systems. Sarina says:

> Up until thirty-odd employees it was possible to keep things in our heads – you kind of know where everyone is, we knew how clients want to in-voice and our accounts department could use spreadsheets to keep track of invoices.

Sarina and the CFO were tasked with finding a software solution, or solutions, to address the challenges that the firm was facing in terms of consistent, transparent and joined-up process and data. Fortunately, her background in Agile and human-centred software design meant that she was well placed to find a solution:

> We started with our requirements and then figured out the minimum viable product - the smallest thing we need right now. We did a LOT of research, reading reviews, considering features, and then going through demos of the top four. We then narrowed it down to two and trialled both of them.

Eventually the duo settled on Avaza, a relative newcomer to the PSA game, but one that had several things going in its favour:

> They were very easy to work with and very responsive. Many PSAs were too complex, and we didn't need all the extra features. It was easy to learn, and Avaza were keen to help us and learn from us as much as we did from them… So, we chose them for their flexibility, their ease of use and their features. It didn't take a lot of training to understand it. Cost was a factor as well.

In terms of implementation, 1904labs started off small, trialling the in-voicing with one company and keeping the old system running alongside for a month. 'Then we slowly increased to resource management, and expense management in different phases. This piecemeal approach allowed us to trial each feature'.

In terms of the business benefits:

> The main one is data at your finger-tips. Whoever needs to see the data can see it in a transparent, reliable and consistent report. It also helps you run the business more smoothly – we now use Avaza to run financial projections – to run different scenarios based upon our pipeline. It saves time, not just in terms of administration, but also going back to old spreadsheets and working out what the calculations were that got you there. I don't see an end in sight for when we leave Azaza – they have been growing with us.

Sarina's advice to new consultancies thinking of using a PSA is to be very clear on what you need:

> What makes you successful? Find a PSA provider where you are more than a number, a firm that will understand your needs. One thing you also need to be aware of is that just because the data is there, doesn't mean that you need to measure it. You need to make sure that it doesn't become a numbers game so that you turn up green on every report. We use the numbers to inform discussions.

To get a better understanding of the opportunities and pitfalls of their experience, I interviewed Avaza's co-founder Behram Kahn. Behram started Avaza with his co-founder Tim Kremer because of their own frustrations with software in other companies. 'We wanted to build something that was easy to use. Many PSA products are overwhelming and too complex. We stay close to our customers and give them great 24 hour report'.

Behram mentions that it is easy to fall into what he calls the 'high quality spreadsheet trap': 'you need a new process, so you start a new spreadsheet. You want to discuss that process so you start a new email thread. You want to capture something, so you start a new work document'. Fortunately for him, the consulting clients he deals with usually understand the benefits of having connected processes and clean data, and so major changes to the PSA processes are rarely needed:

> We often need to come to a consensus as to what a process should look like. We have the flexibility in the product to make custom changes, but you need to be careful that you are not creating a dog's breakfast: something that is hard to use and makes usability compromises.

Behram also confirms something which many other founders and all other PSA interviewees mention: 'adopting a PSA should be part of the initial business set up. You won't need all the features, but it will be useful in terms of managing tasks, client collaboration, time recording and invoicing. As the company grows, onboarding new employees and customers is going to be much easier if you have well established processes'.

Notes

1 Two good books if you'd like more detailed advice are: Bierce, W. (2020) *Smarter Business Exits*. Leaders Press: New York, (written for the US, but 95% applicable to EU & UK); and Alexander, G. (2020) *The Boutique*. AMG: New York.
2 Empson, L. (2012). Beyond dichotomies: A multi-stage model of governance in professional service firms. In: Reihlen, M., & Werr, A. eds. *Handbook of Research on Entrepreneurship in Professional Services*. Cheltenham: Edward Elgar Publishing, pp. 274–294.
3 This diagram is a development of that on p. 128 of Harlacher, D., & Reihlen, M. (2014) Governance of professional service firms: A configurational approach. *Business Research*, 7(1), 125–160.
4 Empson, L. (2012). Beyond dichotomies: A multi-stage model of governance in professional service firms. In: Reihlen, M., & Werr, A. eds. *Handbook of Research on Entrepreneurship in Professional Services*. Cheltenham: Edward Elgar Publishing, pp. 274–294.
5 Gerber, M. (2001) *The eMyth Revisited*. Harper Business: New York, p. 42.
6 SPI (2019) *PSA Buyer's Guide. Service Performance Report*. www.spiresearch.com
7 MacCormack, A., Baldwin, C., & Rusnak, J. (2012) Exploring the Duality between Product and Organizational Architectures: A Test of the 'Mirroring' Hypothesis. *Research Policy*, 41(8) (October), 1309–1324.
8 Wintzen, E. (2011) *Eckart's Notes*. Lemniscaat: Amsterdam.
9 Carman, J. M., & Langeard, E. (1980) Growth strategies for service firms. *Strategic Management Journal*, 1(1), 7–22. p. 7.

8
Managing talent for growth

What are investors and acquirers looking for?

Recruiting and developing strong employees (and associates) not only drives high levels of performance[1] but also sends signals to clients and buyers about the quality of the firm. Done well, it creates a virtuous circle between price, reputation, attraction of talent and performance.[2] When considering a purchase, buyers tend to focus on four qualitative aspects of talent in the firm (leadership is covered in Chapter 2).

The first is the performance of people, which in part reflects the quality of people who are attracted to and stay in the firm, but also the systems through which they are managed, developed, motivated and utilised. The second is risk management during the process of acquisition. Buyers expect the equity in the firm to be shared among key individuals to incentivise their remaining in the firm during the earn-out period. Typically, a minimum of 25% equity is expected to be shared out. Buyers are also acutely aware that people will often leave if they do not feel valued and safe during the sale. This is not just a lesson in communicating well prior to and during the sale, but also that the pay and equity structure is fair and seen to be fair. Third is that there is some congruence between the culture of the acquirer and seller. This can be difficult to articulate (though see Chapter 4 for branding advice) but can be brought to the fore through several conversations as well as by giving buyers or investors face-to-face exposure to employees during the sale process. Fourth is the quality of the senior management team: a high-performing team with a track record of success.

All this said, I am inclined to say that buyers generally see HR management (as opposed to strategy) as a second-line concern. That is, quality talent processes will enable better financial performance via strong delivery, sales, innovation and so on. The reason I say this is because once a firm has been acquired by a strategic or trade buyer, the people management processes are usually (though

DOI: 10.4324/9781003149217-8

not always) supplanted by those of the buyer. This is not to say that your focus should be on financial performance rather than the people because, as Maister pointed out long ago, you can't control financial performance, only its drivers.

People strategy

Taking people seriously

A firm's strategy should, of course, drive HR decisions as much as it does anything else, and when it comes to people, the competences, skills and experience needed will vary considerably on the type of firm. To this end, Figure 8.1 summarises the talent needs for different types of consultancies. It is however a simplification because the challenges for these types of firms differ. Those seeking MBB[3]-type recruits need prestigious partners and high levels of pay which would force a chicken-egg situation if those partners were not typically from MBB themselves. Those recruiting graduates often quickly realise that graduates don't stay long unless there is a strong culture, a defined career path and clear development opportunities.

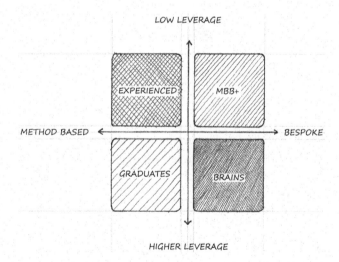

Figure 8.1 Recruitment focus for different types of consultancy strategies.[4]

Yet, in addition all consultancies also have a common need for people that are motivated, have a strong client focus and develop skills in business development. Identifying the core set of skills, values and competences that *your* firm needs to recruit, reward and develop is the first step in building a talent strategy that works.

Roles and hats

Ambitious consultancies are often started by consultants who have left much larger firms. They've usually had a lot of experience at consulting, but many have not had much training in HR. Whilst there may not be time or money to train or recruit for these functions early on, it is crucial that the firm recognises that these are gaps which need to be filled through training, recruitment or outsourcing.

In his great book *The e-Myth*,[5] Michael Gerber outlines three roles that a growing business needs:

- The technician, who loves and is good at delivery.
- The entrepreneur, who drives and leads towards their vision for the future.
- The manager, who measures, creates order and co-ordinates.

Gerber's great insight was not only that all three roles are needed for successful growth, but also that there are fundamental tensions between them (see Figure 8.2). Typically, the technician in charge of growing the business will not develop the systems needed for growth and will focus on great delivery. This means they get run ragged and quality begins to drop. If they are aware of their weaknesses, they bring in a manager type who will be responsible for creating the systems and processes which will allow the company to perform consistently. Yet, neither the technician nor the manager drive growth; in fact, they are both a little terrified of it. For growth to occur, the entrepreneur role is needed to create the business vision and drive change towards it. The conflicts between these roles over time are well described by Gerber and the book is well worth a read. But the fundamental points here are not only that all three roles are needed, but that if growth is left up to a technician (or even a technician-entrepreneur), then the bedrock of the firm will be weak and growth will falter when it gets too big.

Whilst Gerber is completely right concerning key roles, I would also suggest that sales and finance are key capabilities that should be added to the mix. This certainly doesn't mean that partners should not be responsible for sales (far from it), but that the *competence* of sales, marketing and finance (and to a lesser extent talent management) is something that very often entrepreneurs, managers and technicians do not possess and thus needs to be bought in.

The point here is not that you need different people to do these things – although eventually you probably will – but that you should know what you have and what you don't and seek to find what you don't. As above, in the

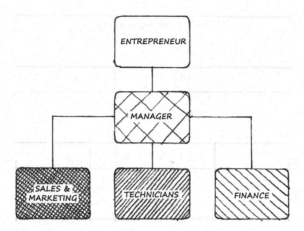

Figure 8.2 Capabilities for the developing firm.

early stages, this does not need to be full-time employees, but might be part-time roles or outsourced functions. As the firm grows and the requirement becomes greater, it makes more sense to bring the capabilities in-house, perhaps with the exception of HR. Certainly, the investment in an in-house finance director (fractional or otherwise) is one of the best investments a growing firm can make, although this usually only becomes affordable when revenue grows above £2 million.

Culture and values

Culture is so important to the growth of most firms that it has a dedicated section in Chapter 3 on strategy. I develop that section here because culture is central to the management of talent. As Louis Gerstner, the former CEO of IBM, puts it, 'culture isn't just one aspect of the game – it is the game. In the end, an organization is nothing more than the collective capacity of its people to create value'. In my interviews, successful firms almost all mentioned their culture or values as a fundamental pillar of their growth. Creating a great culture has huge advantages. It can lower turnover and attract quality new candidates, make the firm more attractive to buyers and reduce the overall need for management and supervision: it guides the actions of employees instead of relying on a host of rules and regulations.

Although I have found little correlation between growing and selling a consultancy and the job satisfaction of the employees within that consultancy,[6] unsurprisingly, those with happier employees had much lower turnover, which is especially important for small firms struggling to attract quality talent.

Generally speaking, it is necessary to treat employees who are highly skilled in a rare area very well indeed, especially if their deliverables are ambiguous and thus dependent upon their goodwill or work 'beyond contract'. This is less about pay, which is generally a hygiene factor rather than a motivator, and more about the way they are enthused towards goals by a passionate leader and leadership team.

A great culture does not happen spontaneously. It is something that has to be fostered and also articulated. In effect, it is a (relatively) Unique Value Proposition (UVP) but for employees instead of clients. It is managed by both hard and soft mechanisms, which include:

- A clear, communicated vision about which the senior team is passionate.
- Clearly articulated and communicated non-negotiable values.
- Consistency between UVP, strategy, branding and marketing.
- Consistency between articulated values and actual practice (rhetoric vs. reality!).
- A clear link between cultural priorities and recruitment, training, reward and promotion.
- Clear symbols, rituals and stories representing and reinforcing your culture.
- Strong emphasis on company and team camaraderie and ethos.
- Leaders who consistently exemplify the desired cultural behaviours.
- Some form of democratic participation of employees in forming and re-forming cultural priorities.

By developing a specific culture, you attract some but also repel others. However, being vanilla is not an option. Vanilla people go to vanilla brands like Deloitte or Accenture, so there is no point competing in that space. You are better off nailing your colours to your mast and attracting people who think like you.

The challenge, however, is how to maintain a strong culture when the firm grows beyond 30–40 employees. The key to this, in my experience, is middle management. All the points above should be maintained, but in addition, middle management need to be incentivised and encouraged to be champions for culture if it is going to permeate a larger organisation.

Of course, there is a risk to a strong culture, which is that it can promote conformity and a bias against change and innovation. I feel this is what happened to McKinsey & Co. in the 2000s, when an incredibly strong traditional culture no longer matched the shifting values of clients and wider public. The series of ethical scandals and how they were handled, to me, showed that McKinsey & Co. did not only have a problem with ethical practice, but were incapable of seeing how bad it was. The cultural and economic dangers of 'groupthink'[7] emphasise the importance of a culture that is both strong, but also reflective and open to change.

Attracting and keeping talent

Recruitment advice for small consultancies

If you have left a large firm, then a steady supply of motivated and skilled talent is often taken for granted. Yet, smaller consultancies rarely have the brand to attract talent and, early on, generally rely on recruiting people they know, sometimes poaching talent from their old firms. However, as firms grow, the connections of the founders are often insufficient to recruit the 10–20 talented people needed each year. This often means that the firm needs to find creative ways to find talent that hasn't been swept up by the large firms. This might include taking similar actions with talent as you do with business development:

- Incentivising new employees to draw on their own networks.
- Using a strong brand and culture to attract non-vanilla talent.
- Researching where the type of talent you are looking for might gather.
- Winning awards which highlight your profile.
- Finding people with the right attitude and potential and training them up in the skills.

Regarding the last point, Tom Hewson at Red Compass[8] tells a great story of watching a cleaner at his offices and admiring the way she threw herself into every task, became the unofficial leader of the other cleaners and interacted brilliantly with everyone she came across. She now works as a consultant for Red Compass.

Often with new firms, in a drive to avoid employing people, the emergence of an associate-heavy firm is often driven by fear rather than strategy. However, as I detail below, using associates for more than 20% of staff is rarely economically efficient (although I do add some caveats below). If you want to continue growing, bringing on employees makes strategic, financial and cultural sense. Employees tend to be cheaper per day, are more likely to conform to your methods and culture, are always available and the value of their work experience and training is accrued internally. Fundamentally, employees enable higher margins, providing your pipeline is relatively full. Even when it is not, employees can be assigned to important internal business tasks: service development, marketing and sales, thought leadership and codifying processes.

Yet, bringing on employees can have its risks. Employees are harder to remove, have a considerable administrative and management overhead and the sense of responsibility can weigh heavily on the shoulders of some founders. The solution involves balance: leaving some flex in the system for when a recession bites and to recruit only when the pipeline history is good and projections are looking consistently positive (six months to a year, depending on whether it's full or over-flowing). The best advice I have heard in this area was from Raazi Imam of Caiman Consulting, who told me, 'Hire slow, fire fast'. I wish I had that advice 20 years ago, as it would have saved me some pain with consultants who was technically brilliant but damaging others in the team and weakening client relationships.

An administrative assistant is the first hire of many growing consultancies. This frees you from relatively simple tasks and allows more time to focus on expanding the business. However, many consultancies simply take on an assistant and leave them to it, rather than seeking to develop their skills and provide strong guidance in the form of direction. A well-supported and well-developed assistant can be incredibly useful in codifying processes, delivering digital marketing, and managing a CRM system as well as all the usual tasks.

Beyond this, the first consultant hires are crucial in cementing the culture of the firm. Several founders told me that it is important to 'recruit on values first', as taking on a person with inconsistent values can 'poison the well'. It is important therefore to have a solid recruitment process. I suggest having (i) a competence interview focused on experience and skills, (ii) a culture/fit interview and (iii) a practical interview, which could involve an assessment exercise such as a presentation. In the assessment exercise(s), get the applicant to work on a task that you have worked on and push them, argue with them and ask them to justify their approach. Throughout, you should try to score the applicant on the attitudes, skills, fit and competences that are important to *your* firm. Tom Hewson looks for the three Cs, 'competence, character and commitment'. For more senior recruits, a detailed understanding of their client network is crucial as this is a key asset which they will be bringing to the table. This should be supplemented by their reputation as a 'visible expert'.

Prederi, who were eventually sold to Bearing Point, had the following criteria for recruiting:

- Heart: will they fit with the values and culture?
- Mind: do they have the right knowledge, intelligence and skills?
- Gut: does your intuition say yes?

Concerning attracting good candidates, a small consultancy may not have the brand attraction, but small firms do have some advantages. Caroline Boston, MD of New Minds – a specialist in recruiting for smaller professional service firms – emphasises three points:

- 'Just as you build buyer personas when thinking about how to articulate your proposition to clients, do the same for candidates. Consider where the people you need might be working now and what you could offer them that is different and appealing'.
- 'Understand your competitors. What are they paying their team, what sort of projects are they working on, what is their culture like? Be prepared to define how your business and employee value proposition are different (and better!)'.
- 'Bring personality! One of the exciting things about joining a smaller business is the feeling of being part of a great team – your culture and values are so important here. Give a sense of your team and culture on your website, in your recruitment materials and throughout the hiring process'.

In addition to this excellent advice, it is also crucial to emphasise to candidates the entrepreneurial nature of your venture. Small firms often have difficulty in the brand wars, but people who avoid the big brands often do so because they have an entrepreneurial spark which is dampened in bureaucracies. The potential to be directly involved in the creation of something bigger and better is a great incentive to motivate potential employees.

Graduate hires

If you, like me, are middle-aged, you would do well not to underestimate the shift in attitudes of younger job-seekers over the last decade or so. The proportion of my MBA classes who would leave a well-paid job because they were unhappy rose each year for 15 years until COVID-19 hit, and since has continued to increase.

I interviewed one US founder who sold his firm recently and when asked about his approach to people management, he stated:

> I say to new people "look, you're not going to retire here, but while you're here we'll try and make sure you learn, are happy, and are a more capable person than when you joined". Whilst you've got those people for maybe five years, you've got to not only develop them but get them to develop you. Their experience and knowledge needs to be captured, they need to mentor and develop others, they've got to leave the firm better than when they joined.

Consultants are by nature ambitious, and the average tenure of a young consultant, even in a large firm, is typically less than five years. Finding ways to keep talent is therefore crucial to minimising the costs and risks associated with recruitment and IP leakage.

The challenge small consultancies have with recruiting is encapsulated in a quote from a very skilled MBA student of mine. When I asked her if she'd consider working for a firm I was advising, she replied: "they don't have the track record or brand, so it would be a major risk for me... especially compared to say Bain". Yet there are ways to attract quality candidates without the benefit of an established track record. Many graduates have heard horror stories about the processing machines that many large consultancies have become, with their 15-hour workdays. Many, though not most, would consider working for a smaller company which gave them personalised development, a wide array of experiences and real mentoring with a partner. There are several things that you can do to maximise your chances:

- build a distinctive culture and brand that is 'sticky';
- develop messaging which is attractive to your target recruits;
- do the footwork: the bigger the pool you target, the greater chance of success;
- anticipate and respond to recruit concerns about your strategy and growth plans;
- sell the benefits of working in a smaller firm

You should also consider who you approach and how. If your target is bright graduates and you have very deep pockets, you can compete with all the other major firms in targeting the top 5% of universities. However, as someone that has taught or guest lectured at these institutions, it is clear that you will have a much greater rate of success, with no difference in the quality of recruit, if you are intelligent in your approach. I recently did the following for a growing consulting firm, who received 163 great CVs, and ended up recruiting four outstanding MSc students:

- Instead of targeting top universities, target top courses. Many of the top 5% courses are not at the top 5% Universities.
- Target MSc students instead of MBAs.
- Don't just focus on business courses. First, consider what your culture and specialism requires (for example, psychology, IT or HRM). Second, consider the skills that are required. Business schools are notoriously bad at imparting transferable skills to students, whereas engineering, mathematics,

IT and even philosophy do much better at this. The best consultants I've met have often been historians by training.

- Target the 'second rank' of universities. Unless you have money to burn, you will find it hard to get in at Harvard, Oxford, Cambridge, INSEAD and the other top institutions. These have strong and expensive gatekeepers, and you will be competing with all of the top firms. Instead, go for the Cornells and Northwesterns (USA), the Warwicks and Bristols (UK) or the IIFTs and SPJIMRs (India).
- Don't rely on the annual careers fair. Find the emails of the course directors and the careers people in the relevant department and contact them. Offer to do guest lectures. Sponsor a prize or a competition.
- Build a relationship with top students by employing them through the University Jobshop for a small project (usually around £20/hour) and/or offering dissertation and research opportunities.
- Once you have a feel for the course and the quality of applicants, it is worth building relationships with two or three key institutions and courses that you think provide you with the best fit.

These approaches also mean that you avoid the incredibly hefty fees associated with recruitment agencies, who, certainly at a junior level, rarely do a great job of selling your unique culture.

Experienced hires

Many founders who had left a large consulting firm often found that ex-colleagues couldn't wait to join them – though only once the new firm had demonstrated its success. Big consulting firms increasingly put client needs a distant third after profit per partner and revenue growth, and indeed are often forced to do so by the short-term requirements of the stock market. This has worsened as profit margins have narrowed, so it is always worth keeping tabs on other alumni from your previous firms.

Whilst pay is generally a hygiene factor rather than a motivator, Damien at Solidiance argues that the same is not true of equity: 'you need to build a family and give people equity. People behave differently when they have equity – they are much more aligned to the firm. If you know how to run the family it is a great self-defence mechanism'. This insight can be combined with that of Raazi Imam at Caiman Consulting, who stresses the importance of having clear and strict metrics for the performance of seniors in the firm. The reward of equity should be linked to the high performance of seniors.

In finding senior hires, it is always worth looking at adjacent industries as well as your own. James Bamford, who co-founded Water Street Partners, told me:

> *It's hard to attract people at the very top consulting firms if you are a smaller firm... We realised that transaction attorneys sitting in big law firms have really transferable skills and many of them are unhappy - people who McKinsey & Co. should have hired but didn't.*

Partners and directors

When ranking factors that impact their purchases, buyers of consulting firms place the quality of the senior management team as joint most important (with a differentiated market proposition).[9] When recruiting and managing the leadership, it is important to be clear about the different roles needed at different stages of the business and how this might evolve over time.

'Recruitment is the most important thing', says Prederi (and Tribal) founder and MD, Stewart Johns. 'The secret by far is to recruit good senior people. Have people who have contacts and know people. You only get work from people you know'.

When seeking seniors, it is common to look for people with complementary rather than overlapping service or market specialisations but fit with your values and ambitions is most important of all. It is also good advice to avoid recruitment and reward schemes, whereby partners create their own fiefdoms and compete with each other rather than co-operate. As Roger Carlile of Ankura warned me:

> *Really great seniors wanted to be in a different culture [to the Big4]. They wanted to be in a place where the firm is sort of client-first, firm-first, not what P&L am I in, what bonus pool am I in, I'd better not tell Susie down the hall what I'm chasing because I might have to share credit. There's a lot of those dysfunctions we know arise from time to time at consulting firms.*

If you have a five- or even ten-year plan to sale, it is likely that the requirement for senior people to manage the growing organization will be greater than your capacity to promote internally. It will, therefore, be necessary to recruit senior people into the company. If your aim is to be in the 10% of sellers that avoid an earn-out, then building a large(ish) diversified team of senior directors is an important step in avoiding a dependency on the founder.

On average, buyers want 23% of equity shared among the senior management team.[10] Of course, equity rewards should be tied to growth and sale targets. In one (anonymised) firm I interviewed, there was a big gap in equity and pay between three extrovert 'rain-makers' and the other seniors who ensured that quality work was delivered every time. The founder told me:

> *During the negotiation phase one of the Directors left because it became clear they were not going to do particularly well out of the deal. This led to a second round of negotiation, during which two other senior people left, so we had to negotiate again...... It not only led to a lower price, but to a longer and more stressful sales process.*

It is sadly, if not unsurprisingly, common for one partner to despair that one or more other partners have lost (or simply never had) the motivation to 'pull their weight'. When this happens, there are three options that require some detailed planning and can be done in the order below:

- Galvanise them to pull their weight.
- Restructure the shares to better reflect outputs.
- Leave and start again.

This is of course easier said than done, especially when long-term relationships are at risk; but there is nothing to be gained by kicking the can down the road, and in my own experience, it is rare for a consistently poorly performing partner to improve unless early, significant interventions are made.

Finally, sometimes founders decide (or discover) that the CEO role isn't where their strengths lie. At Jennifer Brown Consulting, for example, Jennifer Brown has passed on the CEO role and now focuses instead on thought leadership and service development.[11] Another example (one of my own clients) decided that he did not have the skills to take the company to the next level, but one of the other directors did, so managed the transition with new roles for both of them.

Non-executive directors and advisory boards

Consultancies need external advisors for some of the same reasons clients need strategy consultants: providing expert, outside advice that is objective and based on years of experience. Typically, this advice comes in two forms: an advisory board or non-executive directors (NEDs).

Advisory boards are just that. They meet with the leaders, typically once every one to three months, to input into decisions. Advisors do not sit on the board or attend AGMs and do not have formal authority. NEDs generally have a more formal position and input into the running and direction of the firm. They often have a specific specialism that adds value and will sometimes sit on sub-committees which reflect these specialisms. As such, they are often subject to formal appraisals in the same manner as other directors.

In terms of reward, NEDs are often paid roles, although some are rewarded with up to 2% equity depending on what they bring to the table. Board advisors tend to be rewarded with equity, typically around the 1% level, again depending on whether they are simply used for advice or additional activities such as fund-raising or recruitment. Neither should be overlooked for sales. Steve Cardell, CEO at Axon, stated: 'Our most valuable source of leads comes from one of our non-Executive Directors who has masses of contacts'. Both roles are useful also in breaking deadlocks between partners and for settling disputes before they spiral out of control.

Using associates

Wherever you are in the world, using associates always requires you to begin by considering the law. In many Western countries, the early 2020s saw the introduction of laws which sought to prevent companies disguising employees as independent contractors. These practices were profitable for consulting companies who could avoid the employment, pensions and insurance hassles of employees, and also for the contractors who were not only usually paid more, but also often paid lower taxes. It took a long time for governments to catch onto this practice, but many are now banning the use of contractors who are all but in name employees.

The response to this legislation from some corporations has been to ban the use of contractors/associates outright, regardless of whether or not they would fall foul of this legislation. From personal experience, I have seen procurement departments in many large professional service firms, retailers and telcos simply imposing an outright ban on contractors and those firms that might bring contractors in. Now, it remains to be seen if these clients are still going to be able to access the talent they need with these restrictions in place, but at the moment we are beginning to see a reversal of the trend towards a greater acceptance and use of associates in all areas of life.

These legal issues aside, as associates are generally a more expensive option than employees, they should usually only be used in five situations:

1. You are just starting out and don't have the cash needed to hire full-time staff.
2. You need short-term occasional expert resource for projects that do not justify bringing on a permanent employee. As the firm grows, the increasing

frequency of this need will create economies of scale which justify an employee rather than an associate.

3. Despite your best efforts, you cannot recruit sufficient employees who possess the skill sets needed for a project.
4. You need more flexible resourcing for unexpected peaks and troughs.
5. You need high levels of creativity and innovation that you struggle to maintain internally.[12]

These are of course not mutually exclusive, and almost all consultancies have a 15% to 20% associate contingency for unexpected demand fluctuations. Yet, if you are dominated by associates primarily due to difficulties recruiting skilled employees, buyers will be more sceptical about the internal value of the firm, especially if there are competitors in your market which *have* managed to find permanent employees to do the same job. If associates are being used simply because your firm is not competitive in recruiting good employees, buyers will notice.

Although buyers are much more accepting of associates than in the past, strategic buyers tend to get edgy when the percentage of associates gets significantly higher than their own practices. HR consultancies often use a large percentage of associates, whilst highly leveraged buyers that employ large proportions of juniors may be turned-off by high levels of associates. For many buyers, the ideal is around the 20% to 25% mark, but it does depend on the sector. This figure allows periods of expansion and contraction to be managed better, for external skills and perspectives to be brought into the firm and for weak clients to be occasionally pruned without affecting headcount. While some of the companies that I interviewed were up to 75% associate staffed, the vast majority worked between 15% and 35%. If a firm is growing on the basis of associates, I usually suggest that if they want to sell, they should start employing some of the better ones as they get closer to sale, reducing the risk for the buyer.

The pros and cons of using associates are listed below (Table 8.1), but this belies the importance of managing associates *well*. Key principles include:

*   Recruiting quality associates using similar methods to that of employees.
*   Ensuring that intellectual property (IP) is protected both contractually and in the practices of sharing.
*   Having quality assurance processes firmly in place and managed.
*   Integrating associates well with existing teams and processes (see below).
*   Keeping great associates by integrating them into your culture, making them feel they 'belong'.

Table 8.1 Pros and cons of associates

Pros	Cons
Diverse, quality skill set for better delivery	Buyers often dislike high levels of associates
Fresh, external ideas	Little of internal accumulation of expertise/experience
Less hassle than employees	
A good way to test out potential employees	Risk of client/IP theft
	Potential inconsistency in client experience
Easier to remove than employees	
Enable easy contraction during recessions	Low practice development/IP commitment
	Not always available
	Tend to be more expensive than internal resource

The question of whether you tell clients you are using associates is up to you, but either way, the client experience must be seamless. This can be maximised in the following ways:

- Recruiting trusted associates that share your values.
- Training associates in the firm's methods, processes, tools and values.
- Working closely with new associates until they can mirror your practices and values.
- Internal audits of associate work, especially early on.
- Providing firm email and document templates.
- Inviting associates to company events and key meetings.
- Maintaining great communications, even when they're not on assignment.
- Bringing associates in at the start of a project to meld with the team and approach.

In terms of using associates, it is generally good advice not to use them for anything other than delivery. Using associates for business development, account management, practice management, leadership or creating IP creates an unnecessary risk. As an aside, I have seen some consultancies staff poorly performing clients with more associates than employees so that closing the account need not result in employees on the bench.

Given that good associates may often choose between different firms, it is worth treating them well. This means making them part of the family and integrating them with your culture. As a rough guide, associates are typically paid 50% or less of the rate the client is charged, although higher percentages can be used for great associates. Making this explicit can prompt associates to help drive up client fee rates. Negotiations for lower prices with associates can often be achieved through volume discounts (for example, a 10% reduction for a week's work or 20% for a month). It is good practice to pay associates promptly even if the client hasn't paid yet.

Finally, it is not uncommon to pay associates by the project rather than the hour. This can involve sub-contracting the work and paying for a quality deliverable. In the same way as using fixed pricing yourself, it takes time to build up the expertise to know how much a specific deliverable should cost and also understanding the value of this to the client and your firm.

People management[13]

Building an HR competence

HR practices varied considerably among my interviewees. At one extreme, Sarah of Virgo Health told me:

> My previous boss told me if I had to do everything, again, the one thing I would do differently is make sure that I invest in the most high calibre support I can. And we definitely took that advice, but I would add to that, essentially, all problems in business are about people. And all potential in business is about people. Why wouldn't you invest therefore in someone whose specialism is people?

Where Virgo had (part-time) senior HR and finance people right from the beginning, many other firms didn't use HR specialists at all and relied on their own people management. One (anonymised) owner of a firm of nearly 70 people told me, 'I can't stand HR. Gets in the way of running a good firm'. Whilst this may be true for some at an early stage, pretty soon the legal and best practice complexities of running a large team justify specialist expertise. For those not wanting in-house solutions to HR, there are many advisors and outsourced services that were sufficient for many of my sample to grow successfully. Many smaller firms used 'fractional' HR and finance contractors two to three days a week instead of as employees, which appeared to work well for both parties. There appear to be a large number of experienced HR professionals who are balancing childcare with their careers and are happy with part-time or fractional positions.

For those struggling with the people side of their firm, I would recommend reading Tabaccowala's *Restoring the Soul of Business* (2020) and Salacuse's *Leading Leaders: How to Manage Smart, Talented, Rich and Powerful People* (2005). Both argue that, for the top 5% of talent, money is a hygiene factor, and it is culture, sense of achievement, autonomy and personal attention that will keep and motivate great employees.

A final note here concerns alternative, online platforms for sourcing temporary talent. The benefit of these is that you have access to a huge array of global talent, often at reduced prices. The downside is that the relationship is transactional and the experience and learnings stay with them rather than your firm. These types of platforms fall into three areas[14]:

1) Marketplaces for premium talent, such as Cognisium, Toptal, Comatch, Catalant.
2) Marketplaces for crowdsource innovation, such as Innocentive, Kaggle.
3) Marketplaces for digital contractors such as Fiverr, Upwork, 99designs.

Of course, if you are a solo consultant, there is no reason why you should not use the first of these as a supplier to boost your profile and pipeline.

Training and development

Training is an investment. Done properly, it is a short-term cost exchanged for long-term rewards. It is also one of only a few ways to increase the value of your work which, in turn, justify higher prices. Training in small professional service firms is also strongly correlated with greater levels of commitment and innovation from employees.[15] It is therefore unfortunate that so many firms believe that working on client projects is the only way to develop competence.

The balance between training and mentoring will depend on the type of firm and its strategy, but both are important not only for passing on skills, experience and knowledge, but also for enculturing your people into the norms and values of the firm. This becomes increasingly important as the firm grows and the ability of partners to control the activities of juniors diminishes as they become less visible. As consultancy is fundamentally based on relationships and trust, the importance of ensuring that consultants know how to behave with clients when the partners are not there is crucial. Your consultants are your brand.

Training activities for consultants tend to fall into six areas:

1   Culture and values
2   Delivery
3   IP/knowledge creation, capture and management
4   Sales and account management
5   Client market trends and themes
6   Management, governance, technology and administration

In addition, seniors (including partners!) should be trained in pricing, negotiation, project management and mentoring. If they do not take to these, either train up juniors or recruit specialists as a mid-sized firm needs these capabilities. Good project management is something clients will generally pay for, if it means they will be getting better value overall.

How these are delivered will depend on the firm, but they should be systematised and not left to the idiosyncrasies of individual partners and their favourites. This means that the training needs analyses and delivery is done properly and so you can show potential recruits and potential acquirers that you have a thoughtful system which is linked to your strategy. This developmental system will not only include formal training and mentoring, but also a systematic approach to project resourcing such that gaps in consultant's experience are filled by using them in different roles. I would also encourage your firm to develop peer training (for example, monthly sessions where teams share what new things they have learned in client work) and sessions which bring in outside knowledge.

Pay and reward: seniors

In a partnership, partners are typically rewarded through base salary and some form of profit-share. In different types of firms, the equivalent would be the dividend payment or the bonus. In the start-up phase, it is common for partners to forgo some salary in order to invest in growth, and take a minimum out of the firm, often in the form of dividends. Entrepreneurial passion may be sufficient to entice new seniors to take a lower salary in exchange for a mix of equity, performance-related bonuses and future pay rises. Yet at some point, partner base salaries will need to be discussed and things can get a little tricky when there is a mix of experience, business development networks and working hours. There is no best answer here other than to say that the basis for discussion should be clear and agreed before scaling base salaries according to working hours invested.

More complex is the agreement on profit-per-partner at the end of the financial year. Again, when there are a handful of partners, many of whom may have joined within a few years of each other, profits can be agreed and distributed according to shareholding without too much fuss. However, when a firm grows, and new partners are bought on, tensions may emerge. It is worth anticipating these early on. Significant 'rain-makers' will object to a pay-out based on their (low) equity share if they have brought in a significant percentage of firm revenues. Others might rightly argue that they joined the firm first and therefore contributed most to growing the asset that is the firm even if their recent sales work has not reaped rewards. Others still might point out that whilst not major rain-makers they have put more time and effort into increasing the multiple the firm is worth through automation, service development or mentoring.

All of these are valid points. Bonuses or profit-shares should be linked to value creation in the firm, defined as either directly increasing EBITDA or increasing the multiple. The former is often celebrated and rewarded more, but this is a mistake. A significant rain-maker might improve EBITDA by 50% in a year, but a partner working on strong intellectual property might improve the multiple by one to two times. The relative impact of these on the firm depends on a number of factors, but the latter often adds more value to the firm, and both should be encouraged and rewarded.

There are three common archetypes of partner compensation, each of which has pros and cons (Table 8.2). However, in reality, schemes are often mixed, and larger firms also incorporate the 'black box' judgement of a compensation committee who use more subjective measures to assign profits.

Clearly, there is no easy and universal answer, and the outcome is usually a balance between new business development, seniority and capacity development. Whatever balance is reached, aligning rewards to strategy in a transparent, consistent and evidence-based manner is fundamental. Among my interviewees, rewards for partners ranged from 'eat what you kill' through to an equal share for all partners. Benny Cheung at Decision Technologies created a formula based upon a detailed spreadsheet of results which was open to all partners, whereas Chris Gibson at Pen Partnership emphasised the 'art' of compensation planning, arguing that the firm has a flexible model which recognises where people are adding all kinds of value.

A final but important note here is that compensation schemes are also about signalling and reinforcing which behaviours are desirable in the firm. The culture and values of the firm should drive the compensation structure rather than the other way around.

Table 8.2 Partner compensation[16]

	Pros	Cons	Mitigation/conditions
Lockstep (seniority based)	Greater co-operation Higher quality work Stability	Does not incentivise strong junior partners Dangers of free-riding which can lead to low growth	A ceiling is often introduced for senior partner shares. This works better if partners are similar in tenure but also in their values and work ethic to create high levels of trust
Eat what you kill (partners receive what they bring in – minus costs)	Encourages fast growth in fee income A transparent and simple system No detailed reviews are needed	Does not build value in the firm Lack of co-operation or even dysfunctional work Partners accepting work which is not their specialism can lead to poor quality delivery	Suited to heterogeneous partnerships Sometimes introduced for a short period to boost revenues
Merit based (wide range of performance measures)	Balances fee income with other value-building activities Empowers partners to judge best use of their time	Stress over annual performance review Focuses on current performance not past value-add Measurement challenges Punishes a bad year (for example, ill health or bad luck)	Calculating averages over several years Suited to where partners are quite different Sometimes modified by individual negotiation

Takeaways

- Investing in great people, training them and motivating them to perform brilliantly is the most important thing you can do to improve the value your firm provides to clients.
- A strong culture attracts and keeps good hires. It also minimises the need for rules and supervision. Make your culture consistent with your brand and ensure that all management reinforce it with their behaviours.
- Unless your growth is exponential and supply of talent is challenging, be very careful to hire people who share your values.
- As the firm matures beyond 25–30 people, you will need more formal roles and processes for managing people. However, having a strong culture means that expectations of behaviour and decisions can be assured without having rules for everything.
- Using equity as a reward can build a strong family feel with your employees, as long as the distribution is based on achieving clear goals aligned with the firm's strategy.
- Think about partner compensation early on. New firms often reward on the basis of equity share which is not particularly motivating for new but highly able partners.

Case study: Exellys

Raf Seymus learned the limitations of the traditional education system very young. He was suspended from school four or five times as a child and found out quickly that he preferred learning by doing. After a stint in the shipping industry, he worked at coaching young offenders and their families to improve their lives and employment opportunities. In his next job in HR, he realised that good people were leaving the company in droves, less because of higher salaries elsewhere and more because they did not feel they had a say in their own future. Their training was imposed on them and rarely useful, and there was a lack of transparency in how they were being promoted and paid. The programme he established drew on his experience in coaching to create a competence management system that would guide and support employees through the company in a transparent and interactive way.

In 2014 Raf started Exellys to develop the skills of bright technology graduates and integrate them with clients that needed their expertise. Unlike many consultancies that are terrified of poaching, Exellys' business model actively supports clients that want to recruit the consultants they have hired. Realising that growth without funding would be slow, Raf found funding (in three months) from another consultancy, Brainbridge, who saw the idea as complimentary but not in competition with them. Having Brainbridge not only provided finance for expansion, but also support in business development and administration.

There are many interesting, innovative and admirable things about Raf and Exellys, but what stands out most is his strategic prioritisation of his own consultants. The supply of talented technology and IT consultants vastly exceeds supply, so Exellys not only finds them (the firm interviews 60% of Dutch IT graduates) but strategically prioritises the retention and development of these valuable assets. How is this done?

First, through development. Exellys has high quality training, coaching and mentoring programmes which are continually improved through feedback from the consultants. The five coaches ('talent development managers') at Exellys are dedicated, which means that junior consultants seeking development don't have to rely on being in the vicinity of a partner when he or she has a spare hour.

Retention is also improved by putting employees first: 'If they don't have a good experience with the client', Raf says, 'we take them away. We ask for three months to manage the transition, which employees are happy with, but your talent comes first, and the client is a close second'. Of course, all consultancies say that their people are their greatest asset, but how many would end a contract because their consultants were unhappy? Raf continues:

> If they are not happy, we first talk to the client openly and try to change things, but if we cannot change things, we end the contract…We ask them to give us three months to find a replacement and fund a new solution, but after three months they are out because otherwise they will resign.

Raf also emphasises the importance of culture and values as the company grew beyond his immediate control.

> Building a company is harder than starting it. The first people get the culture from working every day from a small team. Systems and processes are important, yes, but you need ambassadors and champions to help new-comers get it in their DNA.

In six years, Exellys grew to 140 consultants and won many awards in this period. It was sold to Projective in 2020. Raf has now started an equally exciting and innovative company, Stellar Labs.[17]

Notes

1 Lee, I., & Cogin, J. (2020) Formalizing the HRM and firm performance link: the S-curve hypothesis. *The International Journal of Human Resource Management*, April, 1–32.

2 Nissen, V., & Dittler, J. (2019). Measuring and managing the reputation of business consultancies. In: Nissen, V. ed. *Advances in Consulting Research*. Cham: Springer, pp. 103–131.

3 McKinsey & Co., Bain & Co. and Boston Consulting Group: short-hand for the elite consulting firms of the world.

4 MBB+: McKinsey, Bain, Boston Consulting Group and other elite firms. Or people these firms *should* have recruited but missed out on.

5 Gerber, M. (2001) *The eMyth Revisited*. New York: Harper Business.

6 One thing I did prior to each interview was to check out employee comments about a firm on websites such as Glassdoor.com. Not the most scientific method, but perhaps more reliable than the word of the Managing Partner.

7 Moorhead, G., Ference, R., & Neck, C. P. (1991) Group decision fiascoes continue: Space shuttle challenger and a revised groupthink framework. *Human Relations*, 44(6), 539–550.

8 Climb in Consulting. *Episode 81: Tom Hewson*. Podcast.

9 Equiteq (2018) *The Knowledge Economy Global Buyers Report* 2018/2019.

10 Equiteq (2017) What buyers of consulting firms look for and how they will determine value in 2018. YouTube. https://youtu.be/GTc9fURaUxI

11 https://jenniferbrownconsulting.com/

12 The downside of a strong culture and standardised processes is that no matter how creative your recruits, they eventually succumb to group-think.

13 I have kept this section short as once your firm gets beyond a certain size you will have expert HR advice on people management and there are many good books on this topic for professional service firms, not least the original by David Maister.

14 Thank you to Dr Dorel Iosif for these categories.

15 Susomrith, P., Coetzer, A., & Ampofo, E. (2019), Training and development in small professional services firms. *European Journal of Training and Development*, 43(5/6), 517–535.

16 For a deeper dive on this, see Wiegmann, T. (2019) *Fairness, Trust and Motivation in Profit Sharing Systems*. PhD thesis, University of Bradford.

17 www.stellarlabs.eu

9
The buying process: preparing for sale

What should *you* be looking for?

In contrast to the beginning of other chapters, this section focuses on what *you* should want. This is not always the same as what buyers want. Putting together a firm that is very attractive to acquirers or investors is the most important thing in a successful sale, but the buying or investment process itself introduces new risks and complexities that can damage the hard work that you have done.

For sellers, the ideal buying or investment process is short, profitable and painless. Most would also like to keep the character, culture and essence of their firm alive, and if an earn-out[1] is necessary, it is important that the targets are realistic and the dependencies and contingencies spelled out. The extent to which these are achievable is dependent in part on how well you have followed the advice in this book, but also how well you manage the buying process.

The ideal situation for a seller is one where there are several potential buyers interested in the firm, where the partners are not overly distracted from their job of filling the pipeline and where the due diligence process unearths no unpleasant surprises and is therefore quick. These minimise the risk not only of a buyer pulling out, but also of the purchasing process being lengthened (with the additional risk that a sales drop during that period leads to a lower valuation next time around).

Two firms I interviewed had disastrous experiences of the buying process, where a cycle of partners being distracted due to the sale, key employees leaving and a stressful buying process resulted in a vicious circle where much of the value of the firm dissipated. In my sample, only 75% of firms successfully sold first time around, leaving 25% who had to renegotiate what was usually a lower value deal.

Think of the selling process as akin to selling a house. You might have a wonderful property but when buyers come looking, you should probably have given it a lick of paint and fix some of those things that have been nagging at you for

DOI: 10.4324/9781003149217-9

some time. Moreover, you can't assume that the buyer knows all the benefits of your house and there is a process of education that you or your intermediary need to undertake. The buyer will need to be taught *all* the benefits of your firm, including why it is just right for *them*.

The big difference between selling a firm and selling a house, as Paul Collins told me, is that a house doesn't get damaged during its sale, whereas a firm is likely to if the process is badly managed. To this end, unless you have buyers fighting over you, I would recommend trying to stick with an interested buyer, even if they're offering up to 15% less than you think the firm is worth. A good advisor will give you a price *range* for your firm, which will be highly dependent on variables you cannot control, including luck. Over the years, I've seen several founders turn down a buyer's price thinking that the economy, their firm and the interest of other buyers will be the same or better in six months' time, only to find that things are worse rather than better.

Two to three years prior to beginning the sale process

An early advisor

Depending on the economic cycle, between 150 and 300 consulting firms are sold each month. Selling a firm at a premium not only requires that it generates sustainable, predictable and growing profits in a niche area, but also that it is packaged and communicated well to a trusted network of potential buyers or investors. For this, there is no substitute for specialist advice. I would recommend your consultancy has the advice of an independent expert experienced in growing and selling professional service firms, and that this advice is sought at every stage of your firm's growth. If you leave external advice to the last year, it is possible that you will have missed something that may take some time to build in and have achieved sub-optimal growth. The advice I give in this section is obviously no substitute for in-depth expertise tailored to your firm, but it does reflect useful insights from buyers and sellers as well as my own experience advising firms.

Advisors tend to fall into two groups: those who advise on growth and M&A specialists. Concerning the former, I suggest avoiding online 'gurus'. As I said in the introduction, their services are more useful for coaches and tend to focus around building a digital sales funnel. I would also avoid people whose advice is based on their own experiences of one firm. Many clients of mine have received advice from people who sold their own firms 15 years ago, only to find that it is completely unsuitable for today's market where expectations of acquirers and investors are higher. Concerning the second group, there are many firms to choose from, but I would focus on a firm that specialises in professional service firms generally rather than your specific type of service firm, because potential buyers will often come from a different service sector. Unless your firm is valued at over £100 million, it is likely that your advisor for the sale will be an M&A professional or a broker. The former tend to focus on deals worth between £10 and 100 million, whereas the latter focus on deals less than £10 million.

At least two years prior to selling, it is worth doing an in-depth audit and valuation of your firm with an external expert. This will achieve several things. It will give you an idea what the firm is worth, the potential buyers that might be interested and how you might tailor your value proposition to better fit their needs. Are you big enough for them to be interested? Do you fill gaps in their service or market proposition? What has happened with previous acquisitions? Would you fit with their culture? You might even start targeting key individuals with invitations to join your steering committee or simply build relationships through networking. An audit will also give you a prioritised list of activities that you should undertake in order to maximise the value of the company. Even if your firm is in prime condition, an M&A specialist will tell you much that will make that preparation period more effective.

Preparing the team

If you (or other partners) wish to have a minimal earn-out period, then it is crucial that you have someone being prepared to take over as CEO/Managing Partner or already have someone in place. Succession planning takes time, but if you have put into place strong systems, the whole process will be less fraught. Whether internal or external, the person in question will need to have strong incentives to stay with the firm at least during the earn-out period and to have shadowed the leadership role for long enough to make the transition smooth.

If you wish to do this prior to a sale, then it should be done at least a year in advance so that the new person has a chance to show that the transition has been successful. A communications plan around succession is also important, to reassure staff and other stakeholders. This can also help you focus on the sale process whilst they take over some of your leadership activities.

In addition, about a year before the planned sale, you should ensure you have solid skills for the team that will be handling the sales process itself. If you can't afford expensive advisors, you must consider who you need for the team. It may be worth recruiting an experienced, well-connected, part-time chair and an M&A-savvy, part-time finance director who are incentivised on sale. When it comes to an external team, this may well be the most important decision you make. Use an independent lawyer and accountant who are experienced in this type of transaction.

Timing of sale

The question of when to sell has a strong personal element, especially if there are one or two majority shareholders that can force a sale. It will very much depend on what their 'number' is, if they are still happy in their work and often how close they are to retirement. However, these factors concern when shareholders might *want* to sell, not when is *best* to sell.

Whilst some sell too early to maximise the value of their work, a few wait too long, wanting to milk the value from their firm to the point where margins begin to reduce. Remember that the sales process can take a year and you may have an earn-out of three years when your earnings will be dependent on growth targets. So ideally, you should be thinking about a sale up to five years before you think growth might peak – not that growth necessarily has to have a peak. This is all very idealistic, and of course many other factors come into play. However, if your firm is following an S-curve, buyers will be less interested when the growth begins to flatten off. The exception is during a recession where buyers are also realistic that most firms will experience some decline. Many of my interviewees sold successfully during a recession. Even during the coronavirus pandemic, M&A activity continued at a reasonable pace.

Preparing key information

As we saw in the chapter on firm design, most firms will have a shareholders/partners agreement and Articles of Association (or similar) which set out the rules by which you operate. Reviewing and potentially amending these long before the sale process is incredibly important, as you may find yourself restricted in what you can do. For example, how you have dealt with minority shareholder rights might hold up the process of a sale indefinitely.

In addition, a year or two prior to a sale, get in the habit of preparing and maintaining a Confidential Information Memorandum (CIM – akin to a marketing brochure a seller provides to entice buyers). I have put one of these for you at joeomahoney.com. It will typically include:

1. Investment summary
2. Firm summary
3. Market and competitor overviews
4. Client base, sales and contracts
5. Services and intellectual property (IP)
6. People

7. Governance
8. Financial history and projections

Two years before a sale, the leadership should use this as a benchmark to track quarterly performance and as a running audit checklist of all the areas that are going to come under scrutiny during due diligence. Doing this early enough will allow you to identify and improve upon weakness that buyers might use to barter down the price.

Who buys, why and how?

Types of buyers

A combination of private equity (PE) and strategic buyers account for around 95% of all purchases, and it is on these that I focus here. PE buyers represent a wide array of individuals and companies that focus on the acquisition as both a stand-alone source of revenue growth and an asset that might be sold on again in the future. PE deals have grown significantly over the last 15–20 years and now account for between 30% and 50% of deals depending on the economic cycle and the cost of debt. One reason for this growth is that PE firms have been taking advantage of cheap debt to leverage purchases for higher returns. Another is that consulting firms are increasingly incorporating recurring revenue IP which offers the potential of high returns and relatively low EBITDA multiples compared to software firms.

PE typically wants a medium-term financial return on investment for their investors. They buy a percentage of the firm (not always a majority) and usually maintain the firm's fundamental operating model, although sometimes combining it with other purchased firms to maximise cross-selling and other synergies. Most of the original board will usually still be involved in governance (depending on the contract). This is attractive to founders who wish their company to remain intact, to boards where one or more partners wish to exit, but also to senior managers who may not have the cash to leave after their earn-out and don't wish to be a middle manager in a bigger, very different company.

Strategic buyers are typically other Professional Service Firms (PSFs) that wish to lever the target firm to improve their own performance. This can happen in four different ways (see Table 9.1), and it is useful to know specifically why potential buyers are interested in your firm as it will give you an indication of their future plans and your leverage in negotiations. Regardless of the primary aim, there are usually a host of secondary benefits which can include acquiring key individuals, technologies, methods, 'star' clients and access to high-growth markets and services. All this said, failure rates of M&A activity are estimated[2] at around 70% in terms of failing to generate value of the price paid (although my own experience is that this figure is much lower in PSFs).

Table 9.1 Why strategic buyers purchase smaller firms

Reason	Focus of performance improvement
Growing international reach	Selling existing services in new high-growth markets; better serving international clients;
Increasing market share	Growth through acquisition; buying up the competition; filling gaps;
Increasing range of services	Cross-selling services in existing clients; vertical or horizontal integration of services;
Differentiating the buyer's existing services	Adding value and pulling power of existing services by adding key individuals, technologies or assets in the same area;

Strategic buyers may not come from your market. Management consultancies are frequently bought by HR consultancies, engineering consultancies, media agencies and IT companies (in order of frequency) usually to create the strategic leverage with their clients for larger projects downstream. Whilst founders and senior management may be promised otherwise, it is rare for a small firm to maintain its independence, culture or systems after a few years of being bought by a much larger firm. This eventuality can prove frustrating for those whose earn-out did not allow them to retire and end up working in a more bureaucratic, less entrepreneurial culture. I saw how disastrous this can be when a large consultancy for whom I was working (young, IT-focused, bureaucratic – the firm, not me) bought an expensive niche boutique (grey hair, individualized, strategy firm). Within three years, the entire workforce of the acquired firm had walked out the door and set up a competing company.

The key point here is that the firm for sale must know and articulate its strategic value to buyers as well as its financial position. What interests strategic buyers foremost is the potential of a firm to add strategically to its specific offerings. This is what should form the basis of your messaging and will likely prompt their initial approach.

Management Buy-Outs (MBOs)

A management buy-out (MBO) was undertaken in only one of the firms I interviewed, and the founder was well aware that he was sacrificing cash to maintain the culture of the company:

I am proud of what we've built together and there was no way that culture and energy was going to remain intact if we sold to a big corporate. I realised early on that there is no way [the team] could match the price of a corporate buyer, but that is the price you pay'.

[Anon]

The pros and cons of the MBOs are well encapsulated in that sentence. As many of my interviewees moved out of their earn-out periods, it became clear that in most cases, their firm was likely to be engulfed by the culture and processes of the larger firm. Whilst there were a few exceptions, where the firms were kept intact as a separate financial and operational entity to the buyers, many purchased consultancies enter a spiral where encroachments on working practices (often swapping long-term investment for short-term reward) lead to people leaving, which weaken the culture and so on.

A MBO is one alternative to this, but if you think that a minimum purchase for a small firm is typically £5–£10 million, a company where the senior team comprises ten people will generally struggle to raise anywhere near this amount, even if they are happy to take the risk! It is of course possible to overcome this obstacle by convincing a bank or other lender to pay the major shareholder(s) for their shares and repaying this as a loan over a period. Other times, the founder may agree to have the equity (plus interest) paid back from future profits. In addition to ensuring the firm is in great shape, a good advisor should provide you with options that match your needs.

Often an MBO will also save you having to spend a huge amount of time making the firm and its numbers look great. It is akin to selling your house to a tenant: they already know where the damp is, and ownership may incentivise them to do something about it.

Initial public offerings (IPOs) and SPACs

As with MBOs, only one of the firms I studied floated on the stock market: Elixirr. The benefit of this is that it allows owners to realize equity whilst still maintaining directive control. An initial public offering (IPO) can generate a lot of money, provide a relatively quick return for owners, allow those who wish to exit to do so and free up capital for investment in big projects. In addition, as publicly traded companies have more stringent accounting and reporting requirements, they can often benefit from a stronger reputation in the market, which can lead to bigger clients and access to reduced cost lending. A final benefit is that shares become liquid so that cash can be realised as soon as the shares are released as opposed to when the firm sells or receives investment.

On the downside, during the IPO itself a firm loses 10% of its value on fees to auditors, underwriters and advisors. You are also likely to need expanded governance, reporting and finance teams as both the preparation for IPO and day-to-day reporting of a publicly listed company is much more work and expensive than any other option. Once floated, there are greater regulatory pressures and disclosure requirements, and often short-term performance targets often take precedence over long-term value. All this result in greater costs, which can have a knock-on effect on margins. More importantly, these pressures can affect the culture in the company which can prompt both employees and founders to leave. Finally, a Managing Partner/CEO can lose control of the company if they do not keep shareholders happy. There are exceptions to the reporting stringency – alternative markets such as the FTSE AIM (on which Elixirr floated) have fewer requirements and are perhaps better suited to more entrepreneurial ventures which still require flexibility.

None of the firms I have interviewed or advised have used a Special Purpose Acquisition Company (SPAC) to IPO – indeed, they are still quite rare in the consulting world as deals tend to focus on medium-sized technology firms. However, if growth rates of SPAC deals continue, it may not be long before they are common in the professional service firm market. A SPAC is typically formed by 'sponsors' to raise IPO funds from investors with a purpose of acquiring a private company and taking the firm public. The investors have two years to find a target firm while the funds are placed in an interest-bearing trust account. If they cannot find a target company within the given period, the SPAC must be liquidated and the funds returned to investors. SPACs are sometimes called 'blank cheque' companies because they are provided with funds to go and find a great investment. As the sponsors have already done the negotiations with investors, the investment deal can usually be done much faster.

The buying process

Many buyers of firms already have existing relationships with their targets, though this is less likely to be the case with firms that are frequent buyers (some buy three or more consultancies a year in pursuit of rapid expansion) and is rarely the case with PE. With 'serial purchasers' and PE, they commonly use an intermediary to find their targets. For firms that have existing relationships, this is most likely to be a large competitor, a firm that you have already been working with on projects or with which you have a reciprocal cross-selling arrangement. It is likely that this firm will be aligned either vertically (for example, strategy to implementation) or horizontally (for example, training to recruitment) and thus the fit is obvious.

I wrote above that the stages of selling a firm are similar to selling a house. Also, as with buying a house, they appear relatively simple but belie what is often a risky, complex and stressful experience, especially for the target. Table 9.2 shows the steps and the potential timelines. The stages don't need to be done consecutively, although there is a critical path, and in reality, these phases often overlap and repeat. Sometimes, a buyer pulls out and timelines get extended, but more commonly something might change (for example, partners leave or profits fall) and the price must be renegotiated.

Table 9.2 Stages to sale (and beyond)

Stage	Details	Duration
Know what you want	It is not as simple as private equity vs. a strategic buyer. Do you want to retain control? Do you want the firm to still exist afterwards? Do your partners want different things (for example, staying on, exit)? Would you rather sell to a private or public company? How long do you want the earn-out to be? What is your target price? Regarding the buyers, it is wise to build a list of the characteristics of buyers that you are looking for and begin building relationships with a shortlist early on.	One to two workshops
Pre-diligence	When you are selling a house, you clean it and give it a new coat of paint. The same is true of a consultancy. Having a great firm is one thing, but making that presentable to attract the most buyers is another. If you have followed the advice in this book, your firm should be in a solid state, but making this attractive to a buyer means further work. Is your share structure clear? Is your Intellectual Property registered? Have you settled your bad debts? Are key contracts, corporate records and governance documents well organised? Have you optimised your sales and costs to maximise profits? Are your governance and management processes clear and readily available? Do you have three years of audited accounts?[3]	Zero to six months

(Continued)

Table 9.2 (*Continued*)

Stage	*Details*	*Duration*
	It is also well worth preparing for the successful outcome: how will the change be managed? What is your communications strategy and plan? Who will know what and when?	
Engage intermediary	If you have not been approached by a buyer (or even if you have), you may engage a third party to help you identify potential buyers and structure the deal.	One month
Search for potential buyers	The seller or intermediary will search the market for suitable buyers. You should aim to find as many suitable buyers as possible, so as to maximise the odds of finding one that shares your values and culture (and a bidding war never hurts....).	One to two months
Initial approaches	Initial conversations are often held with several interested buyers. Additional and clarifying information is typically exchanged. At this stage, an NDA will be signed.	One month
Deeper dive	More substantial information is provided in response to the potential buyers' requests (sometimes called a Confidential Information Memorandum) and an approximate valuation will be generated by potential buyers. If this is on target, a Letter of Intent (LOI) will be signed with one potential buyer, which is usually a mix of binding (typically, exclusivity of negotiations, non-solicitation of employees and confidentiality) and non-binding (for example, the price, deal structure, parties, financing, contingencies and required approvals) terms.	One to two months
M&A due diligence	After agreement on a price, the floorboards are lifted and all aspects of the firm are examined in detail. What is found will inform the detailed negotiations.	One to three months, depending on ease and complexity

Negotiations	The buyer presents an offer based upon its valuation model and due diligence. Sleeves are rolled up and pizzas are delivered. The intensity of this phase can mean that owners get distracted from the main business, such that a deal failure can hurt the potential of a back-up deal. Bear in mind that buyers will often have conducted many purchases and you may not have experienced any. Ensure you use your advisors well!	One to three months
Share Purchase Agreement	A final contract is drawn up for sale. This is often complicated through different partners' needs, conforming to different international laws and preferences on the type of purchase (for example, assets, shares). This culminates in the share purchase agreement (SPA).	One to two months
Completion	Similar to a house purchase, there is a time lag between the signing of the contract and associated payments. This is especially true if the SPA was conditional on any further activities (usually called 'Conditions Precedent').	One to three months
Post sale	Now the hard work begins. The communication plan gets put into effect, the change management plan begins and the earn-out (if included) will start – unless you have negotiated a break (which you should!).	NA

Whilst the average period of sale is between six and nine months, it can last anything from four months to 18 months depending on how prepared you are (and how lucky). The quickest is usually when a buyer is already known to a seller, which renders redundant the first four stages. However, these types of deals are also inherently risky because there is no competitor for the deal and the buyer is likely to be much more experienced in these negotiations. PE deals are usually done quicker than trade deals because they are set up to buy and do these types of deals routinely. In terms of timelines, the big contingencies are 'Pre-diligence' and the 'Due diligence' phases. However, a good PSA that has been used consistently removes much of the organisation needed to demonstrate key metrics to a buyer.

Hopefully, this will help illuminate why many of the owners that contact me wanting to sell soon are disappointed. Doing the most important things in this book (i.e. maximising the potential value of the firm) can take up to two or even three years for a firm that has grown in a haphazard manner. If a one-year sale process and a two-year earn-out are added to the equation, then it can sometimes be five years before the founder realises maximum value. Naturally, some leaders will want to compromise maximum value for a shorter journey to sale.

There may also be some stickiness when it comes to risk mitigation. Most buyers will want some form of risk management around individuals and future performance, so are likely to insist on some deferred payments, earn-out clauses, financial-metric payments, non-compete clauses, clawbacks or payment in shares. Some of these may be preferable to others, but to reiterate: the less the firm depends on you and other shareholders to generate revenue and growth and the more you have managed your succession planning, the easier it is to negotiate a clean deal with a short earn-out.

For every 100 firms that are *considered* by frequent buyers, only around 18 get an NDA, ten get to the Letter of Intent (LOI) and only one gets through due diligence.[4] This doesn't mean, of course, that the other 99 are not eventually bought by someone else, but it does highlight how fraught the process can be. This drop-out rate isn't necessarily due to buyer pickiness but can also be due to sellers dropping out of the funnel intentionally. The average deal will result in 55% of the sale price being paid upfront and the rest acquired through earn-out targets. Around 90% of acquisitions of consulting firms require earn-outs. The smaller the company, the greater the 'people risk' for the buyer and the lower percentage of upfront payments. Greg Alexander founded and sold SBI, and then founded Capital 54, where he is one of the only investors that puts money into very small firms. Greg told me: 'when you are buying into a small firm, you either buy the people or the idea. I buy the people because the idea will usually change'.

The most common targets for an earn-out contract are unsurprisingly profit margin and revenues. In cases where the firm has a unique and valuable skill set (for example, technology consulting), buyers also specify the retention of key employees (who will often, in turn, be offered bonuses to stay). Around three quarters of earn-outs hit their targets, so a CEO should not see the earn-out as guaranteed income.

When buyers don't necessarily want what is best

There are four areas where buyers tend to ask for things that many well-run firms might not deliver, were they not selling. None of these are necessarily a problem, but an adviser may suggest you attend to these areas in the 18 months prior to the sale.

The first concerns service specialisation. Buyers tend to ask for a more focused niche than many firms naturally possess. This is often because firms are looking for a specific service (or sector) offering to add to their portfolio, and a more diverse spread of services may not fit with their plans.

The second concerns profit margins. Whilst buyers like growth and profit margins, firms that have grown quickly will often have invested their profits into people and have little margin to show potential buyers. This is something that can be addressed either in the form of an explanation ('you can see we have invested heavily in people for the last five years; we are now in a position to reap the rewards of the investment we made') or by actually freeing up margins in the 18 months approaching the sale.

The third area of importance is simplicity. As David Blois, founder of M&A Advisory, told me, 'buyers like to keep things simple. If a seller is too complicated or has too many variables, this often scares buyers off'. In other words, you may have a complex company that works for you and other partners, but it may be difficult to sell. An example that springs to mind is an organisation that is a meld of several independent consultancies or has a variety of partners with different exit needs.

The final thing to consider is the possibility that buyers are not actually buyers. They may be larger competitors pretending to be interested in order to access details about your finances, your rates, your clients and your star employees. An NDA here is of limited use, and instead, you will need to do your own due diligence on buyers prior to sending them the CIM and trust your gut instinct.

All this said, I would be cautious about changing the company too much in order to please a potential buyer. The majority of potential deals will fail, and several partners have reported taking their eye off the sales pipeline during due diligence and contracting process only to find the buyer pulls out and suddenly the finances don't look so impressive.

How buyers value your company

The foundation

To illustrate the components of valuation, I have reproduced the diagram from the beginning of this book (Figure 9.1). The firm's EBITDA (and EBITDA growth) provides the basis for calculating how quickly the sale price might be recouped by the buyer. This is used because it is seen as a more reliable estimate of the real profits generated by the firm because it excludes things (i.e. the 'ITDA') that vary depending on country, financing structure or investment decisions. It is by no means perfect and can be depressing in many ways, perhaps the most common being partners taking out large dividends. For this reason, not all multiples should be treated equally (many sellers get multiple envy when I bring up others'). The projected *growth* of EBITDA promises to shorten the expected recoup period, but if perceptions differ between the buyer and the seller, then earn-out targets are a common way of settling the disagreement!

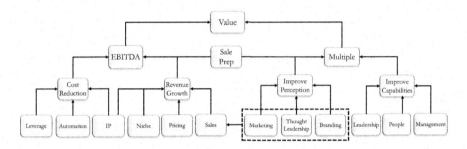

Figure 9.1 The value hierarchy.

It is important to remember that buyers are buying the *promise* of future revenues which are diminished by inflation and risk. As the net present value of firm with static (but healthy) profit margins and revenues reduces considerably even over a ten-year period, it is important for the buyers that the firm is expected to grow. Figure 9.2 illustrates this with EBITDA of £20 million discounted annually at 13%. As you will note, the value of a zero-growth company rapidly diminishes for the prospective buyer. I have put the spreadsheet at

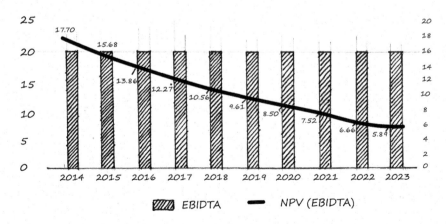

Figure 9.2 Deteriorating purchase value with no growth.

joeomahoney.com, so you can input your own figures. As detailed in Chapter 3, buyers ideally want sustained, growing revenues for at least three years and projections of the same for a subsequent three years. A minimum of 20% EDITDA and 20% growth for the previous three years is the basis for a good price.

I was told by several founders that their advisory firms told them that buyers aren't interested in firms with less than £5 million revenue. This simply isn't true and may be prompted by advisors looking for bigger deal sizes to maximise their own earnings. In reality, over a quarter of deals are for firms with less than £5 million revenue and around 15% are for less than £1 million. Another 35% are for firms bringing in between £5 million and £50 million and another 25% above £50 million.[5] What is true, though, is that EBITDA purchase multiples are lower for firms earning less than £5 million. Multiples then plateau between £5 million and £50 million and then decline with larger deals as the number of potential buyers diminishes. The reason for the low multiples at the smaller end is that buyers here are often simply acquiring teams rather than businesses. As these firms have rarely built sufficient assets to reassure buyers, they typically attract long earn-out periods. Certainly, the smaller end of the market unsurprisingly tends to get deals which rely on firms hitting future targets to secure much of the payment.

If you have a fast-growing firm advising on a high-demand area (for example, AI, robotics, data analytics or cyber security), it is likely that firms will be prepared to relax their requirements as competition for your company will be so high. In the case of very fast-growing firms, it is also likely that the buyer will value the firm on the last few months' profits rather than the last year so as to give a more accurate reflection of value.

The multiple

As an illustration, consider a business that is making £1 million EBITDA and growing at 20% per annum. In terms of its business infrastructure and qualitative assessment, let's say a buyer would value it as a 5× EBITDA company. Next year, therefore, if growth continues on track, the company could be worth £6 million (£1.2 million × 5). But, if instead the team really works hard on the profit growth side (achieving 30% EBITDA growth instead of 20%), they could get the valuation to £6.5 million (£1.3 million × 5). Suppose however that growth rates were held, and managerial effort focused more on improving the qualitative aspects of the firm – thus moving the buyer's multiple offer to 7× EBITDA or £8.4 million (£1.2 × 7). My point here is that once solid EBITDA is achieved, it is often more important to focus on the factors that will help generate a high multiple. Focusing on developing brand, intellectual property, stronger systems and succession planning are likely to generate a higher price for the firm that continuing to focus on additional margin points. Understanding this and having an awareness of the components that make up the multiple are therefore critical to your future business success.

I should also stress here that getting the narrative right during the sales process is a crucial part of managing buyer perceptions. The impact of the story about *why* you are right for them, *why* you have an exciting firm and *why* your growth rates are likely to be high should not be underestimated. As I suggested in Chapter 3, central to this is the category in which the buyer places you: consultancies tend to have a lower multiple than software firms but a higher multiple than training firms. Getting your positioning right is crucial.

Preparation for sale

Secrets, conflicts and hostages

By the time a firm gets to sale, it will typically have major shareholders (usually partners, less commonly investors), minor shareholders (usually employees) and a series of other stakeholders, including clients, the buyers themselves and the families of those most involved with the sale. It is important that these groups are managed and communicated with properly, especially those key individuals who need to be locked in for the earn-out. This can be especially complicated in a firm where partners are at different life stages and thus want different things.

Partners generally keep the sale secret until the deal is done to avoid unnecessary worry, but mistakes often happen. One founder told me of a key document being left on a photocopier, whilst another said suspicions were first aroused when a cadre of suited analysts arrived at a dress down firm for the due diligence. I would suggest assuming that the news will get out and having a contingency communications plan in place.

Generally speaking, only tell the senior managers who need to know about the plans. If you are planning a post-deal bonus, then keeping the deal secret should be part of this. You may feel like a fraud not telling other employees, but if you do tell them, be prepared for some to leave and for others to be distracted. This can affect your performance and lead to buyers pulling out.

Hopefully, you will have followed the advice in the section on governance, anticipated conflict in your partnership charter and communicated your exit strategy clearly to major stakeholders and shareholders. Unfortunately, this isn't always enough to prevent the conflict, which often happens when approaching a sale. Presented with a small purchase pay-out, minority shareholders often find themselves presented with a new job title, a three-year earn-out, a new boss and a contract specifying non-compete and no solicitation clauses. It is perhaps no surprise that they often refuse to sign and can hold the major shareholders hostage in hope of a better deal. I have seen a few deals where such conflict was enough to dissuade a buyer.

The following good practices can help:

- Ensuring that the compensation and equity of influential individuals aligns their interests with those of the firm.
- Winning buy-in and setting expectations of key stakeholders and shareholders concerning the plans of the majority shareholders.
- Building excitement and motivation of the senior team towards the right exit.
- Understanding the minimum requirements of shareholders for a sale, not just in terms of price, but also the type of buyer, terms and conditions.
- Ensuring you have an experienced expert on hand to provide guidance where expectations might be out of alignment.
- Having an independent arbitrator named for potential conflict situations, especially concerning the value of the firm for any unexpected exits.
- Ensuring that the 'back-up' buyer is kept 'warm' when negotiations are progressing with the main buyer. When a deal falls through, it can be shock enough for everyone to readjust their expectations second time around.
- Making sure you have a contingency plan for minority shareholders holding up a sale. Many owners take it very personally and feel they are being held hostage after creating jobs for these people. Regardless of your position, it won't help your cause to cancel the deal and sack them all. It might help more to think about what you are prepared to negotiate on and whether you can act as their advocate in discussions with the buyers.

Peak performance: rhetoric and reality

In the two years prior to instigating the sell process, the entire firm should be focused on maximising EBITDA and the multiple. This may mean shifting the incentive structure in the firm and will certainly mean some crisp communications around accelerating sales. A six-month 'sprint' is a useful tactic here, to focus minds and energy. It is equally important to attack costs wherever possible. This could mean ending subscriptions that are unnecessary, swapping associates for employees, closing offices that are unproductive, removing partners that are simply waiting for the pay-out, and trimming bonuses where possible.

A good advisor and accountant will also help you portray your profit and loss (P&L) accounts in the best light. Approaching sale, it is normal practice to 'adjust' or 'normalise' EBITDA as there may have been additions or subtractions (for example, payments through dividends or bonuses) which do not reflect normal day-to-day financial transactions. In addition, there may have been amortization or depreciation decisions some time ago, which are better adjusted as a one-off cost rather than spread out to adjust the current balance sheet.

Buyers recognise these 'add backs' and expect accounts to be adjusted (either way) in light of one-off payments that might not reflect market rates. It is better to err on the side of additional EBITDA and then have the debate with buyers later for two reasons. First, because the initial presentation of EBITDA puts a marker in the sand which sets buyer expectations. Second, because by the time a buyer comes to have that negotiation, they will have invested significant time and money and are more likely to progress with the deal. Many of us have continued with a house purchase that we've fallen in love with, despite the fact that the survey has highlighted some minor problems.

Negotiating a deal

Whilst this is not a book on negotiation skills,[6] my experience with buyers and sellers suggests there are some key strategies to keep in mind for the best deal:

- Really try to understand the buyer's motivation. How will you fit with them? Have their organic growth plans stalled? Are you a 'nice-to-have' buy or a 'must-have' buy? Be pushy and ask for their five-year plan. Dig into them as much as they dig into you; this is especially justified where there is an earn-out as they are asking you to back their future.
- Don't reveal too much too early. Information is power in negotiations and you must be in control of what is revealed and when. To this end, try to avoid getting cosy with one buyer too early on. Don't go for dinner. Definitely don't go for drinks.
- More than one interested buyer is crucial to getting a good price. If there is one buyer, and they know it and know that you really need to sell, they are in control of the deal. Wherever possible, get more than one buyer interested, even if you have to mix up PE and strategic buyers.
- Once the LOI is signed, you are usually prevented from courting other potential buyers. It is crucial that before you sign the LOI, you have the best possible terms. An experienced M&A advisor will help you a huge amount here. One told me to always insist that they 'show you the money' before you sign, to ensure they actually have the funds ready to go.

- Once the LOI is signed, buyers have the upper hand. They will generally seek to renegotiate the price based on things they've discovered. One tactic they use is to draw out the due diligence until the seller is sweating. This can be prevented by specifying a time limit prior to signing the LOI.
- Be open to earn-outs. Saying no upfront means turning your back on many potential buyers and potentially losing out on a higher total price for the firm. Earn-out payments tend to provide a higher return than upfront deals, despite having less guarantee of success.
- Quantify your value to them. Make a list of all the ways you will help them. For example, most buyers focus on how they will sell your services to their clients. Try to quantify this, but also quantify how you can sell more of their services to your clients and any other benefits you can think of.
- Don't start spending, or even planning the spending, of the money before the deal is done. You are more likely to accept last minute renegotiations by the client (which is a common phenomenon) if you've already told your family about the new yacht.
- Don't take your eye off the business during negotiations. Get your team focused on business development and operations so that sales don't slip during negotiations. Your advisory firm and the expert team you have put together should do the majority of the work for the sale.
- Focus on the terms of the deal as much as the price. A lower price with better terms is usually preferable to the opposite, as bad terms will dent the price ultimate anyway. Terms are likely to include the earn-out period; the percentage paid upfront; whether the price will be paid in cash or shares; whether assets are being purchased or shares; non-compete clauses; earn-out targets; earn-out conditions (for example, resources); your role and power in the post-deal company. You should have a clear idea what you will and won't accept here and what your preferences are.

Negotiating a good earn-out

Earn-outs tend to be used when there is a gap between the buyer's and seller's price expectations or when the business is still dependent on the owners (usually for sales). A good earn-out isn't necessarily a short one. It is one where there are no surprises, and both parties end up happy because the goals of the earn-out are realistic, reasonable and supported. The details concerning the earn-out are usually hammered out in the negotiation. There are certain things interviewees tell me tend to go wrong during an earn-out, and these might focus your attention on the negotiations:

The first is lack of financial resources. A few sellers have told me that once they sold, they were disappointed with the amount of cash available for investment in their firm's (or more accurately, their department's) growth and that this had corresponding effects on their ability to hit targets. Whilst it is important to recognise that, as part of a bigger firm, you are one of many hustling for additional budget; this is something that should be covered in the negotiation. You should have a good idea what investment is required to hit your targets and seek to get this agreed.

Things can also go wrong in the area of human and other resources. Often, a newly acquired firm will rely on the functions of the larger firm in order to succeed. From a buyer's perspective, this is crucial to achieving economies of scale. Yet, for the seller, it can mean that decisions take longer, bureaucracy slows things down and the new team isn't as capable or doesn't understand your unique needs. A common complaint is when the acquired firm needs to use the buyer's sales team who don't really understand the new services and products.

Another challenge that often arises during an earn-out is central expenses being inserted into your P&L account. Frequently, the buying firm will add an expense line around 'Head Office Expenses' or similar. These can be significant and will eat into your reported profits, which is likely to impact your ability to hit earn-out targets. Again, this should be discussed upfront and detailed in the contract.

A problem also arises if the individuals that led the purchase of your firm leave (or worse, the buyer is taken over themselves) and your political influence diminishes. One seller told me that he struggled to make the new owners of the company honour the original agreement. A related challenge concerns your decision-making power. It is hard to hit targets if your ability to take and enforce decisions is highly circumscribed.

Bear in mind that early missed targets have knock-on effects on later ones, and which can mean year three targets are virtually impossible to hit by the end of year one. This can be a very depressing scenario!

With all this in mind, my advice for negotiating a good earn-out is:

- Be clear on what you want. Not just the minimum price, but all the details from support, earn-out, the type of work you will be doing and the decision-making power you will need.
- Don't just focus on the money. A match in values and chemistry makes the next two to three years much more likely to be enjoyable and successful.
- Get as much cash as you can upfront, unless you are pretty certain that you are going to be hitting some high-growth targets in future years.

- Put a time delay on when the earn-out starts. This will give you a chance to recover from negotiations, settle in, educate the sales force about your services and execute your communications plan.
- Specify the details you expect concerning investment, access to decision-makers and be clear on what processes of theirs you will expect to use (and the risks associated with these). If they want you to use their sales team, ensure that you have time to train and brief them.
- Insofar as possible, identify contingencies for specific scenarios. For example, a recession, the buyer being bought or a personality clash.
- Remember that the buyer or investor is likely to have much more experience than you in M&A deals. Invest well in experienced advisors to help you in the process. If you are not a great face-to-face negotiator then bring someone in who is.

Takeaways

- Prepare for a sale or large investment at least two years in advance.
- At least two years in advance:
  - Ensure the shareholders are clear on what they want from an exit or investment. Discuss the minimums needed (for example, cash, earn-outs, exits) with everyone that can hold up the event. Have this facilitated by an advisor.
  - Seek to maximise recurring and non-headcount-related revenues (see Chapter 5.)
  - Ensure you have reduced the dependence on key individuals by having strong IP and processes in key areas.
  - Have a clear idea of what firms might be interested in buying or investing in the firm and the gaps that they would want you to fill. Align your strategy with these gaps.
  - Ensure your Articles of Association and Partnership Agreement are not going to get in the way of a sale.
  - Have a strong succession plan.
  - Set expectations of the senior team and link sale targets to their reward structure.
  - Audit the firm from a perspective of a buyer and create a plan to deal with weaknesses.
  - Maximise EBITDA growth for two to three years before the sale, unless you are investing in activities which will maximise your multiple
  - Anticipate and deal with any court cases, debts and problem individuals.
  - Ensure your accountant and lawyer are aligned with your goals. Ideally, both should be experienced in M&A deals.

- At least a year before a sale:
  - o Research and begin building your value proposition for buyers or investors. Why should they buy (or invest in) you and not a competitor?
  - o Build a team of internals and externals to deal with the sale. Assess potential M&A advisors or brokers. Recruit fractionals or board members who can help with specialist skills, knowledge or connections.
  - o Focus everyone not involved with the sale on business development. Shift rewards to ensure that sales are maximised whilst the sale is progressing.
  - o Ensure that you have quick access to all the key data and facts that will be needed for the CIM and the due diligence process.
  - o Assemble all the key documents, metrics, reports needed for the due diligence and CIM.

Good luck

As someone who has grown three firms and sold one, I'd like to end with two pieces of personal advice which I wish I had more closely heeded.

The first is that the growth journey is a marathon, not a sprint. Ignoring your health, loved ones and hobbies in pursuit of a business is a quick way to end up successfully unhappy.

The second piece of advice is to think deeply about your motives before embarking. If you are motivated by solely wealth, you *may* find that the things it buys do not create happiness. If you are driven to create security for your family, you *may* find that they'd rather just spend time with you. If you are spurred by the high expectations of (perhaps long gone) parents, you *may* find that deep down they would have preferred you were less stressed.

However, if you love creating good things and the experience that comes with it then you are unlikely to be disappointed. As T.S. Eliot wrote:

> We shall not cease from exploration
>
> And the end of all our exploring
>
> Will be to arrive where we started
>
> And know the place for the first time.

I wish you good fortune on this journey.

Notes

1 Where shareholders are contracted to remain with the firm for a period and hit specific targets to earn the remainder of the purchase price.
2 Christensen, C. M., Alton, R., Rising, C., & Waldeck, A. (2011) The new M&A playbook. *Harvard Business Review*, 89(3), 48–57.
3 There are several benefits to having all your key documents ready to go. Not least, the impression the buyer is given that you have done this before and there may be competition for their bid.
4 Equiteq (2014) *The Knowledge Economy Global Buyers Report 2014/2015*.
5 Equiteq (2018) *The Knowledge Economy Global Buyers Report*.
6 A good book on negotiation is Malhotra, D., & Bazerman, M. (2007) *Negotiation Genius: How to Overcome Obstacles and Achieve Brilliant Results at the Bargaining Table and Beyond*. New York: Bantam. Try to avoid books written by hostage negotiators.

Index